The Percehay Family of Ryton

Hope you find this interesting!
Best Wishes
David.

Published in 2017 by the South Ainsty Archaeological Society on behalf of David Brewer

Copyright © 2017 Author

British Library Cataloguing-in-Publication Data

A catalogue record for this book is available from the British Library

ISBN 978-0-9567168-2-8

Typeset by Lesley Collett Graphics

Printed and bound by Henry Ling Ltd, Dorchester

Front cover: Coat of Arms and Crest as declared by the Percehay family at various Visitations

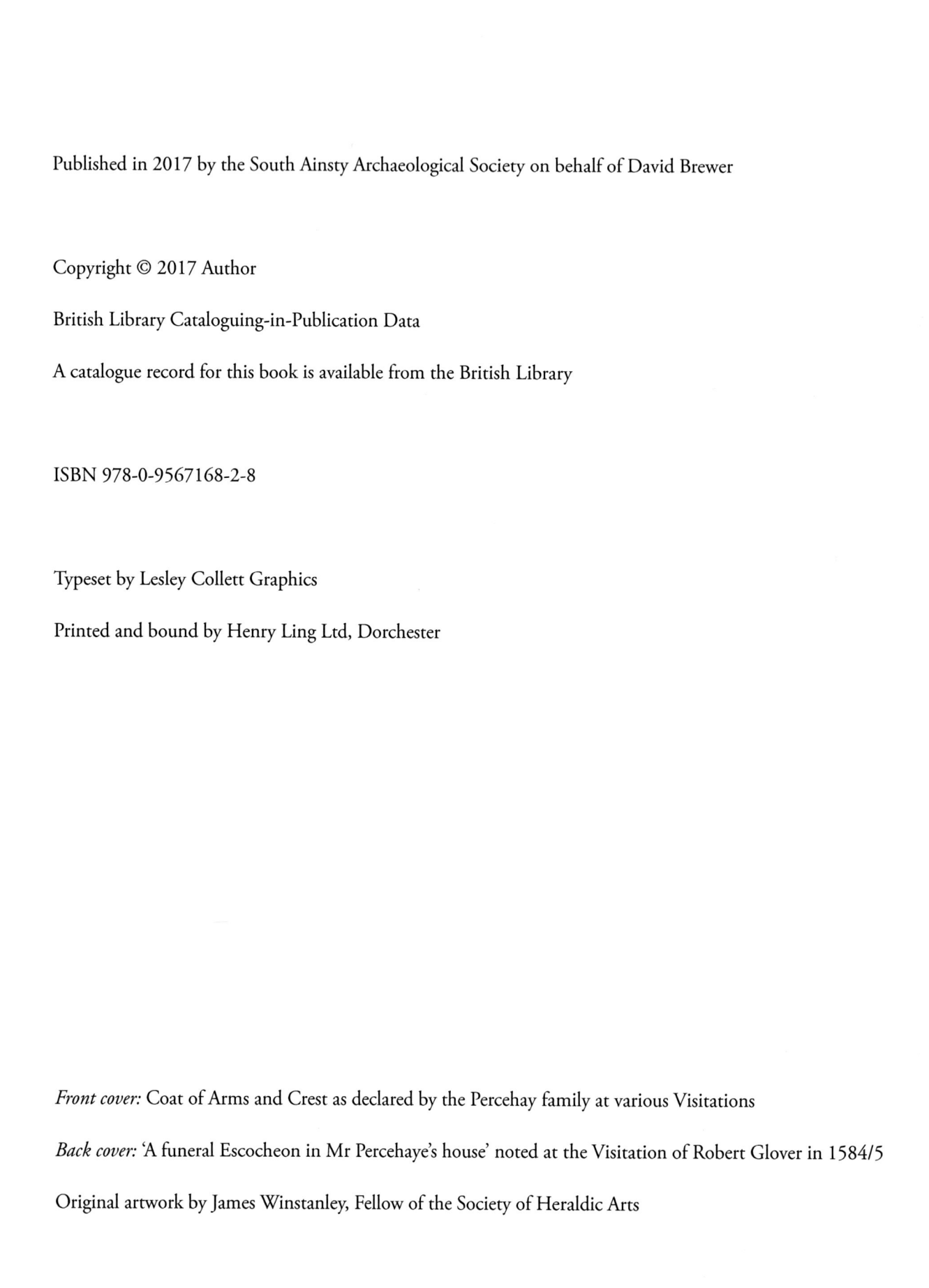

Back cover: 'A funeral Escocheon in Mr Percehaye's house' noted at the Visitation of Robert Glover in 1584/5

Original artwork by James Winstanley, Fellow of the Society of Heraldic Arts

The Percehay Family of Ryton

Forgotten Lords of a Deserted Ryedale Township

David Brewer

2017

This book is dedicated to the memory of
Les and Amy Brewer
who made Ryton their home,
and to Marjorie Harrison
who sparked my original interest in researching the past.

Contents

List of Figures vi
Acknowledgements vii
Abbreviations viii

Chapter 1: Introduction 1

Chapter 2: The Percehay family: Lords of the Manor of Ryton 3
    Foundation 3
    Pillars of the Community 7
    Decline 12
    The True Faith 15
    Death, Debt and Inheritance 17

Chapter 3: Pedigree of Percehay of Ryton 25
    Key to abbreviations used in the Pedigree 26
    Notes on the Pedigree 26

Chapter 4: Ryton: a 'Deserted' Township of Ryedale 31
    Ryton before the Percehays 31
    Ryton during the time of the Percehays 34
    Ryton after the Percehays 36
    Ryton – a Deserted Village 38

Chapter 5: Place-Names of Ryton 61

Appendix 1: Key Sources 89
    Barstow Plan of 1744 and later Valuations and Rent-books 89
    Plan of Lund Forest in the Township of Ryton 1849 89
    Yorkshire Archaeological Society – MD 92 Nos 1 to 28 90
    The Garforth distribution of 1655 90
    Note regarding other sources 91

Appendix 2: Percehay of Ryton – Coats of Arms..93
    Percehay Coats of Arms – References 95

Appendix 3: The Chapel of St Oswald at Ryton in Ryedale..99

List of Figures

Figure 1: Aerial view of the site of the deserted village of Ryton..41

Figure 2: Aerial view of the land distributed in 1604 and re-distributed in 1655 42

Figure 3: The chalice – 'The Gifte of Christopher Percehay of New Malton Esq. and Susannah his wife to the Church of St. Michaels' 1705 43

Figure 4: The pewter alms-dish celebrating the Chapel of St Oswald in the Percehay house at Ryton 43

Figure 5: Casual prehistoric finds from Ryton..44

Figure 6: (top) The original deed dated 1356, complete with Sir William Percehay's seal attached, held in the Merchant Adventurers Hall in York; (below) seal matrix and imprint........................45

Figure 7: Surviving part of 'The Map of all the Land situated at Ryton in the Parish of Kirby-Over-Carr in the County of York belonging to Thomas Barstow Gent. Surveyed in the year 1744 by Rt. Bewlay. Copied from the original Map by Robert Gilson 1787' 46

Figure 8: Names of Closes from the Rent Book of Thomas Barstow 47

Figure 9: Possible early routes through Ryton 48

Figure 10: Ryton circa 1500 49

Figure 11: Ryton circa 1700 – Known dispersed farmsteads 50

Figure 12: 1655 Plan 1 – Names of Closes prior to distribution; Plan 2 – New Closes created in 1655 with new owners...51

Figure 13: 'Terrar of Lund Lordship in the Marishes'. Part of 'A Terrar of Newburgh's Lordship', pre-1683..52

Figure 14: 'A Survey & Valuation of the Right Honourable Henry Earl Fauconberg Estate situate at Lund Forest in the East Riding of the County of York. Surveyed & Valued September 1796 by us Ed. Watterson Tho. Rodwell'...53

Figure 15: 'Plan of Lund Forest in the Township of Ryton and Parish of Kirby Misperton in the North Riding of the County of York the property of Sir Geo. Wombwell Bart. 1849'..................54

Figure 16: Plan of the Lund Estate at 1849 with field-names added..55

Figure 17: 'Plan of the Township of Ryton in the Parish of Kirbymisperton in the North Riding of the County of York. 1842 Robt. Wise Surveyor Malton.' Map for the 1842 Tithe Award for Ryton 56

Figure 18: Names of Closes from the Tithe Award for the Township of Ryton of 1842................57

Acknowledgements

The production of this book would not have been possible without access to original documents, specifically those held by North Yorkshire County Records Office at Northallerton, referred to throughout as NYCRO; those held by the Yorkshire Archaeological and Historical Society, referred to as YAS since most of their publications pre-date a recent change of name, now housed in the Special Collections Department of the University of Leeds Brotherton Library; and those in the Borthwick Institute for Archives at the University of York. The staff at these venerable institutions have been extremely helpful and encouraging throughout. Some documents, such as the records for Malton Priory, are still in the original mediaeval Latin, and sincere thanks go to Margaret Elsworth who has kindly helped by translating a number of these documents. Her work also revealed important ancient place-names and these have helped to clarify the situation in Ryton before the time of extant written records.

Deciphering the possible origins and meanings of place-names would not have been possible without the considerable research that has taken place under the guidance of the English Place-Name Society, based in the School of English Studies at the University of Nottingham, and Dr Paul Cavill of this organisation has been very patient and encouraging and nurtured my original interest. Other original documents are held at the National Archives at Kew, and their efficient copying and postage service has saved both travelling time and hotel expenses. One key document is held at the Merchant Adventurers Hall in York, together with the Percehay seal matrix, and images of both are included with the kind permission and assistance of The Company of Merchant Adventurers of the City of York. Images are also included of the pewter alms-dish from the Church of St Laurence at Kirby Misperton, and of the silver chalice from the Church of St Michael in Malton; the permission and assistance of both churches is very much appreciated. The very important discovery of the Barstow estate map of 1744 and associated rent books would not have been possible without the enthusiastic assistance of the Barstow family. Specific thanks are due to Michael Barstow of Sherburn and Roger Beament of St Albans, husband of Ann Barstow, for their invaluable assistance and encouragement. Very special thanks must go to Mrs Catherine Bevis, née Barstow, for helping to preserve all the Barstow family papers and documents and making them available. Without these the true story of Ryton could not have been unravelled. Local knowledge has also been critical in understanding the information available, and the active assistance of a number of local families has been appreciated, as has access to particular locations.

Special thanks must go to John and Margaret Raines, David and Jane Raines, Mr and Mrs Richardson, Ken and Pauline Wilson, and George Featherstone, who have all contributed and assisted with local knowledge and experience. A resistivity survey of the old manor site was only possible with the assistance and guidance of Dr Jon Kenny, community archaeologist, and the physical help of Roger Weatherill, a dedicated amateur archaeologist. My fellow members of the Yorkshire Heraldry Society have offered enthusiastic advice and guidance, and the work of Barbara Mulroy, who kindly made sure that the information on heraldry was credible, and of James Winstanley, whose stunning artwork is on the cover of this book, is very much appreciated.

Transforming my original electronic manuscript into this book was well beyond my capabilities and has been left to professionals. I am indebted to my long-time friend and mentor Catrina Appleby, whose extensive knowledge and experience of editing publications for the Council for British Archaeology made her the ideal person to edit this book. She was my guide throughout the whole process of researching and writing, and suggested alterations and corrections as necessary. The finished look of the book has been greatly enhanced by Lesley Collett, who transformed the document ready for the printers. These final processes of editing and typesetting have made such a difference to the presentation of this book.

Special thanks must go to my long-suffering wife, proof-reader and constant 'sounding board', Joan, who must have wondered if 'The Book' would ever be finished! It did take rather longer than anticipated, mainly due to the sheer volume of information available – at least it kept me quiet.

Abbreviations

Aveling N/R: Hugh Aveling O.S.B. (1966) *Northern Catholics, The Catholic Recusants of the North Riding of Yorkshire 1558 to 1790*

B.I.: University of York, Borthwick Institute for Archives – www.york.ac.uk/library/borthwick

Cause Papers (CP): Cause Papers in the Diocesan Courts of the Archbishopric of York 1300–1858 – www.hrionline.ac.uk/causepapers

CofCR: Calendar of Close Rolls – www.british-history.ac.uk

CofPR: Calendar of Patent Rolls – www.british-history.ac.uk

D/R: Deeds Registry at North Yorkshire County Record Office (NYCRO)

Harl/Soc: Harleian Society

KMBT: Kirby Misperton Bishop's Transcripts at B.I.

KMPR: Kirby Misperton Parish Registers and 'The Green Book' at NYCRO

Merchant Adventurers: The Company of the Merchant Adventurers of the City of York

mic: microfilm

NA: National Archives (Kew, Richmond, Surrey) – www.nationalarchives.gov.uk

NRRY/NS: North Riding Records Yorks, New Series. Volumes 1 to 4, The Honor and Forest of Pickering – vol.1=1894, vol.2=1895, vol.3=1896, vol.4=1897

NYCRO: North Yorkshire County Record Office (Malpas Road, Northallerton) – www.northyorks.gov.uk/archives

OED: Oxford English Dictionary – www.oed.com

OMPR: Old Malton Parish Registers at NYCRO

OS: Ordnance Survey

Place-Names: Items in italics can be found in Chapter 5, Place-Names

PRS/NS: Pipe Roll Society, New Series

S/Soc: Surtees Society

VCH: Victoria County History

YAJ: Yorkshire Archaeological Journal

YAS: Yorkshire Archaeological Society (now Yorkshire Archaeological and Historical Society)

YAS/RS: YAS Record Series

YAS/RS EYC: YAS Record Series, Early Yorkshire Charters

Y/F: Yorkshire Fines – www.british-history.ac.uk/Yorkshire Fines

YHS: Yorkshire Heraldry Society

ZDV: Fauconberg (Belasyse) of Newburgh Priory Archive at NYCRO

Chapter 1

Introduction

Hiding in the hundreds of documents still available concerning both Ryton and the Percehays are stories of murder (at least three); rebellion (a number of times); knights; dedicated service to king, country and county; religious persecution; exploitation of the poorest by both the church and the monarch; pillars of the community; powerful and influential ladies; child brides; mediaeval mansions; fortunes lost; family feuding and betrayal; and even an imposter who tried to steal someone's identity half a millennium before the internet made it commonplace. But why begin the search for the history of Ryton, today just a scatter of farmsteads that barely qualifies for the description of hamlet, and why agonise over the associated Percehay family who are locally long forgotten and written-off by scholars as an insignificant branch of another totally unrelated family? Coincidence has played an uncanny and recurring part and created the circumstances that caused the initial interest. Another project included researching maps of Yorkshire, and it soon became apparent that Ryton was invariably depicted on each one, making it impossible to ignore by someone who was brought up there. It raised many questions, such as why was Ryton shown when some of the other, now much larger settlements, for example Kirby Misperton, were absent and why was Ryton bridge always marked but not necessarily the ones at Howe or Newsham?

Very quickly it became obvious that it was not possible to understand the history of Ryton without understanding the fortunes of the family that were Lords of the Manor for over 500 years. They not only dominated events in Ryton but were also one of the key families in Ryedale, in North and East Yorkshire, and in north Lincolnshire, having interests in some 21 manors (or parts of manors) and properties spread over a further 42 settlements. They even had lands in Scotland, and more down in the West Country centred on Devon and Dorset, showing a degree of mobility that had not been anticipated considering the means of transport then available. They were real knights in feudal times and were fully entitled to display their crest and coat of arms as shown on the front cover. Their position meant they held many public offices, serving as Foresters of the Fee in Pickering Forest on behalf of the king, justices of the peace and collectors of taxes, as well as being responsible for mustering militia on behalf of the king to defend the realm, with the result that at least one of the Percehays was at the Battle of Crecy. Their influence resulted in one Sir William Percehay being appointed High Sheriff of Yorkshire, although this was only one of the many public duties he performed. He was also appointed Knight of the Shire, required by the king to represent Yorkshire in Parliament, which he attended on at least four occasions. Having been around for such a long time it was inevitable that there were occasions when the family backed the wrong side: another William Percehay's support for the Pilgrimage of Grace could have been disastrous, but being brother-in-law to Henry VIII's Solicitor General seems to have saved this William from any real punishment. In fact their power and influence was disproportionate to their relatively modest position as knights; this was due principally to their family contacts. They were one of the few families who could trace their roots back to Normandy and they were resident in Ryedale for so long that they became *the* family to be associated with, resulting in marriages with many of the local gentry, as detailed in the enclosed pedigree (see Chapter 3).

With such an influential family resident in Ryton as Lords of the Manor it is not surprising that for most of their tenure Ryton was an important settlement. But was Ryton important before they arrived; did any other family or institution have any influence in Ryton while the Percehays were resident; and for how long after they had gone was Ryton a thriving township? Eventually Ryton became what is now termed a 'Deserted Mediaeval Village', but why did it disappear? A history of the township is given separately to try to understand all the influences that made it initially successful, but ultimately led to its desertion (see Chapter 4). The local knowledge of both the author and Ryton residents has played a key part in understanding how the geography and topography of the area have affected agriculture, the key economic activity throughout Ryton's recorded history. Knowing where the remnants of ancient ridge and furrow were located before they were farmed out of existence has been instrumental in pinpointing the lost Domesday village of Salescale, and knowledge of old paths and tracks that were in use into the 20th century has caused a rethink about the original direction of early routes that may have influenced the location of the settlement that became Ryton. The demise of Ryton as a township is clearly documented, but these documents need to be interpreted carefully and understood as some of the raw statistics are quite misleading. The documents also record many place-names and knowledge of their possible meanings gives a deeper understanding of particular areas and events. The chapter on place-names (Chapter 5) gives the opportunity to include some brief histories and descriptions that are relevant to the overall picture of Ryton, but may not otherwise be included in the main text, although the details about Salescale and the bridge over the Costa (Frerebrigg / Lundbrige / Tranmer's footbridge) are key to the whole story and would have had to have been included at some point. The chapter also allows the real origins of the confusingly named Lund Forest, Ryton Grange and Abbott's Farm to be published for the first time, and who wouldn't want to know the reasons behind the naming of Jerry Bridge, Dicky Ground and especially Glisterpipe!

Maps provided the initial stimulus to discover more about the history of Ryton, and they have been one of the key sources of original information; consequently it is not surprising that so many maps have been reproduced both for reference and clarity. Coincidence again played a part in locating one of the most significant maps, being from the original Barstow survey of 1744. This was discovered directly because of jury service in York Crown Court where half a day was spent waiting in the High Sheriff's dining room. On the wall is a list of all the previous High Sheriffs including Sir William Percehay, but it also included a modern Michael Barstow from Sherburn, near Scarborough, and he eventually found the family member who was the last owner of the Lordship of Ryton. Without his kind assistance it is unlikely that this map would ever have been discovered, hidden as it was at Sheringham in Norfolk. The Newburgh Priory estate map of 1849 with the associated survey details from 1683 (estimated date), 1796 and 1858 have all been critical in understanding the Lund estate, the involvement of Rievaulx Abbey, and especially the paths and tracks that cross the area. Information from these estate maps, coupled with that from the Tithe Award survey of 1842, means that nearly every location can be identified with a high degree of certainty, especially when combined with information from the Deeds Registry at Northallerton going back to 1736.

Appendix 2 on the Percehay coats of arms is very specific but is included as it contains the source of some of the knowledge about the Percehay family and may be of general interest. It is of necessity very detailed, even academic, as it needs to stand up to scrutiny by those interested in Heraldry. The information gained reinforces the status and influence of the Percehay family and enables their pedigree to be completed as accurately as possible. Appendix 3 on the Chapel of Saint Oswald was researched in order to ascertain whether the extant pewter alms-dish that suggests the presence of a Chapel dedicated to St Oswald at Ryton was either genuine, in which case the Chapel really did exist, or was some sort of fake, as has been suggested. Its continued existence is both remarkable and fascinating, and yes, it really does appear to be exactly what it says on the pewter.

Chapter 2

The Percehay family: Lords of the Manor of Ryton

Foundation

The Percehay family of Ryton was well connected, especially by marriage, its members being trusted public servants of both king and county and extremely influential throughout the whole of the 500 and more years that they lived at Ryton. During that time they were one of the key families in Ryedale, with William Percehay being described as 'one of the very few genuine squires in the (Pickering) Lythe' at the turn of the 17th century.[1] Their importance and antiquity was also recognised by William Camden during his 1582 survey for his book *Britannia*. When describing the course of the River Rye from Helmsley to Malton, the only township he mentioned was Ryton: 'hard by the river side standeth Riton, an ancient possession of the ancient familie of the Percihaies',[2] so even by this early date they were already 'ancient'. They were knights in the days of the feudal system, when they rendered military service as a condition of holding their manors and lands, although 'Knight's Service' later became little more than a means of taxation. They lived in very uncertain times, with the constant threat of raids by marauding Scots, although as will be seen, raids and disturbances by their own neighbours were just as likely. Over a period of 625 years (1086 to 1711) they are mentioned in well over 250 public documents, which itself gives an idea of their importance, and a surprising number of original documents still exist specifically concerning the family. Some documents are general lists recording who was taxed, when and by how much, but others are legal documents highlighting the conflicts that arose in the days before an effective police force. Many documents concern land transactions, emphasising just how important it was to be able to prove ownership of a particular property. This became very relevant when someone falsely claimed to be a Robert Percehay and tried to take over the manor of Ryton.[3] By their very nature surviving documents could give the impression of a family in constant conflict, but of course documents do not exist covering the majority of the time when life continued 'as normal'; then, as now, good news was rarely recorded.

The Percehays came over from France some time before Domesday, but it is not known when, or from where they originated. In the Great Domesday Book, Ralph Percehaie was recorded as having seven sites worth 50d (old pence) at Newington, near Oxford,[4] but that is the only reference. There is not enough information to follow the dispersion of the Percehay family across the country, but the next records show them in Yorkshire when a Percehaie was a witness to a grant of land at Flaxton to St Mary's Abbey in York.[5] This has been dated to the period 1129 to 1135. This shows that by then they were already of some importance in the area, since the use of someone as a witness not only gave the document that person's seal of approval (literally if his seal was attached) but it also implied that person's full support, both moral and physical, in the event of a dispute. It is, of course, possible that the Percehays were already in Ryton at that time, but it is not until the record of the annual audit of accounts for the Crown, known as the Pipe Rolls, for the 14th year of the reign of Henry II (1167–68) that it is possible to make the connection with Ryton.[6] By then Walter Percehaie already had five manors in the area, some held from Alan Neville who was chief lord of at least part of Ryton. From that time on, the Percehays consistently referred to themselves as being 'of Ryton' rather than of any other of their many estates in the area. From the turn of the 13th century there are occasional records of the Percehay name in other parts of the country, but it is only in Devon, Dorset and Somerset that some of the family are known to have settled for any length of time, and this line dies out in 1380. The Yorkshire Percehays have a direct link with this branch, confirmed by the use of the same coat of arms, but with a minor addition to show both the 'difference' and their kinship.[7]

It is not possible to say when the Percehays were raised to the status of knight. It is probable that the title was assumed in documents such as the Pipe Rolls, as anyone who held manors would have been knights, if only by default, due to the feudal obligation of Knight's Service that went with the holding of a particular manor. At a later date (1240–41)[8] it was decided that anyone who held estates worth more than £20 (later £40) a year in total was automatically liable to compulsory knighthood, so stating the title was almost unnecessary. Each knight was expected to serve the king, and in time of war had to provide his own armed retinue. As late as 1539[9] William Percehay takes his men from Ryton to the Muster at Barton Cross – as this was for the whole of Ryedale this would probably have been located at today's Barton-le-Street. The group of armed men would probably have looked very informal, consisting of the local peasants, equipped with any agricultural implement that could be utilised as a weapon: a pitch-fork, axe, or bill hook could inflict horrendous wounds, and it was armies made up of these workers that protected the realm. This was well before the existence of a national standing professional army – that only really began with Oliver Cromwell's 'New Model Army' in the mid-17th century – although there was a small force of around 5000 regular troops employed to guard the king and his palaces. This system of local militia is referred to below, when it may explain a reduction in the number of taxpayers in Ryton. The presence of knights does not necessarily mean that jousting and other knightly tournaments took place at Ryton, although they may have done. However, there certainly would have been archery practice as this was compulsory for every man below the rank of knight. Another indication of the feudal era is the debt of five marks owed by Robert de Brideshale (Birdsall) for an agreement by duel with Walter Percehaie in 1167–68 concerning land.[10] This was at the very end of the period when disputes were settled by combat or judicial duel, and in this case a duel may not actually have taken place. Henry II could ill afford to lose his knights in this way, so he was already in the process of introducing the King's Court and associated jury – the birth of our current legal system.

The first Percehay to be recorded as a knight was a Sir Walter, who was witness to a grant of land to the Chapter of York (the governing body of St Peter's cathedral) dated to the period 1213–20,[11] which was just before work began on the construction of the Minster. He had a number of manors and parts of manors held by Knight's Service, including half the manor of Crambe, where he was in dispute in 1219 with the prior of Kirkham, who held the other half, concerning right of access to his lands at Whitwell.[12] It is possible that this Sir Walter even had a castle at Ryton, befitting his position. Malton Priory Chartulary records the gifts to St Mary's Priory at (Old) Malton, and the locations of two of these gifts at Ryton are referenced in relation to a 'casteldich' (castle ditch).[13] The dates of the gifts are not given, but most are believed to have been made during the 12th or 13th century, although by then any castle (whatever that may have meant) may well already have been ancient history. With no other documentation to confirm this 'castle', the references have to be treated with caution. However, we do know a great deal about the Percehay manor house at Ryton, which may, or may not, have been built on the site of an earlier 'castle'. It is clearly shown on the 1744 plan of the Ryton estate that was carefully surveyed for Thomas Barstow, where it appears as a building approximately 100ft (30m) long by 20ft (6m) wide. Numerous earthworks are still clearly visible at the location, although there are no other physical remains. A recent resistivity survey did not add anything to the information already known; it has since been established that all the materials from the old manor house and buildings were comprehensively cleared in 1821 and re-used to build today's Manor Farm, a few hundred metres to the west. This information is confirmed in letters from the Barstow Archive at NYCRO, and the report of George Willoughby, the appointed builder, from his survey carried out on 7 August 1820, summarises the situation:

The house and the whole of the outbuildings are so much dilapidated that they are altogether unworthy of repairs, so much so that it is absolutely necessary that the house should be propped or secured otherwise it will not be safe to inhabit over winter. There is a great quantity of bricks and stone of various sorts which may all be made use of again in rebuilding.

He then lists all the considerable amounts of materials including various types of stone, 'a great

Chapter 2: Lords of the Manor of Ryton

quantity of bricks', tiles, flags, slates (probably stone), old timber, and even glass; with each material he suggests their re-use in the proposed new house. A recent survey of Manor Farm confirmed that the planned re-use of the materials was indeed carried out.[14] Obviously it is not possible to date the building of the old manor house from the materials alone, but the presence of a distinctive stone that is likely to have come from a nearby quarry at Hildenley (just to the west of Malton) is significant. The Percehays held the manor of Hildenley from 1287[15] through to 1522[16] and during this time it is likely that at least part of the manor house would have been built using their own stone. In fact, the few finds there have been from the site indicate habitation from around the end of the 13th century through to the beginning of the 19th century, so perhaps the building of the manor house began shortly after the acquisition of Hildenley. Certainly after 1522 it is unlikely that the family could have afforded to build the grand 'mansion' that is implied from the Hearth Tax return of 1673 when it had 13 hearths, making it larger (at least by this measure) than any property in Malton or Old Malton, and on a par with the Grahams at Nunnington (12), the Cayleys at Brompton (12), and even the Watsons at Helmsley castle (14). (This was long before Castle Howard or Hovingham Hall even existed.) Only Lord Fairfax at Gilling Castle, with 21 hearths, seems to have had a larger property. The sheer quantity of re-used materials confirms just how large the original manor house must have been, as today's Manor Farm comprises a substantial six-bedroomed farmhouse, plus a range of outbuildings. There would have been few houses in Ryedale more impressive than the Percehays', sitting as it did on top of Ryton Rigg, dominating the vale and making their power and importance apparent to everyone.

Surviving as a significant family in the area for such a long time is, in itself, remarkable, demonstrating resilience, flexibility and a degree of pragmatism that could be said to encapsulate a dogged 'Yorkshire' common sense. This is typified by another Sir Walter who, in 1280, along with John of Ryton, was in dispute with William of Habton about grazing rights on some of the moorland between the villages of Habton and Ryton.[17] The land was within the boundary of Ryton but adjacent to Habton village, making it difficult for Walter (and John) to police effectively. At the same time there appears to be other on-going disputes concerning the boundary between Ryton and Habton, so eventually a compromise was reached. The boundary of the limited grazing for the residents of Habton is agreed, but with the ownership being retained by Walter. As a result, 'all the said disputes were forever settled'. The family's pragmatism is even more apparent when they clearly retain 'the old faith' (Catholicism) but manage to go virtually undetected (see below). By the time of this Sir Walter it is clear that the Percehays were already at the very top of the local social hierarchy. His closest neighbour of any standing was John de Vesci (1244–89[18]), Baron of the fortress of Alnwick and Lord of the Manor of Malton. According to the Percehay family, who presented appropriate written proofs (charters) at the Visitations of the Heralds of the College of Arms when claiming their right to bear their particular coats of arms,[19] Walter's son and heir Robert Percehay married Joan, daughter and sole heir of this John de Vesci. Unfortunately current histories of the Vesci family are not consistent, but most have this John dying without heir, resulting in his inheritance passing to his brother William, so this situation requires explanation.

A perennial problem when researching any particular gentry family is the tendency of antiquarians to follow only the male line, with younger sons sometimes ignored, and daughters rarely mentioned, but this only partly explains the lack of records mentioning Joan de Vesci. Her mother, John's first wife Agnes, is supposed to have died 'of grief on hearing of the imprisonment of her Lord' after the Battle of Evesham, giving her death as 1265 (of whatever cause!). John was only born in 1244, and he is unlikely to have fathered offspring before the age of 15, putting Joan de Vesci's birth somewhere between 1260 and 1265; it is clearly possible that Joan's birth was the actual cause of her mother's death. However young she was when she married Robert Percehay, her children can have been little more than infants when her father John died, probably in early 1289, but again there is doubt and it may have been slightly earlier. It is also distinctly possible that at John's death, Joan was herself already deceased, so the statement that he died childless would in fact be true. It is clear from one of the Percehay charters that Joan is not alive in 1292, as her son Walter has to declare that he is son and heir of Joan de Vesci and that he has good memory of her. This suggests that her husband Robert is also deceased. A charter signed by John de Vesci confirms that he had given this Robert his house in York, presumably as part of the marriage settlement. Another charter quoted by the Heralds records that Joan Percehay, Lady of Ryton, gave her son and heir Walter 'the whole of my manor of Strudightyn Martyn in county Forfard in Scotland that is held through hereditary descent'. Scottish contacts suggest this location is likely to be Strathmartin, on the outskirts of Dundee, in the county of Forfar. This is probably part of the inheritance brought to Eustace de Vesci, grandfather of John, by Margaret, an illegitimate daughter of William the Lion, King of Scotland, with the inheritance specifically going down through the female line. The conclusive proof that this Walter Percehay really was the son and heir of Joan de Vesci is that at the first declaration of his arms in 1319 he bears the Percehay coat of arms with the Vesci shield added, exactly as a son should display when inheriting arms from both his father and mother.[20] Another clear indication of this Vesci connection is the fact that Walter Percehay was one of the executors of the will of William de Vesci of Kildare, the last male of the line, who died at Bannockburn on 24 June 1314.[21] William was the illegitimate son of Joan Vesci's uncle, another William, probably making Walter Percehay his nearest relative at that time.

The confusion at this time is exacerbated by the presence of another Joan Percehay. The available information indicates this one to be the sister of Robert Percehay and daughter of Sir Walter. Her father was 'summoned to serve against the Scots' on 24 June 1300[22] but does not seem to return because the Lay Subsidy of 1301[23] has her husband, Roger of Wrelton, paying the tax at Ryton (and Wrelton and Crambe) as head of the family. This also seems to confirm that her brother Robert is already deceased, and his son and heir, another Walter, is not old enough to take over. However, at the recording of Knight's Fees in 1302,[24] Joan has taken over from Roger, who has presumably died, and she is then referred to as Joan Percehay. It seems to have been usual for a widow to revert to her highest status on the death of her husband, and as the Percehays were much more influential and higher up the social ladder than the Wreltons, she reverted back to her maiden name of Joan Percehay.[25] The role, power, and influence of females in previous generations obviously requires a serious re-think … It is clear from numerous documents that a husband required his wife's permission to do anything with her possessions. In fact the lands and all the goods that formed a woman's dowry came with a lot of strings and expectations attached, and in the absence of a male heir, her possessions may well have reverted back to her original family on her death. Not only does Joan take over all the Percehay family responsibilities, initially on behalf of her nephew Walter, but even when he is old enough to be listed as a 'vill holder' (responsible for the settlement or township) at Crambe in 1314/15,[26] she is still the vill holder at Ryton. Clearly this Joan continues to be active and influential, and it is this lady who left a legacy for the Percehays that still has a physical presence today. In 1311, when she was described as 'Joan de Percehaye relict of Roger de Wrelton', she petitioned Archbishop Greenfield to be allowed an oratory in *her* manor of Ryton because of the difficulty in attending the church at Kirby Misperton due to her weak disposition; the distance to Kirby Misperton (although at the time they were just as likely to attend church at St Mary's Priory at Old Malton); and the inaccessibility during frequent flooding. Her request was granted but 'the chaplain, who should serve the oratory, was to make oath to restore to the rectory of Kirby Misperton all oblations and obventions made there'.[27] This grant was limited to three years, but the oratory (chantry) was still there at the Dissolution,[28] and is almost certainly used (very discretely) until 1705. The grant is commemorated by the pewter alms-dish, dedicated to the Chapel of St Oswald at Ryton (see Figure 4 and Appendix 3), which is still in use today at Kirby Misperton.

Joan and Roger did produce at least one child, Alan de Wrelton, who seems to die a relatively young man. As a result, all the de Wrelton lands (in Wrelton and Lockton), and the important hereditary position of 'Forester in Fee' in the area known as Pickering Forest, pass to his nearest relative at the time – William Percehay, Joan's great-nephew.[29] This very lucrative position of Forester in Fee remains with the Percehay family for nearly 200 years.

Chapter 2: Lords of the Manor of Ryton

Pillars of the Community

Sir Walter, son of Robert Percehay and Joan de Vesci, gradually took over the family responsibilities from his great aunt and seems to have become a typical mediaeval knight. He is lord of various manors including Ryton, Hildenley, Wrawby, Crambe (part) and Potto (part), and is called on to perform many public duties. Among the positions he held it is recorded that he is Commissioner of Array in Yorkshire in 1322[30] (effectively in charge of mustering the able-bodied men from the whole of Yorkshire ready to protect the realm, in this case probably against the king's own cousin), summoned as a Knight of Yorkshire to the Great Council at Westminster in 1324,[31] and a collector of the tax on wool in the North Riding in 1338.[32] It had been assumed (probably correctly in view of the above position held) that he was involved at the Battle of Boroughbridge in 1322, when the family feud between Edward II and his cousin the Earl of Lancaster was finally settled. Lancaster made the serious mistake of asking Robert Bruce to come to his aid with a Scottish army, but this was always going to be opposed by the gentry in the north of England who were under constant fear of raids from the Scots, so they joined with Edward and Lancaster lost his head. After the battle the king's supporters were thought to have registered their coats of arms on what became known as the Boroughbridge Roll; Sir Walter's entry shows the Percehay family coat of arms as a silver shield with a red cross flowered at the ends (see Appendix 2), to which he had added a small shield in the top right quadrant with his mother's Vesci arms. However, recent research[33] suggests that this Roll of Arms was actually recorded for a tournament held during the Berwick campaign of late 1319, suggesting this Sir Walter did indeed participate in knightly pursuits. An agreement[34] Walter made with the monks of Rievaulx, allowing them free passage over all the moors of Ryton with carts and carriages as well as on foot, suggests he was as pragmatic as his grandfather. The monks were Sir Walter's neighbours to the north of the Aykeland beck (today's Ackland, previously Tacriveling) in the area they called Lund; this was probably the location of the 'lost' settlement of *Salescale*. They already had a bridge over the Costa (see *Frerebrigg*) to communicate with their possessions in the Marishes, and needed to transport all their goods back to Rievaulx, which they did via the river crossing at Little Habton. They thus needed to cross the moors of Ryton between today's West Farm and land to the north of Shotton Hall. The entire length of this east/west route was still shown as a footpath as late as the first Ordnance Survey map of 1850. Sir Walter wished to be on good terms with the monks, since he needed to cross their land at Lund, both as his preferred route to Pickering via the bridge over the Costa, and as his shortest way to the family lands at Wrelton via Kirby Misperton.

This Sir Walter leaves a will dated 21 December 1344, with probate granted on 6 December 1346 at York; this survives in the archives of the Borthwick Institute.[35] Perhaps surprisingly, at least from our 21st-century perspective of the role of women in earlier times, his wife Agnes also leaves a will, written appropriately on the feast of Saint Agnes the Virgin (21 January) 1348–49, with probate granted on 26 February 1348–49. These wills have been invaluable in helping to construct the Percehay family pedigree (see Chapter 3). Their daughter Joan has progressed from 'nun of Yedingham' to 'Prioress of Yedingham', demonstrating yet again that the female Percehay line cannot be ignored. Interestingly, Walter's will includes the phrase 'my body to be buried in the Abbey church of St Mary at Malton, if I die in England', rather implying he was still an active knight, at a time when the old enemies of France and Scotland were a constant threat. The year of his death may therefore be significant: 1346 was the year of the decisive battles at Crecy (26 August), when Edward III defeated the French, and later at Neville's Cross, near Durham (17 October), when William de la Zouche, the fighting Archbishop of York, defeated the Scots, capturing their king, David, who had tried to take advantage of Edward's absence. The records suggest that Walter was almost certainly involved at Crecy as he is listed, with his coat of arms, in the 'accounts kept by Walter Wetewang, treasurer of the (king's) Household, of the wages of those present at the siege of Calais in 1346–1347'.[36] This siege began in the first week of September 1346, only a few days after the Battle of Crecy. Sir Walter Percehay clearly did not live to see the end of the siege as it continued until August 1347; while the date and the cause of Walter's death are not known, by December 1346 he was dead. He may have died of injuries from either engagement, but it has to be remembered that most soldiers involved in campaigns were just as likely to die from diseases associated with the unsanitary conditions of camp life as they were to die of their wounds. All that is known is that his body was buried at the Abbey church of St Mary as requested, since his wife Agnes asks to be buried next to him there when she later made her own will. This will also shows that Agnes was in charge of her own affairs and possessions, leaving clear instructions that her own debts are to be cleared, her funerary expenses paid, and gifts distributed in accordance with her wishes. Clearly she was not just a 'chattel' of her husband!

After the death of Sir Walter, his son and heir Sir William takes over his estates and some of his public duties. In fact William seems to spend most of his life serving king and county.[37] By the date of his father's will (December 1344) William is already married with three children: Walter, John and Agnes, although by the time of his mother's will (1348), John has already died. Little is known about his first wife, Isabell, although she is probably a daughter of Sir John de Melsa who grants the manor of Levisham to both William and Isabell in 1352–53.[38] William is already active during his father's life and the Sir William de Percehay who is Forester in Fee in Pickering Forest in 1340[39] is probably the same, having taken over by 1334 from his father's cousin, Alan de Wrelton. The family connections in York are already known by the gift from John de Vesci, and Sir William acquired other estates from the executors of Henry de Belton 'lately citizen and merchant of York'. Part of Henry's estates was 'given, granted and confirmed' by Sir William to 'John Freboys, John de Crome and Robert de Smeton, citizens and merchants of York' in a charter dated 'the Friday next after the feast of St Lucy the Virgin in the year of our Lord 1356'.[40] This group of business men later became known as The Company of the Merchant Adventurers of the City of York and their impressive Hall, dating from that time, is believed to stand on the land given by Sir William Percehay. The original charter still exists in a remarkable condition, complete with Sir William's original seal attached (see Figure 6). The Percehay family coat of arms are quite distinct, as is the family's crest of a bull's head. By a truly remarkable coincidence, the archive at the Merchant Adventurers Hall also contains a seal matrix (the implement used to make the impression of the seal in molten wax) belonging to a 'William Percehay knight', that was found at Levisham, the manor given to William and Isabell. While it does not quite produce an exact match, it is very similar; it is thought to be of a slightly later date (see Appendix 2). Credit must be given to the members of the Dunelme Metal Detectorists Club who not only recognised what they had found, they did some research and made sure the seal matrix was presented to The Company for safe-keeping at the Merchant Adventurers Hall.

Sir William Percehay has official duties in the North and East Ridings, both collecting taxes and sitting as a justice of the peace,[41] from the time of his father's death right through the next 36 years. In addition, he serves abroad during 1366[42] and, as he has to appoint attorneys to look after his affairs in his absence, it is probable that his eldest son Walter is already dead (known to die in his father's lifetime); his future heir, Robert, would only have been 10 or 12 at that time.[43] Sir William was also entrusted with the responsibility of representing Yorkshire as a Knight of the Shire when summoned to Parliament at Westminster, where he attended on four occasions: 1373 (Nov/Dec), 1377 (Jan/March), 1382 (May) and 1383 (Feb/March).[44] Each journey to London at that time would have been quite considerable; the payment for his expenses shows that his shortest time away from home was 25 days (1382), which is not surprising considering the state of the roads and the distance travelled. His longest stay was for the Parliament that sat from 27 January to 2 March 1377 when he was paid for 47 days absence. If he attended for the whole period, as he almost certainly would have had to do, then this suggests that he made the journey from London to York in as little as six days; no mean feat if true. However, as Sir William also had estates in Lincolnshire, perhaps that was his base for the journey. Unfortunately it is this Parliament of 1377 that is remembered as the Bad Parliament, because it is thought that some of its actions contributed to the unrest that culminated in the Peasants' Revolt of 1381.

Sir William was appointed High Sheriff of Yorkshire for the year 1374–75,[45] at a time when this was effectively the role of Chief Justice for Yorkshire, rather than the ceremonial position it is today. He continued as a justice in the East Riding and, as a Commissioner

Chapter 2: Lords of the Manor of Ryton

of Array there, was instructed to be prepared to resist invasion in 1377 and 1380.[46] England, as ever, lived in troubled times, but the situation was made even worse by the death of Edward III and the succession of his ten-year-old grandson Richard II. It was this absence from Ryton, with as many men as he could muster, that may explain the low numbers recorded paying the 1377 Poll Tax at Ryton (relative to adjacent villages and compared to earlier and later tax returns). Sir William continued his public service, and as late as November 1382[47] he was appointed to collect the 'fifteenth and tenth' (more taxes, which perhaps had been the real underlying cause of the Peasants' Revolt) in the East Riding. By now Sir William must have been an old man by the standards of the day. His younger brother Walter is cited as being present at Scampston at the baptism of Sir William Latymer, who was born on 24 March 1329/30.[48] As Walter seems to be one of the god-parents, it is unlikely he was under 21, suggesting that he was born before 1308, so our Sir William's birth must pre-date that. This would also tie in with the fact that William is old enough to be listed in Wrelton and Amotherby at the Lay Subsidy of 1327–28,[49] so conservatively he is at least 76 years old when, in September 1383, he was excused further appointments 'and during the remaining few months of his life no further duties were imposed upon him'.[50] Sir William Percehay, son and heir of Sir Walter, died on 15 August 1384, having been probably one of the best-known members of the gentry in Yorkshire, certainly in the North and East Ridings. His Inquisition Post Mortem[51] examined his properties, for tax purposes of course, and these included the manor of Wrawby with property in Kettilby, Elsham and Glanford Brigg in Lincolnshire, as well as the manors of Ryton, Hildenley and Levisham, and parts of the manors of Crambe, Lockton and Wrelton with property in Amotherby, Low Hutton, Newton, Kirby Misperton and Potto, all in Yorkshire.

During the lifetime of Sir William there are very few references to any other Percehay in Yorkshire, although his brother John, who had the family's interests in Swinton, is given as a witness to a land transaction in Aymondersby (Amotherby) in 1364.[52] This John leaves a will, signed on the eve of the festival of the Apostles Simon and Jude (their saints day is 28 October, so this is the 27th) 1391, with probate granted 10 November 1392.[53] This will provides an interesting insight into the total commitment of people at that time to their faith, as well as showing that his horizons were much wider than just 'Swynton in Rydale'. He leaves his soul 'to God and Holy Mary and all his saints' but he asks for his body to be buried in the cemetery of the parish church of 'holy Peter in the Welughs' within York. This probably refers to Saint Peter-le-Willows on Walmgate, near today's Willow Street, one of the many York churches to be lost at the Dissolution. John's residence in York, for at least part of the time, is confirmed later when his wife asks in her will to be buried at St Mary's in Castlegate.[54] In addition to leaving the rector of St Peter's a suitable fee (20s), he also asks that 13s 4d be distributed to the poor on the day of his burial, thus ensuring a suitably large congregation. He also makes bequests to the vicar of 'my church of Apilton in Rydale' and to John of Swinton, rector of St Edward in the suburbs of York (probably St Edward the Confessor on Tadcaster Road). Even his treasured possessions reflect his devout faith, leaving the Prior and Convent of Murton a set of 'Decretalium' (papal decrees), being 'letters emanating from a pope and making known a rule or decision concerning religious doctrine, Christian morals or church law'.[55] John Newton receives one book called Blessed Peter, and John Byot receives a breviary (a book of psalms, hymns, prayers etc. to be recited daily by clerics). John Percehay is obviously well educated, to the point where he is in the process of writing a book called 'Trevet', also left to John Newton, and described as 'not yet fully written'. The majority of his goods go to his wife Isabell, who he is quite happy to appoint as his executrix. Sadly neither of their wills mentions any children, either because they never had any, or because they are already deceased.

The family's dedication to their faith continues with the nephew of John and Isabell, Sir Robert Percehay, son and heir of Sir William. Sir Robert and a Robert de Newby (a chaplain) apply to the crown for a licence[56] to found a chantry (a chapel or altar within a holy building endowed for the celebration of masses for the founder's soul) with one chaplain to pray for the king, the said Roberts, John of Ryther, and for the souls of Sir William Percehay, Margaret of Ruston and others.[57] This chantry was dedicated to St Mary Magdalen and situated within the Charnel in

9

the parish of Scarborough.[58] It is not known why this particular location was chosen for a second, or even third, Percehay chantry, the first still being in use in their house at Ryton, and another created at some point before 1516 when Lyon Percehay's will mentions 'my chauntry in Kirkeby Mysperton'.[59] There is also no information to say why the king, Richard II, also founded a chantry in the same charnel a short time later on 16 June 1395.[60] He arranges for 6 marks (mark = 13s 4d) to be granted 'from the issues and profits of that county' to Robert de Newby and his successors to pray for him and the souls of his father and mother, his late queen, Anne of Bohemia (died 1394), and others. Whatever the circumstances, there can be little doubt that Richard II was at least aware of the existence of the Percehays. It has to be noted also that Henry IV continued to grant the payment to the chaplain of the day for prayers to be said for Richard etc.[61] This may have been an act of contrition in view of the suspicious death of Richard while in the care of Henry in Pontefract castle – still a matter of some debate. The king of the day, at least up to 1460, and the Percehays continued to support this chantry until the Dissolution. By that time it is referred to as Percehays' chantry, and the Chantry Surveys for Henry VIII in 1546 show that there are still lands associated with it, originally provided by the Percehays, giving a yearly living of 15s.[62] It had also contained 'certen goodes and plate to the value of lvis. iiijd' (56s 4d), but William Percehay had the foresight to remove these well before Henry could get his hands on them!

Sir Robert Percehay no doubt continued in some of his father's various positions as a public servant, but in May 1398 the Sheriff of Yorkshire was instructed to organise the election of a new coroner as Robert Percehay, knight, was too sick to perform his duties.[63] Whatever his ailment, he is alive and well in 1402 when he is appointed as one of the collectors of yet another tax.[64] Robert should have had a nice quiet life living off his many sinecures and taking advantage of his father's legacy but unfortunately, for some unknown reason, he decides to style himself Persay rather than Percehay. It is possible that he still intended this to sound like 'Per-s-ay', but it is also possible that he was trying to appear 'English' rather than having French ancestry, especially in view of the continual conflict with France. Whatever the reason for the name, and why this variation was chosen (many others were tried later), it was simply the wrong name to be called when the king was looking for anyone even vaguely involved with the Percy Rebellion in 1405. An examination of the public records, especially the Calendar of Close Rolls from Henry IV dated 24 November 1407 at Gloucester, clarifies the events involving Robert Percehay. The main point is that Robert almost certainly was not involved in the rebellion in any way. The example of Richard Scrope, Archbishop of York, and his execution for treason, and the pursuit of Henry Percy, Earl of Northumberland, and his eventual death three years later in battle against the king's forces at Bramham Moor, can leave no doubt that if someone calling themselves Persay (however it was pronounced) had been involved in the rebellion he would have lost his head. The records show that Robert came very close, despite the fact that he must have been innocent. Initially 'Robert Pershay knight who on 1 May 6 Hen IV [1405] raised an insurrection against the king contrary to his allegiance' lost his manors of Levisham and Wrelton, but behind the scenes some frantic negotiations must have taken place because 'by letters patent of 17 February following the king pardoned him, by name of Robert Percehay knight'. It was not until 24 November 1407 at Gloucester that the king's hand was formally removed from Levisham and Wrelton and 'Robert Percehay' regained all he had forfeited, including the office of a Chief Forester of Pickeringlythe, once 'the matter fully understood'. Perhaps Sir Robert was not the brightest knight, or perhaps he was just stubborn, because despite the clear insistence by the king that he should be known as Percehay, he seems to continue to use his own version, leaving his will of 1426 in the name of 'Robert Persey' knight.[65] There can be no doubt that this is Robert Percehay, as the brief will does mention Ryton, and he names his wife as Elizabeth (confirmed by Agnes of Lockton, his sister, in her will[66]) and his sons John and George.

One legacy that Robert did leave was confusion about the name Percehay, although his son and heir John does stick with Percehay, the name used for all the members of the family in the 'tax returns' of 1428,[67] and still in use by the same 'John Percehay of Riton esq.' in 1451.[68] However, between John and 'Leo Percye' in 1511,[69] there are many name variations including Persay, Persey, Parsy, Pershey, Perche, Pershay, Parchay and Perchay, but everyone of them can be connected to Ryton and are of the Percehay family. By 1518[70] the family return to Percehay, Percehey, or some very close equivalent, and the last male of the line leaves 'Christopher Percehay' clearly engraved on the chalice he gave to St Michael's church, Malton in 1705.[71] The confusion regarding the name has not been helped by previous translators and transcribers who decided that the above variations must surely indicate some connection with the Northumberland Percys, even though they had no idea what the connection might be. The evidence clearly shows however that they were a totally separate family with no mutual connections, but unfortunately a number of references to the Percehay family have been permanently written into the Percy index of history and are effectively lost.[72] It is perhaps because of this that there are so few books or papers with references to the Percehays (or Percys identifiable as Percehays of Ryton) for the period from 1450 to 1499. In fact during that time, our knowledge of the family is dependent almost exclusively on the Duchy of Lancaster Records, as transcribed in the four volumes of the North Riding Records Yorkshire, New Series (NRRY/NS) printed from 1894, concerning the Forest of Pickering. This was a very large administrative area and need not necessarily have contained forest as we understand it today, a 'forest' being, according to the OED, 'an area typically owned by the sovereign and partly wooded, kept for hunting, and having its own laws'. It was primarily yet another implement used to extract taxes from the area.

The position of Forester in Fee in the Forest of Pickering came to the Percehays by Roger de Wrelton's marriage to Joan Percehay. The early death of both their son, Alan de Wrelton, and of Roger himself, without other heirs, resulted in the position being passed to the Percehays. The position is shared between William de Percehay (who then holds the estate of Alan de Wrelton) and Lady Parnell de Kingthorpe (yet another female with real power) who jointly confirm their claims to these positions in October 1334.[73] The right to pass on this hereditary position to another family by marriage must have been agreed with the appropriate court because in 1340 Sir William Percehay's position is confirmed.[74] However, although the Percehays are still active in the running of the Forest of Pickering during the 15th century, by 1494 Lionell Percehay's title is 'keeper of our Park of Blandesby', being just a part of the Forest north of Pickering, so perhaps by then the importance of both the role and the 'Forest' has reduced and the family only look after that part of the Forest. The area had its own courts and rules specifically intended to protect the Earl's (of Lancaster) interests, especially the game and 'vert' or (green)wood. The Forester in Fee was in overall charge of the Forest, paying a yearly rent entitling him to certain privileges. William and Parnell both claim, among other things, 'escapes … browsewood, drywood and nutgeld [a tax on nuts] throughout their whole bailiwick in the Earl's demesne', paying each 'the yearly rent of £1 to the Earl and his heirs'. However, despite being in overall charge, the Forester in Fee was subject to the same rules and courts as everyone, and occasionally the Percehays had to answer for their actions. In 1340, 'Sir William de Percehay, forester in fee, is found guilty of cutting off more than the browsewood, which he was allowed as a perk, and the verderers and regarders say he took much larger branches.'[75] He is sentenced to be imprisoned and his office seized. Afterwards, at his request, he is 'permitted to compound for his offences and for the restoration of his office at the sum of 13s 4d'. There are several occasions when the Percehays 'take too much wood', and in 1488–89, 'Raufe Persey took viij [8] loade of woode without licence'.[76] They even have the effrontery to kill the Earl's deer: '20 January 1503 Item a hind slayn in Hirkom [Horcom] by Roger Cholmeley and Thomas Pershay'.[77] Initially the position of Forester in Fee would have been very profitable, with minimal duties and responsibilities, and although some of the traditional customs are recorded as late as 1622,[78] the management of the estate of the Duchy of Lancaster eventually reverted back to the Crown.

The only other reliable source of information regarding the Percehays of Ryton during the period 1450–99 is the pedigrees declared at the Visitations of the Heralds as detailed in the references for their coats of arms. Although these are not recorded until some time after the events, they do seem to agree with other, earlier records when they can be cross-referenced. From these Visitations it is clear that, despite their ups and downs, the gentry of the area always desired to be associated with this family that had mingled with royalty and married daughters of barons; even today there is serious social kudos associated with marrying into 'old money'. It is known that Sir John Percehay married Alice, a daughter and heir of the Lound family who could also take their lineage back to Edward I at least, and John and Alice produce a son and heir Edmund who was born before 1427. He does not seem to be based at Ryton as an adult because he is 'of Flixborough Parke', having married Isabell Fauconbridge (Falconberg/Fauconberg), a marriage that recombined the lands of Sir Robert Darcy in north Lincolnshire that had been divided between his two daughters.[79] In fact both Edmund and Isabell were great-grandchildren of Sir Robert Darcy, being the nearest known direct blood relatives to marry; the introduction to the Percehay pedigree explains some of the confusion caused by the use of familiar terms such as 'cousin' having very different meanings in earlier times. Edmund's son and heir, Sir Lyon, is well documented in the Forest of Pickering records, so it is assumed he moved back to Ryton on the death of his grandfather, Sir John, his father Edmund already being deceased. Sir Lyon also marries well, being matched with Anne, daughter of Sir Ralph Babthorpe, although it would appear that his uncle, another John, brother of Edmund, had married Anne's widowed sister Elizabeth, so he was already related to this notable East Yorkshire family.

Decline

The fortunes of the Percehay family begin to deteriorate just after the death of this Sir Lyon (sometimes Lyonell or Leo)[80] who is 'late' by 10 December 1494.[81] No reason is known for this deterioration, although as will be seen, serious financial problems occur again when the head of the family is more generous with his dowries and bequests than his estate can support, so perhaps there was a similar occurrence at this time. Unfortunately this is one of the periods when little is known about females in the family. The Forest of Pickering records show that Sir Lyon had at least five brothers, but it has not been possible to name any of his sisters. While in theory he may not have had any, and indeed the only offspring named by the family are Leo and William, it can be deduced from the pedigrees of others that he had at least one married daughter. The desire to look after the non-inheriting children, both male and female, may have been at least part of the reason that his son and heir, another Lyon (usually Leo, but also Lyon and Lionell), is having

to sell 'a messuage [dwelling] with lands in Beverley' in 1499.[82] Sometime after 1504 this Lyon is trying to recover money he is owed, and his son and heir, Walter, is also in dispute with Sir James Strangways concerning the deeds for the manor of Potto that they both part-own.[83] This latter problem seems to be resolved by the marriage of Walter's sister, Ann, who becomes the second wife of James, second son of Sir James Strangways, but ultimately it results in the loss of their part of Potto. The Yorkshire Fines also confirm that Leo and his wife Katherine, daughter of Sir John Hotham of Scorborough (near Hull), sell the manor of Brantingham with lands there and in Thorp, Ellercar, North Cave, Swynton and Hull in 1507, and shortly afterwards (1510–11) they sell the manor of Hessle, with a mill and land in Hessle and more land in Hull. These were significant possessions worth a considerable amount of money by any standards. This reduction in the number of properties belonging to the Percehay family of Ryton is in addition to losing all the Lincolnshire possessions which seem to have gone to Leo's brother William, who has married Elizabeth, daughter and sole heir of Walter Hynd of Barton upon Humber.[84] This Lincolnshire line eventually distances itself from the Ryton family, ironically adopting Percy as their preferred surname.

The situation becomes even more complicated on the death of the second Lyon Percehay of Ryton whose will is proved 20 May 1517.[85] For some unspecified reason, a device known as a 'Common Recovery' is used to hold his lands in trust. It was believed that this 'legal process … by which entailed estate may be transferred from one person to another, based on a legal fiction involving the collusive default of a third party' would permit his second son, William, to inherit ahead of his first son, Walter. By this date Walter has probably already lost his wife Joan, daughter of Sir John Pykeryng. Their marriage had been contracted as early as 14 July 1487[86] and the family's declared pedigrees always show Walter as 'died without issue'. If it was the case that he had no heir, then every effort would have been made to break the 'entail' to the first male (i.e. Walter) that the possessions were supposed to pass down to, although the Common Recovery is now thought to have been unnecessary. In the case of the Percehays, similar situations had arisen before, and would do so again, without impacting the succession to the second (and even third) son. All that is known is that Lyon's will includes reference to an agreement made earlier (Easter term 1516) that 'Lorde Willuthby, John Vavasor, Jambs Mallyver and Peter Percehay [his youngest son] … recovered all my manors, landes and tenements agaynst me, Lyon Percehay and Kateryn my wyffe and Walter Percehay my son, by wright of entre only for thentente [the intent] of performance of this my last will'.[87] Effectively these trustees oversee the distributions he specifies in his will, with the residue being held for the benefit of his son William, as specified in the marriage contract agreed with John Vavasor of York (dated 20 February 1511/12) relating to his daughter Joan and William Percehay.

Having engineered the situation where everything passes to William, but is held in trust, something goes seriously wrong. As early as May 1518 William is being summoned for a debt of £200 owed to Robert and William Constable.[88] Unfortunately, as is usual with these documents, the reason for the debt is not given, but there seems little doubt that the money is owed by William (perhaps on behalf of the family). He is arrested, escapes,[89] but is eventually tried, although the sentence (again as is usual) is not recorded. To put this debt into perspective, at the court hearing William is only held to have the manor of Kingthorpe in his own name. This consisted of the manor, '10 messuages, 40 acres of land, 100 acres of meadow, 100 acres of woodland, 40 acres of pasture, and a rent of 4s', with the manor deemed to be worth 40s (£2) a year, and the messuages, land etc. another 40s a year, meaning he had a yearly income of just £4 against a debt of £200. Although the Common Recovery kept most of the Percehay possessions nominally separated from William, the family must have wanted to protect their good name, and perhaps he was not really responsible for the original debt. Consequently, between 1519 and 1522[90] William and his wife Joan are permitted to sell manors and lands to clear the debt, including Wrelton, Aislaby, Middleton, Crambe, Swinton, Hildenley, Over Howton, Wolfreton, Hessle, Kirk Ella, West Ella, and Swanland. In fact, by the end of 1522, the Percehay empire has been reduced to little more than their manor of Ryton. The court case also has consequences for the Strangways family. Thomas is Sheriff of York at the time and his brother James is under-Sheriff, and between them they are in charge of the jail at the Castle in York. Not surprisingly, Robert and William Constable ask them to explain in the Court of Chancery why William Percehay managed to abscond.[91] Sadly the document is partly illegible to the point of being of little use, so it is not known if the family connection between prisoner and gaoler is mentioned, but of course all concerned would have known that William Percehay's sister Ann was, at the time, the second wife of this James Strangways![92]

Life was clearly difficult for the Percehay family, but their troubles were compounded by the actions of their immediate neighbours who took advantage of their difficult situation. The fact that the worst of these troubles were caused by church institutions that considered themselves above the law perhaps shows why the teachings of people like Martin Luther were gaining ground. Some of the details of three pleadings to the Court of Star Chamber at the time of Henry VIII still exist and give an indication of the problems. The Percehay family had, for centuries ('tyme oute of mynde of man'),[93] had certain rights in the common called 'Mares More' (Marishes Moor) below Pickering. These rights included the digging of turves for fuel, but on 20 June 1519, over 30 men from the 'house and monastery of Revale' (Rievaulx) had 'with force and armes in ryottouse maner' used seven waynes (wagons) to steal the turves the Percehays had already 'caused to be dygged'. This type of crime would normally have been dealt with locally at a lower court, but William Percehay clearly thinks the Abbot and his servants would exert undue influence. Whatever the outcome, the case was taken seriously enough for the parties to be summoned 'by writs of privy seal to be before the King and his council at Westminster', with a penalty of £100 for non-attendance. Clearly there was a case to answer and the principle of the monasteries having to obey the laws of the land had to be tested.

The next case is much more serious and shows a total disregard for human life by the monastery at Rievaulx and its servants, and how law and order at a local level had effectively broken down.[94] The case is listed as 'Tailour v Chomley' and again concerns rights and traditions relating to the Forest of Pickering.[95] Unusually, some of both the complaint and the replies are given, but not the verdict. By the time of this case the Abbot of Rievaulx, via his tenant Roger Cholmeley,

13

seems to be renting out the profits from the Forest and is trying to recover the payment of 'Hungeld'[96] from the Percehays and the inhabitants of Ryton. The records for the Forest clearly show that Ryton (among others) 'these do only sute unto the honor but yelde no rente',[97] which is hardly surprising as for most of the past 200 years the Percehays had been Foresters in Fee. However, to get round this the Abbot petitioned the courts for this tax to be applied, knowing he was effectively asking the same Roger Cholmeley, who was also bailiff for the area. Not surprisingly the Abbot won the case, so when the Percehays refused to pay, Roger Cholmeley arranged for the payment to be taken by force in the form of cattle. When challenged, his men said to the people of Ryton 'they would thrust them yn wyth ther daggers and other wepons', and 'so in ryottous manner they drove furth ther cattall'. During the attempt to rescue their cattle Robert Tailour was first shot with an arrow and then 'one of the morderas, whos name ys called John Forman, cam unto the said Robert, lying upon the grounde, wyth pyked staffe, not feryng God nor Youer lawes, but ther strake his nekke boune a sowndre [asunder]'. Six other men of Ryton were badly injured 'and are like to die'. To compound this situation, the inquest the next day was conducted by the local coroner, none other than the same Roger Cholmeley, who not surprisingly concluded that Robert Tailour was killed by misadventure with stray arrows from his own riotous company. The friends of Robert cried foul and asked the coroner for Yorkshire to hold an independent inquest, but Roger Cholmeley imprisoned half the jury that had been formed before they could give their verdict. Whatever the outcome, it is clear that Ryton never did pay the Hungeld!

The final case from the Star Chamber refers to an incident in August 1533[98] when William Percehay is attacked by men on behalf of the Prior of Malton 'beryng inward malyce and dyspleasor' to the said William. During this disturbance William is saved by one of his kinsmen, Roger Percehay, who was 'sore bette and woundyd, and hym utterly for ever maheymyd [maimed] in cutting of his thye assonder, and hym then and their lefte for dede'. Again the position of the perpetrator, this time the Prior, is used to accuse William of actually causing the disturbance. Once again William has to complain to the Justices of the Assize to have the case heard in the Star Chamber. Of the three accused, one says he was there by coincidence and didn't know what was going to happen. Canon John Jackson agrees that one of his colleagues, Robert Cremer, was involved but knows nothing about any payment after his death to Cremer's brother by the Prior. William, Prior of Malton, just says he knew nothing about anyone called Robert Cremer. Again, whatever the reality, it is clear that the rule of law and order could be manipulated by those with power and position, with the law of the country now concentrated in the hands of a few people who felt they could do as they pleased, and frequently did.

In addition to all these incidents, the financial problems of William Percehay never seem to be completely resolved and he continues to sell property, but now it diminishes his holdings in Ryton itself. In 1527 he sells land to the east of Ryton (the area of today's Rye House, Abbott's Farm and Swan Nest) and in 1533 he sells the rest of the land to the east of the village (today's Longlands, Sleightholme Farm and Bulmer Farm).[99] By 1535 he and his then wife Elizabeth even have to sell the whole of the West Field to his sister and her husband, Robert Crayke.[100] This last transaction may have been required to pay the legal fees for a very odd court case that William had to pursue in order to retain any of his property. William goes to the Court of Chancery, pleading directly to Sir Thomas Audley as Lord Chancellor, to stop an imposter who is claiming to be the rightful heir to William's now deceased brother, Walter. The original court document is faded, difficult to read, and unfortunately a strip has disintegrated down the right-hand side meaning no line is actually complete.[101] However, when read with all the other information available, especially the Percehay pedigrees, it becomes clear that someone called 'Robert Maunsell otherwise namyng hymself Per[cehay]'[102] is asked by William Percehay to provide the 'Charters and Evydences' to support his claim to the manor of Ryton (etc). This Robert clearly fails to do this, and the Yorkshire Fine of Trinity 27 Hen VIII (1535), whose original is still preserved,[103] shows that 'Robert Percehey de Potto Gent', now thought to be this Robert Maunsell using an alias, has to quitclaim to William and Elizabeth the 'Manor of Riton and 30 messuages with lands in Riton, Kirby Misperton, Barght, Habton, and New Malton; also the advowsons of the chantries of Holy Trinity in Kyrby Misperton and St Marie Magdalene in Skarborghe'. However, this Robert continues to cause problems by going to the Yorkshire Star Chamber in October 1535,[104] this time referred to as Robert Persey, but almost certainly the same Robert Maunsell, complaining of being evicted from the manor of Potto by Anne Strangwythe (Strangways), who is, of course, William's sister and entitled to Potto from her father's will; and from the Manor of 'Hyldyngley' by Sir Roger Cholmeley, who legitimately bought Hildenley from the Percehays in 1522. Once again this Robert fails in his attempt and has to quitclaim both manors,[105] but it serves to emphasise just how important it was to be able to prove ownership, and is the reason that so many records concerning land transactions still exist. Although it is not known who this Robert Maunsell really was, it may be significant that some time later a Robert Maunsell, using the alias of Robert Rouff, is also involved in a similar dispute about the tenancy of the manor of Roundhill in Wincanton (Somerset),[106] suggesting Robert Maunsell was simply an opportunist.

With all these problems William had had a difficult life, so it is surprising to find he is still a well-respected, active member of the Yorkshire gentry. Unfortunately this meant he became involved with the unrest, partly caused by Henry's Dissolution of the Monasteries, that culminated in the Pilgrimage of Grace. There was much more to this uprising than religion and royal divorce, and it was probably the greatest threat encountered by Henry VIII in his entire reign. Not only were the northern rebels conservative by nature and reluctant to move from the 'true faith' and its associated traditions, but there was a real feeling that the region was ignored by a remote government in Westminster (has anything changed?). There was also the realisation that Henry's motives were more financial than religious, leaving the north even more depleted financially after the wealth of the church institutions had been effectively taken south to London. Whatever the background, it would appear that William Percehay of Ryton was one of the rebel leaders[107] and he was instrumental in persuading Sir Thomas Percy to join the rebels in October 1536.[108] Thomas had been trying to return secretly to his wife and children at their home in Prudhoe Castle and had met William Percehay by chance. The rebels were desperate for leaders of stature and the much-quoted phrase 'thousands for a Percy' gives an indication of the importance placed on persuading a reluctant Sir Thomas to join the rebel cause. It is suggested that William Percehay pressurised Sir Thomas, threatening the well-being of his mother at her home in Seamer, resulting in him joining Aske, Latimer, Neville, Fairfax and others to lead what is now known as the Pilgrimage of Grace.[109] Little more is known about William's involvement, except that he does not lose his head. This may have had something to do with the fact that Henry Bradshawe, Solicitor General (later Attorney General) to Henry VIII, was married to Joan, sister of William's second wife, Elizabeth. In fact William seems to suffer few if any consequences of his involvement, and is next mentioned when he brings his men from Ryton to the muster at Barton Cross in 1539, suggesting he had already regained any positions he may have lost, and is certainly a free man.

The True Faith

William's second wife, Elizabeth, seems to come complete with a daughter, Anne, from her previous marriage to William Tyrswick (or Tynswyke), a Merchant Adventurer of London. This Anne eventually marries Robert, son and heir of William Percehay by his first wife Joan, so they are not related by blood, but he is actually her step-brother. While this connection is not specified in their pedigrees, it can be deduced from other documents, including Elizabeth's will of 1566[110] which is a valuable source for the Percehay family's connections at that time. Their relative poverty compared to earlier times, and the eventful life of William, do not seem to have affected their standing in society. Elizabeth and William's son Leonard inherits the family possessions from his half brother Robert, who died young without heirs, and he marries Prudence Spencer. She is a daughter of Thomas Spencer from Bedfordshire (a branch of the same family eventually produce Princess Diana) who had purchased extensive properties throughout Yorkshire, including Old Malton from Martin Anne,[111] another Percehay relative. (Martin was the son of John Anne of Frickley, whose second wife was Catherine, widow of Leon Percehay and grandmother of this Leonard.) Elizabeth and William's daughter, Christian, initially marries Richard Wood of Pickering (that family move via Copmanthorpe to Hollin Hall near Ripon), and after his death she marries Gawin Pollard (of the Pollards of Brompton). In fact the 'quality' of the gentry wanting to marry with the Percehays remains undiminished throughout, reflecting their significant position as the senior gentry of the area. It is no coincidence that the Percehay shield, depicted on the frieze by Sir William Fairfax in the Great Chamber at Gilling Castle in the 1580s, is in the most prominent position (top centre) on the heraldic tree for the gentlemen of the Wapentake of Ryedale cum Pickering Lythe.[112] It is remarkable that this Great Chamber still exists, almost in its original condition despite its chequered history over more than 400 years, making it one of *the* historic treasures of Ryedale and probably one of its best-kept secrets.

Another significant common cause binding the gentry of the area together was Catholicism. The break from Rome by Henry VIII not only removed the ultimate authority of the Pope, it outlawed many practices that a very conservative northern gentry considered sacrosanct, with the result that many (if not most) families found their own ways to continue these practices. Henry's son Edward, or rather his advisers, took a very reformist, protestant, anti-Catholic course, but he was followed immediately by his half-sister Mary's persecution of protestants and reunion with Rome. Elizabeth I tried to navigate a middle course of toleration for all, with herself as Supreme Governor of the Church of England, content that 'outward conformity by attendance at (her) church of a Sunday was enough; if men chose also to hear Roman mass privately or attend a sectarian meeting there would be no harm done'.[113] Unfortunately for the Catholics, the Pope seriously upset Elizabeth by excommunicating her in 1570, having supported her rivals during the Northern Rebellion of 1569 when an attempt was made to replace her with the Catholic Mary, Queen of Scots. As a result, it became an act of treason to be a Catholic priest in England and from this point all Catholics had a difficult time. However, despite everything, and especially the Percehays' earlier problems with the Abbot of Rievaulx and the Prior of Malton, most of the Percehay family and a large proportion of the gentry of the area secretly adhered to their faith, even if outwardly they complied with the demands of the Church and state. This mutual secret had the effect of binding the Catholic gentry together and was another reason to marry into like-minded families.

However, it has to be remembered that not all members of a family adhered to the old ways, and relatively few saw the need to express their Catholicism openly. Consequently, the available lists of recusants do not give a complete picture.[114] The Percehays kept a very low profile, rarely coming to the attention of the authorities. In 1590 William, third son of Leonard and Prudence, was reported for his infrequent attendance to church.[115] His fate is not known, but he is not mentioned in his mother's will of 1594 or any later document.[116] His younger brother Richard 'was admitted to the English College at Valladolid'[117] in Spain in 1604 at the age of only 14, to train as a missionary priest (Catholic of course) with the intention of returning to England. He moved on to the English College at Douai (between Lille and Arras) in 1610[118] to continue his Catholic education, but it is not known if he ever returned to England – he would have faced serious consequences if he had. The eldest brother of William and Richard, Thomas, may well have been a practising Catholic all his life, but he only confesses his faith and is prepared to take the consequences when he knows he is about to meet his maker. He was visiting his daughter Mary in York when he died and was buried at St Martin's Coney Street on 6 February 1625/6.[119] He had 'ended his days with a short burst of defiant open recusancy which landed him in gaol in 1626, the year of his death';[120] these dates suggest that he may even have died in gaol. The eldest son of this Thomas, another William, also felt the need to be committed to his faith, but he died before his father in 1620 while training to become a (Catholic) priest at the English College in Rome.[121]

One off-shoot of the family steered a very different course. By the time of the death of Lyon Percehay in 1517, the Lincolnshire possessions had passed to his brother William, then resident at Barton upon Humber. This branch of the family gradually changed their name to Percy, although they are still referred to as Percehay at the Visitations of 1584/5 and 1612. Information from these Visitations, and 'The Visitation of Yorkshire in the years 1563 & 1564 made by William Flower esq. Norroy King of Arms', published by The Harleian Society,[122] where extensive footnotes are added, shows that Richard, a grandson of this William, became a distinguished lawyer at the Exchequer Court of York, and the Rector of Settrington from 1591 to his death in 1598. He was educated at Christ Church College Oxford from 1552 where he gained his BA in 1556 and his MA in 1558.[123] He went on to qualify as a Bachelor of Civil Law and Doctor of Civil Law, being described as 'the best qualified York ecclesiastical lawyer of the day and a strong Protestant' by Aveling. In fact this Richard, now calling himself Richard Percy, was connected at the highest level, helping to educate Archbishop Sandy's eldest son Edwin[124] and becoming Vicar General,[125] the Archbishop's representative in matters of jurisdiction. Fortunately his Catholic relatives at Ryton do not seem to have come to his attention!

There were many reasons why the Percehays went to great lengths to conceal their Catholicism, not least the expense of the associated extra 'taxes' imposed on recusants. The family were already in much-reduced circumstances and could ill afford to lose what little they still had. They also benefited, both socially and financially, from holding public offices, a privilege denied to Catholics until 1829 and the passing of the Roman Catholic Relief Act. Leonard Percehay still had some influence within the administration of the Forest of Pickering, being listed as a juror in 1577[126] and no doubt held other sinecures considered to be his birthright. The Percehay who left most records of his public offices was Leonard's grandson, Christopher, son of Thomas. His career didn't have the most auspicious beginning, with the first record showing that he had to pay the notorious composition for not taking his knighthood at the coronation of Charles I.[127] This had been a devious plan by Charles to obtain revenue without the need to go through Parliament. The quoted reference gives full details of the ruse employed, but all freeholders with an income of more than £40 per annum were invited to attend a ceremony in London on 31 January 1626, but this proclamation was not published in Yorkshire until 30 January 1626, making it impossible to attend. All those not present were fined for this insult to the sovereign. A foolproof plan, but it may explain why the date for the execution of Charles was later set by Parliament as 30 January (1648). Despite this, Christopher Percehay served as a Justice of the Peace under Charles and he was 'one of the few pre-1642 Justices who came back to serve the Parliament'.[128] In fact Christopher was very active during the Interregnum, serving for the whole period.[129] Among his many duties he was a member of the Committee in Yorkshire complaining about the 'oppressions and exactions of the Scots army' in 1645;[130] he was added to the Committee for the North Riding for the 'Assessment of the Ninety Thousand Pounds' in 1649;[131] appointed to the Committee for the County of York to raise £5217-6-8 in 1652;[132] one of the Yorkshire Commissioners of Sequestrations in 1655/6;[133] and a Commissioner for the assessment of £3043-8-10 for Yorkshire and the City at the end of the Interregnum in 1660.[134] This Christopher must have been quite a diplomat because he continued in public office after the Restoration of Charles II, when he was appointed 'Receiver General of the rents of delinquents estates sequestered and two thirds of the estates of the Popish recusants for Yorkshire', an office he still held in October 1661.[135]

Appointing Christopher to this latter position may indicate that he had embraced the new religion, but his inclusion with his son in the list of non-communicants at the parish church of Kirby Misperton in 1663 does require some explanation as there are a number of possibilities.[136] An obvious one is that the family were temporarily resident in York, perhaps with his sister Mary's family in Coney Street, as all his positions were based in York. In fact it is possible that Christopher had seen very little of his manor house at Ryton for the previous 20 years. Even if he had been at Ryton at Easter (the date mentioned by the Rector and the one time, of the minimum three in the year, when communion was supposed to be taken[137]), he may well have attended the parish church of St Mary at Old Malton. This church is nearer to, and more accessible from Ryton and had been the family church for centuries. There was also a developing problem concerning the payment of tithes to Kirby Misperton, which were meant to be paid at that service, although it was not until 1671 that this dispute went to court.[138] Whatever the explanation, no action was taken and the Percehays are not mentioned again in this context.

Death, Debt and Inheritance

This Christopher Percehay encountered considerable personal losses at around the time of the Restoration. The Kirby Misperton parish registers for

1658–72 record the burial of 'Mrs. Frances Percehay wife of Christopher Percehay of Riton esq.' on 11 January 1658/9. His grandson Christopher Percehay (no.4), the first and ultimately the only son of his second son (Christopher no.2), is born on 30 December 1660 but does not survive infancy and is buried on 9 February 1661/2. From the same registers it can be seen that he loses another grandson, Percyhay Hayme, son of his eldest daughter Frances (wife of John Hayme of Wrelton) in March 1660, and she is also buried at Kirby Misperton on 2 March 1662/3. Only 11 days later he buries another grandson, Christopher Dove, son of his third daughter Ursula (wife of William Dove of Appleton). A later document[139] shows that he also lost his eldest son Walter, who died intestate in February 1660/1, having previously lost his second daughter Milcah (wife of Arthur Jegon) – 'dyeing about Michaelmas 1657'. Thus in just over five years Christopher Percehay has lost his wife, his eldest son, two daughters and three grandsons, and by the time of his death (buried at Kirby Misperton 20 September 1669) he has only one surviving grandson with the Percehay name. This is yet another Christopher (no.3 of the four alive in 1661) who is only 15 years old. By then the continuation of the Percehay line rests entirely with him as he has no brothers, and although his uncle Christopher (no.2) remains married for a further 30 years to Susannah, daughter of Robert Gere of Barugh and already widow to Thomas Vaughan of Whitwell, the records show that they did not produce any more children after the death of Christopher no.4 and none is mentioned in his will.[140] All this responsibility at such a young age cannot have been easy for Christopher no.3 to deal with, and life is made even more difficult when he becomes embroiled in expensive litigation. Barely a year after his grandfather's death, and at the age of only 17, the issue of tithes comes to court in 1671.[141] Leonard Conyers has just taken over as rector at Kirby Misperton and he is trying to make his position more lucrative. A search of the Cause Papers, being the record of the Diocesan Courts of the Archbishop of York 1300–1858,[142] shows that between 1671 and 1700 ten parishes in Ryedale generate only three cases for this court between them.[143] Leonard Conyers instigated nine from Kirby Misperton, and all were attempts to generate more tithe income than any previous incumbent. Perhaps his low point was when he took Jane, the widow of Thomas Harrison, to court to recover (among other things) his fee for the burial of her husband – 'the sume of 1s 2d according to the custome or prescription'[144] – despite the fact that he clearly didn't perform the service and he could say only vaguely when Thomas died ('in or about the months of September, October or November 1680'), suggesting that he was not even resident at the time. It has to be noted that despite making an agreement in 1671 with the Percehays through an arbitration panel for a composition (fixed payment) of £8 per annum to cover all the disputed tithes, Conyers still brings it back to court again in 1673, 1674 and 1675, although he must have failed in his attempts to increase the payment as £8 is the amount still being paid when tithes were abolished in the 20th century.[145] At this time Leonard Conyers was running what amounted to his own equivalent of the hearth tax, charging every parishioner one *ob* (half a penny) per annum for his smoke tax in lieu of tithes on fuel,[146] and he made a similar charge on every person over 16 years of age, being the equivalent of a poll tax;[147] neither of these taxes can possibly have been legal and even at the time must have seemed indefensible and particularly avaricious.

However, even more critical problems were brewing for Christopher no.3 with his own relations. Over the previous century the Percehay family had married well: his great-grandfather Thomas had married into the Wyvill family (twice); his grandfather into the Strickland family; his father into the Staveley and Grant families from the Ripon area; and Christopher himself made a very good match with Elizabeth Tankard (see Chapter 3). These alliances would have improved the Percehays' financial position, but in return they provided the status of being associated with a family whose lineage went back to Domesday. Consequently, grandfather Christopher had bought back some of his ancestors' Ryton properties, specifically Longlands and its associated 'Mansion House', but they were still relatively poor, and the problem of providing 'settlements' for the daughters of the Percehay family had been accumulating for some time. Grandfather Christopher had three sisters and two half-sisters who survived into adulthood and married (see Chapter 3), and they would all have received some settlement as their 'portion' of the family possessions. The next generation was also predominantly female

– son and heir Walter had four sisters but only one brother. It is his grandfather Christopher's settlements for these daughters that seems to be more than Christopher no.3 can afford to pay from the Ryton estate, especially as the then-deceased Walter's wife, Barbara, is receiving an extremely generous settlement on her re-marriage. Even worse, Walter's brother, Christopher no.2, also has to be provided for despite marrying a woman of substance.

Three surviving court documents provide some of the details concerning Christopher no.3's difficulties, but the information is not complete so care must be taken before conclusions are drawn.[148] Even at the time not all the relevant documents were produced, either because they were lost, or to give an advantage as is alleged in one of them. The first document (NA C10/491/137) is from 1670 and seems to be the result of a claim from Anne Jegon, second wife and widow of the then-deceased Arthur Jegon who had previously been husband of the also deceased Milcah Percehay, who wants the £200 still owing to her dead husband from Milcah's original marriage settlement. The document is actually a counter-claim from Christopher no.2, as administrator for grandfather Christopher and Barbara, mother of Christopher no.3 and the widow and administrator of Walter, who both say the money has already been paid, or should have been, by Christopher no.3. Consequently they make the claim 'that the said Anne Jegon and Christopher Percehay the younger combyneing and confederating themselves to defeat and defraud' them of the £200. These are strong words to use against your own nephew and son, especially as he is then just 16 years old. However, the next document (NA C10/139/37), from 1680, rather suggests they were right, as Christopher Percehay no.3 has had to pay the outstanding £200 by Lady Day (25 March) 1673. Perhaps it is best not to speculate about the true relationship between Christopher no.3 and the (young?) widow Anne!

Document NA C10/139/37 also concerns a claim from the heir of another deceased aunt, Frances Hayme,[149] against Christopher no.3. Christopher Hayme, son of Frances nee Percehay, thinks he is entitled to his mother's £30 p.a. until her marriage settlement of £300 is fully paid. This document very conveniently also lists all the other outstanding commitments on the Ryton estate. These included £100 p.a. to his widowed mother Barbara, despite the fact that she was already re-married to yet another Wyvill; £50 p.a. to his uncle Christopher no.2; £30 to the Hayme family that was clearly not being paid; £40 p.a. to each of the families of the other two aunts, Ursula Dove and Elizabeth Sympson; and at least £8 p.a. in tithes, giving a total of £268 p.a. This has to be viewed against the income from the whole of the Ryton estate of only £250 per annum. Clearly Christopher had an annual shortfall and zero income for himself, although he does have other income from properties brought to the family by Barbara, his mother, but these are conveniently ignored (and they may not generate the £100 p.a. going back to Barbara anyway). This situation eventually resulted in the need for a loan, so he turned to gentlemen from the Merchant Adventurers, as it was businessmen like them who provided such services in the days before high street banks. The loan of £1556–5s is detailed in NA C5/590/48, dated 23 October 1705, and it is this third document that catalogues the ensuing downward spiral. The original loan is made by a John Ramsden in 1685 who took all Christopher's possessions as collateral. In February 1687/8 the debt is transferred to Michael Barstow who extends the loan by another £943–15s, making the total outstanding £2500 (plus interest). In July 1690 the debt is extended by another £600, and by yet another £730 the following March. By now the debt is rapidly getting out of hand. Christopher Percehay dies a relatively young man some time between 1691 and the death of Michael Barstow in 1699, 'leaving onely two daughters viz. Barbara and Elizabeth his coheirs in their minority', indicating that his wife Elizabeth is already deceased. By 23 October 1705 Thomas Barstow, who was left the debt as his inheritance from his father Michael, realises he is never going to recoup either the original sum of £3830 or any of the interest that by then exceeds £1400; he also has the expense of effectively acting as guardian to the daughters, a situation which suggests that the rest of the Percehay relations have either disowned Christopher no.3 or they are avoiding being responsible for his debts. Consequently Thomas forecloses and takes possession of all the Percehay estates, and thus their connection with Ryton that had endured for over 500 years comes to an ignominious end …

But not quite! Christopher no.2 is still alive, although he has avoided being involved with the problems at Ryton. As noted earlier, he had his own problems since he had no children to carry on his line, although his wife Susannah had come complete with a daughter, Mary, from her first marriage to Thomas Vaughan of Whitwell. Mary should have inherited her late father's estate, and he had drawn up a document to make sure this happened,[150] but in 1660 other members of the Vaughan family possess the manor of Whitwell and refuse to hand over this document. The outcome is not known, but whatever happened, Christopher no.2 becomes a relatively wealthy man, and (ironically or perhaps significantly) in 1705 he and his wife can afford to give a stunning chalice to their local church in Malton (see Figure 3). It is inscribed 'The Gifte of Christopher Percehay of New Malton Esq. and Susannah his wife to the Church of St. Michaels 1705' and includes a shield with the Percehay coat of arms complete with the crest of a bull's head. It is hallmarked and has been identified as being made in York in 1702 by William Busfield. This would have been seriously expensive at the time, and consequently today it has to reside in a bank vault, but it is still used on special occasions. Christopher's will of 1708,[151] proved after his death in December 1711, also shows just how wealthy he had become. The cash bequests alone total £655 [multiply by 100 for approx current value], in addition to his real and personal estate. Included in his bequests were two donations of £10 each 'to be bestowed in a piece of plate in remembrance of me'. It is probable that one of these was used to purchase the pewter alms-dish still in use at Kirby Misperton church, actually commemorating the Chapel of St Oswald in his family's manor house at Ryton (see Figure 4 and Appendix 3). As well as being comfortably off, Christopher still circulated with the highest in society, although it helped that he was related to most of them (see Chapter 3). He quoted Sir William Strickland 3rd Baronet (son of his cousin Thomas) his 'particuler good friend', and one of the pieces of plate in his memory went to 'Sir William St Quintin and his good lady mother'; she just happened to be another cousin. The Palmes family, heirs to the Eures of Malton and noted Catholics, are also mentioned, again being related. He also provides for his late wife's daughter, Mary, now Mrs Brookes, and her married daughter, Hannabell, is then living with him; she is left the largest bequest of £300. Touchingly he also requests 'that my body may be buryed in St Michael's Church in New Malton aforesaid under the Communion table next to my dear wife a place being reserved of purpose'; here they both still rest.

The last known Percehay from Ryton would appear to survive until 1755. According to Aveling,[152] who was quoting 'Henry Maire the lawyer-genealogist', 'Barbara, the sole daughter and heiress of Christopher Percehay Esq of Ryton in Yorks by his wife a sister of Sir Thomas Tankard of Brampton bart.' was buried at St Pancras, London in 1755, aged 75. The marriage is known to have taken place on 2 July 1676,[153] so a birth date for Barbara in 1680 is feasible. The fact that Maire considered her the *only* daughter suggests that he had reason to believe Barbara's sister, Elizabeth, did not make it to adulthood. Not surprisingly, Barbara married a Catholic, one Thomas William Selby, and it is thought this Thomas and Barbara sold their interest in the manor of North Otterington to Sir Hugh Smithson in 1712.[154] This manor, along with Christopher no.3's interests in other properties in the area (Pickhill, Aynderby Steeple, Rocksby, Leeming, Exilby, Newton alias Scabbed Newton and Osmotherly) had all gone to Thomas Barstow in 1705, so it would appear that he not only became guardian to Barbara but he may also have provided her with some form of settlement on her marriage. One other possibility, however, is that the benefit of all these additional properties reverted back to the heirs of Barbara Staveley/Percehay/Wyvill on her death as she had provided them on her marriage to Walter Percehay, one of those heirs being Barbara Percehay/Selby.

Other Percehay lines may have emanated from the Ryton family, but none is known to survive. The Percehays who became Percys at Barton upon Humber have already been noted and some of their descendants may still exist but with the name Percy. There is a clear connection to the Percehays in the Devon, Dorset and Somerset area, with the Harleian Society connecting Caundel Haddon in Dorset in 1316 with Sir Walter de Persehay, who also had Crambe (his mother still held Ryton at the time).[155] This line dies out by the end of the 14th century, but not before 'Sir Henry Percehay Knight, born at Kitton in the parish of Holcombe Rogus, Sergent at Law, Baron of the Exchequer, Justice of the Common Pleas'[156] makes a significant (and much recorded) impact in the area. Relations also move to the London area, Robert Percehay, second son of Leonard and Prudence, being 'of Blackhurst Sussex, gent' when making his will in October 1625, although sadly he does not mention any children.[157] He also moved in august circles, having leases in Beauly Park and The Great Park of Petworth, and included Lord St John, Lady Wallingford, Sir Basil Brookes and Lord Viscount Montague among his friends. It is possible that his younger brother, 'Henry Citizen of London',[158] did produce male heirs, but none can be confirmed. A Stephen Percehay of London, Gentleman, who made his will on 1 September 1658 may have been one of his sons.[159] If so, then other Percehays likely followed and this line may still exist. If not, then Christopher Percehay no.2, who was buried under the Communion table, next to his dear wife Susannah, on 4 December 1711 at New Malton at the venerable age of 75, was indeed the last of a very long and illustrious line, being Lords of the Manor of Ryton for well over 500 years.

Notes

1. Aveling N/R; p184
2. William Camden, *Britannia* (1610 edn), p722
3. See Robert Maunsell later
4. NA E31/2/1/1628; folio 56V Great Domesday Book. Original spellings retained if quoting from documents.
5. YAS/RS EYC (Early Yorkshire Charters) vol.2; p368 First name may have been Walter, but not confirmed.
6. 'The Great Roll of the Exchequer' became known as the Pipe Rolls because the original documents were rolled up to be stored so they resembled pipes.
7. See Appendix 2
8. YAS/RS 61, p85; Compositions for not taking a knighthood.
9. Letters and papers Foreign & Domestic, Hen VIII, vol.14, part 1; Jan to July 1539
10. YAS/RS EYC vol.2; p395, from Pipe Roll 14 Hen II p85
11. YAS/RS EYC vol.1; p472 Bigod Fee
12. YAS/RS EYC vol.2; p43 Brus Fee
13. B.I. MF(E) 44 BM Cotton MS Claudius DXI f.102/3 – original in the British Library
14. Kindly conducted by Edward Waterson FRICS.
15. YAS/RS 121; Feet of Fines for the county of York from 1272 to 1300, p82, no.13; John Chambard gives Walter Percehaye all Hildingleye.
16. Y/F 1522, Easter term 14 Hen VIII; William Parcehay & Johanna sell manor of Heldyngley etc to Roger Cholmeley.
17. YAJ 69; Yorkshire Deeds vol.5, p72
18. From the *Oxford Dictionary of National Biography*. John may have died as early as 1287 but his Inquisition Post Mortem was 1289.
19. The Visitations of 1584–85 & 1612 by Glover & St George recognised six separate family coats of arms that they were allowed to add to their own, including that of the Vescis, so they seem to have been convinced of the connection. The 'Carta' (charters) were also recorded by them – probably Glover.
20. See Appendix 2
21. Calendar of Inquisitions Post Mortem: Vol 5, Edward II, pp307–12
22. Parliamentary Writs, from Harl/Soc Knights of Edward I (P-S) p45
23. YAS/RS 21; Yorkshire Lay Subsidies, p50
24. S/Soc 49; p380 Johanna Percehay is responsible for Crambe and Hildenly, but Ryton is not actually mentioned.
25. This tradition is also highlighted by Dame Elizabeth Beckwithe who retained this name despite being re-married to Christopher Kenn (NYCRO mic 3989 p169) as did Dame Elizabeth Compton when later married to both Walter Walshe and Philip Hobbey (NA C1/1005/45).
26. S/Soc 49; *Nomina Villarum*, p324 Walter holds part of Crambe, and p320 Joan holds Ryton.
27. S/Soc 151; Register of Wm Greenfield Lord Archbishop of York 1306–15 part 3, p60, no.1274 dated 7 April 1311. Oblation = offering, Obvention = income.
28. S/Soc 91; Yorkshire Chantry Surveys, vol.1, p128
29. NRRY/NS vol.3; Duchy of Lancaster Records (Coucher Book), pp82/3
30. Harl/Soc Knights of Edward 1, vol.4 (P–S), pp45–6 from the Patent Rolls
31. Harl/Soc Knights of Edward 1, vol.4 (P–S), pp45–6 from Parliamentary Writs
32. CofCR Edw III vol.7; 1343–46, p441 refers back to his appointment in 1338
33. Wells-Furby, B. (2013) *The Boroughbridge Roll of Arms reconsidered*
34. S/Soc 83; Rievaulx Chartulary, p289
35. S/Soc 4; Wills Registered at York part 1, pp6–7 (Walter) and pp53–4 (Agnes)
36. Known as the First Calais Roll; Textmanuscripts.com p1, and detailed on p160 of 'Some Feudal Coats of Arms' on the openlibrary.org
37. YAS/RS 91; Parliamentary Representation in the County of York, pp121–3 details over 30 references to Sir William.
38. NA C143/306/12; John de Melsa, knight, grants the manor of Levisham to William Percehay and Isobel his wife.
39. NRRY/NS vol.3; Duchy of Lancaster records, p23
40. In 1356 St Lucy's day (13 December) fell on a Tuesday, so the Charter was granted on Friday 16 December. Original charter still held at the Merchant Adventurers Hall.

41 Calendar of Patent Rolls (CofPR), 1346–49 p356 & Calendar of Fine Rolls (CofFR), 1347–56, p21
42 CofPR 1367–70, p200
43 Estimate from YAS/RS 91, p122
44 CofCR Edw III; Dec 1373 / CofCR Edw III vol.14 pp523–28 / CofCR Richard II vol.2 pp125–35 & pp283–96
45 Full list is on the wall of the High Sheriff's dining room at York Crown Court
46 CofPR 1374–77, p498, 1377–81 pp39, 301
47 CofFR 1377–83, p337
48 Calendar of Inquisitions Post Mortem, Edw III file 113, no.671
49 YAS/RS 74; p113, 1327–28 Lay Subsidy includes William Percehay at Wrelton who may well be this William.
50 YAS/RS 91; Parliamentary Representation in the County of York, p123
51 NA C136/36/10; Inquisitions Post Mortem, Series 1, Richard II
52 S/Soc 186; York Memorandum Book, f52
53 S/Soc 4; Wills Registered at York, p164
54 B.I. mic 913; York wills vol.3 fol 63, will dated 3rd September 1400 with probate 30th July 1401
55 *Mediae Latinitatis Lexicon Minus*, J F Niermeyer (2001), p309
56 NA C 143/423/30; Inquisitions *Ad Quod Damnum*, Henry III to Richard III, 17 Richard II (1393/4)
57 YAS/RS 129, pp113–14, and S/Soc 91; Yorks Chantry Surveys, p138
58 OED: charnel – a building or vault in which corpses or bones are piled
59 S/Soc 106; York Wills vol.6, p1
60 CofCR 20 Richard II part 1; membrane 33, 25 June at Westminster 1396 referring back to this date
61 CofPR 1 Hen IV; m15
62 S/Soc 91; Yorkshire Chantry Surveys, p138
63 CofCR Richard II vol.6; May 6 139
64 Feudal Aids 1284–1431 vol.6, 1923, p261
65 B.I. York Wills, mic 912, vol.2, fol.505
66 S/Soc 4; Wills registered at York, part 1, p165
67 Feudal Aids 1284–1431 vol.6, 1923, pp310, 314, 316, 317
68 YAS/RS 83; Yorkshire Deeds vol.7, p149
69 Y/F 1510–11, Hilary Term, 2 Henry VIII
70 NA C131/104/39; Chancery: Extents for Debts, Series 1, William Percehey vs Robert and William Constable
71 YAS Extra Series, no.3; Yorkshire Church Plate p133
72 e.g. *The Lord Lieutenants & High Sheriffs of Yorkshire 1066–2000* (2000) W M Ormrod (ed), p72 gives Sir William Percy as High Sheriff 1374–75 despite being clearly recorded as Sir William Perciehay of Ryton, who is easily identifiable.
73 NRRY/NS vol.3; p82
74 NRRY/NS vol.3; p23
75 NRRY/NS vol.3; p23
76 NRRY/NS vol.1; p162
77 NRRY/NS vol.2; p210
78 NRRY/NS vol.2; pp1–12
79 Full details in notes for Chapter 3
80 In all cases the name used on the document is the one used in this text.
81 NRRY/NS vol.1; p170
82 Y/F 1499, Easter term, 14 Hen VII
83 NA C1/346/4; Leon Persy of Ryton vs Guy Dawney, NA C1/154/68; Walter Parchay vs Sir James Strangways
84 Harl/Soc, Visitation of Yorkshire 1563 & 1564 by William Flower
85 S/Soc 106; A Selection of Wills from the Registry at York (vol.6), pp1–2
86 YAS/RS 45; Yorkshire Star Chamber Proceedings, pp181–4
87 S/Soc 106; A Selection of Wills from the Registry at York, pp1–2
88 NA C131/104/39; Chancery: Extents for Debts, Series 1, William Percehey vs Robert and William Constable
89 NA C1/486/61; Chancery pleadings: Robert and William Constable vs Thomas and James Strangwysshe
90 Y/F Hilary 10 Hen VIII, Trinity 12 Hen VIII, Hilary 13 Hen VIII, Easter term 14 Hen VIII
91 NA C1/486/61; Chancery pleadings: Robert and William Constable vs Thomas and James Strangwysshe
92 See Potto connection earlier, and will of James Strangways dated 8 Sept 1532, pr. at York 3 Mar 1534/5
93 YAS/RS 45; Yorkshire Star Chamber Proceedings vol.2 p180–1 no.LXIX
94 See *The Council of the North* by F W Brooks (1966), The Historical Association pamphlet no.25, p7.
95 NA STAC 2/30/109 and YAS/RS 70; Yorkshire Star Chamber Proceedings, pp62–8 Tailour vs Chomley
96 A payment to allow dogs to roam free
97 NRRY/NS vol.1, pp35–6 ('they acknowledge the Honor [of Pickering] but yield no rent')
98 YAS/RS 45; Yorkshire Star Chamber Proceedings, pp137–9 and NA STAC 2/20/59; William Parcehey vs Prior of Malton
99 Y/F 1527 Michaelmas term 19 Hen VIII to the Todde family, and 1533 Easter term 24 Hen VIII, to Roger Cholmeley
100 YAS MD92-3
101 NA C1/873/24; Chancery pleadings: Percehay v Maunsell
102 The part of the document with the 'cehay' disintegrated and is now missing.
103 YAS MD92-1
104 YAS/RS 45; Yorkshire Star Chamber Proceedings, p181, Robert Persey vs Strangwythe
105 Y/F 1535, Hilary term 27 Hen VIII, Ryton, and 1536, Easter term 28 Hen VIII, Potto
106 See NA STAC3/7/100; John Whyte vs Robert Maunsell alias Rouff
107 Letters & Papers Hen VIII vol. XII(I), p393
108 Full story related by Madeleine Hope Dodds and Ruth Dodds in *The Pilgrimage of Grace 1536–7 and the Exeter Conspiracy 1538* (1915).
109 Ibid
110 B.I. York Wills; mic 927, vol.17, fol.518
111 Y/F 1557–58, Hilary term 4&5 Philip & Mary
112 *The Great Chamber at Gilling Castle*; Hugh Murray for Ampleforth Abbey Trustees (1996); photo between pp28/29. This is highly recommended as it gives the remarkable history of this building and its contents.
113 *The Lives of the Kings and Queens of England*, Antonia Fraser (ed), (1975), p205

114 OED: recusant – a person who refused to attend services of the Church of England. These lists also included devout protestants who thought that the C of E was not puritan enough.
115 Aveling N/R; p184
116 York Wills; B.I. mic 940, vol.27, fol.167
117 Aveling N/R p184 has this Richard as William's son, but records now available suggest that he was his youngest brother (see Pedigree). Valladolid, the former capital of Spain, is just north of Madrid.
118 Catholic Record Society no.10 (1911): Douay Diaries vol.1, 1610 15 February
119 KMBT; 1625/6 Feb 6 Thomas Percehay of Ryton esq buried att York
120 Aveling N/R; p272
121 *The Yorkshire Gentry from the Reformation to the Civil War*, J.T. Cliffe (1969), p197
122 Harl/Soc, Visitation of Yorkshire 1563 & 1564 by William Flower, p238
123 *Alumni Oxoniensis 1500–1714* (1891): Percy, Richard, Christ Church 1552, BA 1555/6, MA 1558 son of Walter Percehay of Barton on Humber
124 *The Church Under the Law – Justice Administration & Discipline in the Diocese of York 1560–1640*, Ronald A Marchant (2008)
125 *Catholic Recusancy in the City of York 1558–1791*, J C H Aveling (1970), pp49 & 315
126 NRRY/NS vol.1, p7
127 YAS/RS 61; Compositions for not taking knighthood at the Coronation of Charles I, pp 84–107
128 Aveling N/R; p305
129 See p102 in 'County Government in Yorkshire during the Interregnum', G C F Forster (1976), *Northern History* vol.12, pp84–104.
130 House of Lords Journal vol.7; 15 October 1645, pp638–44
131 House of Commons Journal vol.6; 1 August 1649
132 Acts & Ordinances of the Interregnum 1642–1660; pp653–88
133 YAJ 6; Letters of the Yorkshire Commissioners of Sequestrations to Cromwell, by Sir George Duckett, pp92–3
134 Acts & Ordinances of the Interregnum 1642–1660; pp1355–1403
135 Calendar of State Papers Domestic CII Addenda 1660–1685; July 1660, with receipts to October 1661
136 Aveling N/R; p417
137 *Book of Common Prayer*; rubric at the end of the Order for the Administration of the Lord's Supper
138 Cause Papers CP H 4668; 1671 Leonard Conyers vs Christopher Percehay re Tithes
139 NA C10/491/137; Chancery pleadings: Percehay and Wivell vs Jegon and Percehay
140 York Wills; B.I. mic 988 W67 no.313
141 Cause Papers CP H 4668; 1671 Leonard Conyers vs Christopher Percehay re Tithes
142 www.hrionline.ac.uk/causepapers
143 Appleton, Barton, Brawby, Hovingham, Ness, Normanby, Nunington, Salton, Sinnington, Slingsby
144 Cause Papers CP H 5689; Leonard Conyers vs Thomas Harrison deceased
145 NYCRO TD 194/2; Barstow Archives, Rent Books
146 Cause Papers CP H 3814; Leonard Conyers vs William Moone
147 Cause Papers CP H 3032; Leonard Conyers vs Thomas Halliday and others
148 Documents held at the National Archives
149 Hayme in the parish register and in this document, but also Haimes and Hame in this same document and Hames on the Dugdale Visitation.
150 NA C5/537/83; Chancery pleadings: Percehay v Alured and others
151 York Wills; B.I. mic 988, reg67, fol.373
152 Aveling N/R; p399
153 Dugdale's Visitation; Notes from Clay vol.1, p71
154 VCH; *A History of the County of York North Riding*, Vol.1 (1914), pp439–44, Parishes, North Otterington
155 Harl/Soc, Knights of Edward 1 vol.4 (P–S), pp45–6
156 Plymouth and West Devon Record Office; ref 373/2 1716
157 NA PROB 11/150/417; will of Robert Percehay
158 S/Soc 36; Visitation of Yorkshire by Sir William Dugdale 1665
159 NA PROB 11/288/482; will of Stephen Percehay

Chapter 3

Pedigree of Percehay of Ryton

This pedigree is a compilation of the known pedigrees declared by the Percehay family at the Visitations of Yorkshire by Thomas Tonge (1530), William Flower (1563–64 & 1567), Robert Glover (1584), Richard St George (1612) and William Dugdale (1665), with additional information published by the Harleian Society and J.W. Clay. This base information has been enhanced by the considerable number of references to the Percehay family in various public archives. Well over 250 documents have been consulted, including 14 family wills; these confirm the names given in the pedigrees and also contain cross-references to many gentry families in the area. In addition, the Parish Registers (NYCRO) and Bishop's Transcripts (Borthwick Institute for Archives) for Kirby Misperton give specific dates for baptisms, marriages and burials from 1600, although the records are not complete. The volume of information means there is a high degree of certainty for each person listed and additional information is given in the following notes. The pedigree suffers at times from a lack of information concerning females, due mainly to the obsession with the eldest male child, rather than a lack of actual females. Even non-inheriting sons are sometimes ignored, and only rarely are there details about their marriages or offspring. It must be remembered that every single member of the family, either male or female, cannot possibly have been recorded, especially in earlier times. English versions of names are used throughout, although some of the records are in Latin and have Latinised versions of names. This in itself can cause confusion as Johanna, the Latinised female version of John, can be translated back into English as either Joan or Jane. In the case of the Percehays, Joan was a very popular name, and while none of the original documents gives any Janes, some translators do.

An effort has been made not to overcomplicate this already complex pedigree. In this area the Percehay, Anlaby, Anne, Babthorpe, Constable, Conyers, Crayke, Hotham, Hercy, St Quintin, Strangways, Stickland, Vavasour, and Wyvill families frequently intermarried, so there are more connections than those shown. However, what is very surprising is the total lack of direct blood relatives marrying. The closest seems to be when Edmund Percehay marries Isabell Fauconbridge: both are great-grandchildren of Robert Darcy. The belief that the gentry frequently married their cousins seems to stem from the use of that term to mean any general family member, or relative of a relative. An example of this use of the word 'cosen' is found in Robert Percehay's will of 1626 when he frequently uses the term when referring to relatives of his late wife who have no blood connection to him whatsoever. It is also used by Isabell Crayke (nee Percehay) in her will when she refers to Sir William Babthorpe as 'cosen'. It is even more confusing in this case, as he is the father of Frances Babthorpe, who married Isabell's grandson William, and thus qualifies as a general family member; however, reference to both family pedigrees shows that Isabell and Sir William do have the same great-grandfather, Ralph Babthorpe, making Isabell and William second cousins, not cousins, by our nomenclature of today. A similar difficulty is encountered in Elizabeth Percehay's will of 1566 when other family terms are used in unfamiliar ways. Elizabeth refers to her 'sister Bradshaw', being Joan Bradshaw who really is her sister, and then to 'Lady Beckwith my sister' who is Elizabeth Cholmeley and is only distantly related by marriage – in fact in this case the term 'sister' is more likely to mean her very close friend rather than a relative. In the same will 'my daughter Prudence Percehay' is wife to her son Leonard; 'Anne Percehay my daughter' really is her daughter (by her first marriage) who married Elizabeth's step-son (from her second marriage) Robert Percehay (her second husband's son from his first marriage) so Anne and Robert were not actually related by blood; 'my sonne Richard Wodd' is her daughter Christian's husband; 'my brother Spencer' is father of her son Leonard's wife; and 'my brother Wodd' is the father of her daughter Christian's husband. The term step-son (or daughter) seems to be actively avoided, perhaps because the term 'step-' originally meant orphan rather than having only one living parent (which of course is not what it means these days), and the term 'in-law' is not encountered until Leonard Percehay's will of 1593 when he refers to his brother-in-law Robert Bower, but even after this date the term is not generally used. Other potential confusions are hopefully clarified in the following notes concerning specific people.

Key to abbreviations used in the Pedigree

First spouse 1 Name 2 second spouse

af. = after; al. = alive; b. = born; bapt. = baptised; bf. = before; bur. = buried; d. = deceased; dau. = daughter; d.i.f.l. = died in father's lifetime; n.r.i. = no recorded issue; pro. = probate;

Notes on the Pedigree

1. In 1167–68 this Walter had at least five manors in the area, and some of these were held of Alan Neville (Pipe Roll 14 Hen II, p85). The Neville family (Ralph) had given part of Ryton (now thought to be the original 'lost' Salescale from Domesday) to Rievaulx Abbey shortly after Henry I gave them the 'wastes below Pickering' on the other side of the Costa. From this date the Percehay family are mentioned in documents relating to Ryedale, and are referred to as being 'of Ryton'. It is not possible to say just how many Walters there were between 1166 and 1300 as all lords of the manor between those dates seem to have had this name. The previous Walter shown is known to be in Yorkshire, but not specifically where.

2. In the period 1166 to 1202 Latinised versions of Walter, Alan, Arnold, William and John are mentioned in this area in the YAS/RS Early Yorkshire Charters. The use of brackets indicates that there is some uncertainty about a particular name; either the actual name is uncertain, or the relationship within the family cannot be confirmed.

3. From the Byland Chartulary (S/Soc 208) it appears that Lady Hugeline Percehay became Hugeline of Laysthorpe (between Stonegrave and Oswaldkirk) and produced Emma of Laysthorpe. This was before the general use of surnames, so it is not unusual that Emma of Laysthorpe married Samson of Laysthorpe. Unfortunately this system gives no clue as to who Hugeline or Emma actually married, except that both husbands were 'of Laysthorpe'. What can be deduced from the Chartulary is that at the time there were direct links between Laysthorpe and Ryton, so it is reasonable to think that Lady Hugeline Percehay had some connection with the Ryton Percehays.

4. This Sir Walter was 'summoned to serve against the Scots' on 24 June 1300 (Parliamentary Writs, from Harl/Soc Knights of Edward I vol.4, p45). Edward I had defeated William Wallace at Falkirk in 1298, but again felt the need to invade Scotland. He eventually withdrew after intervention by the Pope and a truce was agreed. However, Walter appears not to have made it back to Ryton as he is not mentioned in the 1301 Lay Subsidy.

5. The de Wrelton details are deduced from the references in the 'Coucher Book' (NRRY/NS vol.3, pxvii); the Lay Subsidy of 1301 (YAS/RS 21, p50); the Knight's Fees of 1302/3 (S/Soc 49, p380) and the Register of William Greenfield (S/Soc 151, pp59–60).

6. This connection was accepted by Thomas Jenyn about 100 years later, and the charters presented to Robert Glover confirmed this link to the Vesci family. Joan seems to have pre-deceased her father John who died in 1289 and husband Robert is deceased by 1292.

7. Henry is named as Forester in Fee 'for William' in 1335. He could be either Walter's brother as shown, possibly his son, or even a 'cousin' from the south-west.

8. This Walter may not be 21 at the Lay Subsidy of 1301 as he is not mentioned, but by 1314/15 he was joint Vill holder at Crambe (Nomina Villarum S/Soc 49 p324) while his aunt Joan was still the Vill holder at Ryton. He signs a charter dated 1292 to say he is 'son and heir of the late Joan de Vesci with clear memory of her' so he must be more than a toddler by then and obviously she died some time before. It is clear that his father Robert is also deceased by that date.

9. This connection was made by Dr J.S. Purvis in his 'Notes on Old Malton Church 1941–45' (copy in Malton Library – ref 942.846 Y) and it is implied in Walter's will (S/Soc 4, pp6–7).

10. This Robert is not mentioned in his father's will, written in 1344, so he may have been too young to be included, but he is in his mother's (January 1348/9).

11. Elizabeth is mentioned in her father's will of 1344 but not her mother's. However, her mother does leave one mark to Agnes, daughter of William de Bylton and another mark to Joan, sister of this Agnes. The order and value suggests these could be Elizabeth's children but

with Elizabeth herself already deceased.

12. John de Melsa is sometimes given as John de Meux. He passes his manor of Levisham to William and Isabell in 1352–53 (NA C143/306/12) and is probably father of Isabell, but he could also be just a close relative.

13. Agnes of Lokton's will gives part of this information and the rest is from VCH (Huttons Ambo) and the Inquisition Post Mortem of her husband Thomas. Because of the lack of surnames it is not possible to say if Mary Bolton married a relative.

14. Darcy pedigree given in Visitations of the North 1567 by William Flower (S/Soc 133, p14). The footnotes referring to the Percehay connection are incorrect and do not reflect either the Darcy pedigree or the Percehay pedigree referred to. However, an earlier Visitation by Flower (1563/4) refers to the Percehay pedigree (Harleian Society, p238) and explains this descent in extensive footnotes by cross-reference to an indenture of 1437.

15. Robert's wife is named as Elizabeth by his sister Agnes of Lokton in her will of 1391 (S/Soc 4, p165) and in his own will (S/Soc 4, p412) written 10 December 1426. However, the Feudal Aids of 1284–1431 (vol.6) for 1428 refers to 'Joan recently wife of Robert Percehay knight' on both p294 (for Hildenley and Crambe) and p316 (for Ryton). The record gives 'Pro. 17 Feb following', suggesting probate was granted less than two months later, unless it actually means February 1427/8 being the following year in the terminology of the day. This would allow just enough time for Elizabeth to die and Robert to re-marry a Joan.

16. Noted by Dugdale (Clay vol.2, p3) in the Scrope pedigree.

17. At the Visitations the Percehays recorded their right to bear the Lound coat of arms 'Argent Fretty Azure' (sometimes given as Azure Fretty Argent), being that noted for Henry Lound by Jenyn. This Alice de Lound is thought to be the last of the line that included Sir Peter de Lound from Bukethorp (Bugthorpe) as detailed in Knights of Edward I (P–S) by the Harl/Soc (p63).

18. This marriage brought the Darcy lands in Lincolnshire back together, having been split between the two daughters of Sir Robert Darcy. This marriage of direct blood relatives (great-grandchildren) is one of the few in this pedigree. This Lincolnshire connection continued with the marriage of Edmund's granddaughter (not named) to Sir Gerard Southill (Suthill) who lived at Redbourn, just to the south of the Percehays' lands (Harl/Soc Lincolnshire Pedigrees (P–Z), p915). Her father is actually given as Sir Lyon Percy by the Harleian Society, but the date, location and the tendency of the Barton upon Humber Percehays to prefer Percy all suggest that her father was the Sir Lyon Percehay shown in this pedigree.

19. Thomas could be the incumbent recorded at Kirkbymoorside as Thomas Persay in 1501.

20. Usually Lyon, sometimes Leo or Lyonel, with his son usually Leo, but both very variable.

21. The Barton upon Humber line eventually becomes 'Percy', as detailed in Flower's Visitation (1563/4).

22. Alice gives her husband as Nicholas Anlaby (YAS MD335/13/2/3 'Indexed Coat of Arms and Pedigrees vol.3, p327'; Harl/Soc 'Yorkshire Pedigrees part 1, A–F, p12). It is at this time that there is least information about daughters.

23. It is distinctly possible that this John Pykering was the father of Joan, Walter's wife. Detail from YAS MD92-2, S/Soc 106, pp1–2 and YAS/RS 45, p181.

24. This marriage was noted in the will of Lyon Percehay (S/Soc 106, pp1–2). Anne was second wife to James Strangways of Whorlton. This clears up Clay's query (p310) about Anne being named in James' will rather than Elizabeth (Ratclyffe), who had been his first wife.

25. Tynswyke at Flower (1563–64) and Tyrswick at Glover (1584–85). Neither of these names cross-references with other documents. However, among the Percehay properties declared on the death of Robert in February 1426/7 is Kettilby in north Lincolnshire. By coincidence, the Tyrwhit family also lived at Kettilby. The record for the Tyrwhits is not detailed enough to confirm the possible connection, but both families were in this area at the relevant time.

26. From Yorkshire Star Chamber Proceedings (YAS/RS 45, p137) it is clear that in 1533 this Elizabeth had been previously married and had at least one daughter called Anne, aged 6; her will later confirms that she had also produced Elizabeth (who became Elizabeth Atwood) by this earlier marriage. Her husband in 1533 is William Percehay who already has a son, Robert, by his first wife. Various documents confirm that this Robert's wife was named Anne. By the time of Elizabeth's will in 1566 Robert is dead, but his wife Anne is still alive and is the only person known at that time who could be referred to as Anne Percehay. Elizabeth refers to her as 'Anne Percehay my daughter' and in this case it is most likely that she really is her daughter, rather than just the wife of a deceased step-son. The order of the gifts in the

The Percehay Family of Ryton

Pedigree of Percehay of Ryton

1129–35   (Walter) Percehaie

1166–1200 **Walterus Percehaie**[1]   (Alano Ernaldo Willelmo Johanne)[2]

1213 **Sir Walter Percehay**

(Lady Hugeline Percehay d. by 1268)[3]

Eustace de Vesci = Margaret dau. of William,
1169-1216   Lion King of Scotland

William de Vesci d. 1253

John de Vesci, Baron of Alnwick, Lord of Malton
1244-1289

Sir Walter[4]
d. 1301

Roger of Wrelton[5] = **Joan**   **Robert** = Joan de Vesci[6]
d. by 1302   L of M 1302 - 1315   d. by 1292   d. bf. 1289
                                       d.i.f.l.
            Alan d. by 1334

Henry[7]   **Sir Walter**[8] = Agnes   Joan   Alice   Isabell = John des Arches[9]
al. 1335   b. bf. 1289   pro. Feb 1348/9 al.1344   al.1344
           pro. 6/12/1346   Walter

Robert[10] George   Thomas   Walter   John = Isobell   Elizabeth[11] = Wm of Bylton   Joan   Agnes
           al. 1348 al. 1348 b. bf. 1308 pro. Nov pro. July al.1344 d. by 1348   Prioress of Nun of
                               al. 1348   1391   1401   Yeddingham   Watton
                                                                  Agnes   Joan   by 1348   1344-91

Mary 2 (af. 1368, by 1374) = 2 **Sir William** 1 = Isabell dau. of Sir John de Melsa[12]
dau. & heir of Henry Moreby   b. bf. 1307
wid. of Wm de Acclum   d. 15/8/1384

Walter   John   John of Lokton = 2 Agnes[13] 1 = Thomas Bolton   Sir Robert Darcy[14] of
al. 1344   al. 1344 d. bf. Agnes   al. 1344   d. 20/5/1374   Flixborough Parke in Lincs
d.i.f.l.   d. by 1348   pro. Oct 1391

                                      Mary = Wm of Lokton
                                      b. 1373

                         (Joan)[15] = 2 **Sir Robert** 1 = Elizabeth   Margaret = Sir Roger
                                        b. 1354-6   Fawconbridge
                                        pro. Feb 1426/7

         George   Elizabeth[16] dau. of = 2 **Sir John** 1 = Alice[17] dau. &   Walter = Matilda
         al. 1427   Robert Scrope   b. bf. 1407   heir of Lound
                     son of Henry   al. 1462/3
                     4th Lord Scrope   d. by 1485
                                                                                   Isobell[18]
         John = Elizabeth dau. of   Ralph   Edmund of Flixborough Parke   Fawconbridge
         al. 1489 Sir Ralph Babthorpe b. 1427, al. 1494 b. bf. 1427, d.i.f.l.

Edmund   William   Henry   Oliver   Thomas[19]   **Sir Lyon/Leo**[20] = 2 Anne dau. of   1 = Salveyn
al.1492 al.1494   al.1494   al.1492   al.1491   L.of M. by 1485   Sir Ralph Babthorpe   of Duffield
                                                     d. bf. Dec 1494   sister of Elizabeth

William[21] = Elizabeth dau.   **Leo/Lyon** = 1 Katherine 2 = John Anne   Alice[22] = Richard Anlaby   (dau?) = Gerard Southill
of Barton on Humber & sole heir of pro. May 1517 dau. of Sir John Hotham of Frickley of Etton   of Redbourn
                     Walter Hynd   of Scorborough   d. 28/8/1544
                     of B on H

A

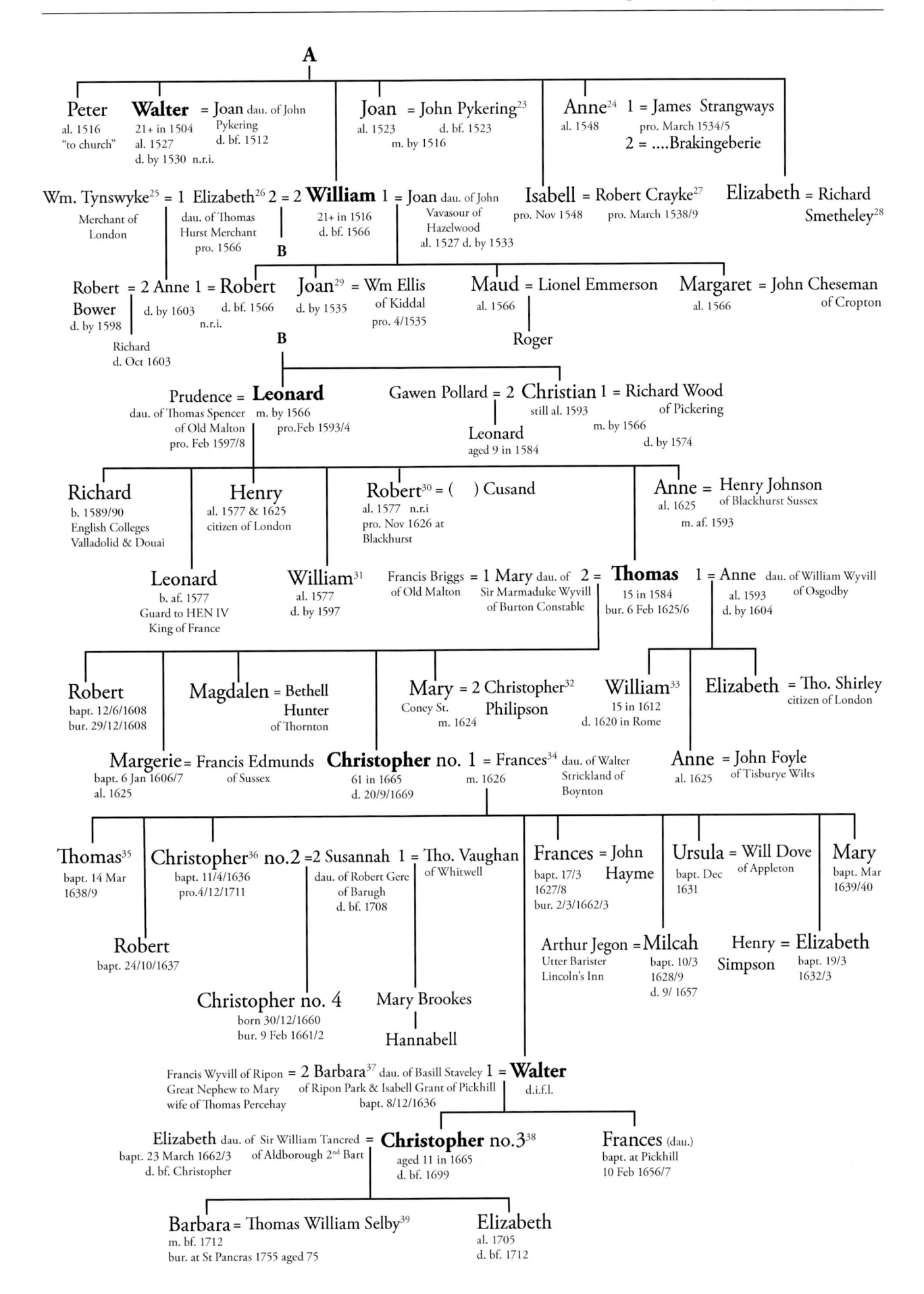

Chapter 3: Pedigree of Percehay of Ryton

A

Peter — al. 1516 "to church"

Walter = Joan dau. of John Pykering
21+ in 1504
al. 1527
d. by 1530 n.r.i.
d. bf. 1512

Joan = John Pykering[23]
al. 1523
m. by 1516
d. bf. 1523

Anne[24] 1 = James Strangways
al. 1548   pro. March 1534/5
2 = ...Brakingeberie

Wm. Tynswyke[25] = 1 Elizabeth[26] 2 = 2 **William** 1 = Joan dau. of John Vavasour of Hazelwood
Merchant of London   dau. of Thomas Hurst Merchant   21+ in 1516   al. 1527 d. by 1533
pro. 1566   d. bf. 1566

B

Isabell = Robert Crayke[27]
pro. Nov 1548   pro. March 1538/9

Elizabeth = Richard Smetheley[28]

Robert Bower = 2 Anne 1 = Robert
d. by 1598   d. by 1603   d. bf. 1566
n.r.i.
Richard
d. Oct 1603

Joan[29] = Wm Ellis of Kiddal
d. by 1535   pro. 4/1535

B

Maud = Lionel Emmerson
al. 1566
Roger

Margaret = John Cheseman of Cropton
al. 1566

Prudence = **Leonard**
dau. of Thomas Spencer   m. by 1566
of Old Malton   pro.Feb 1593/4
pro. Feb 1597/8

Gawen Pollard = 2 Christian 1 = Richard Wood of Pickering
still al. 1593
Leonard   m. by 1566
aged 9 in 1584   d. by 1574

Richard
b. 1589/90
English Colleges
Valladolid & Douai

Henry
al. 1577 & 1625
citizen of London

Robert[30] = ( ) Cusand
al. 1577 n.r.i
pro. Nov 1626 at Blackhurst

Anne = Henry Johnson of Blackhurst Sussex
al. 1625
m. af. 1593

Leonard
b. af. 1577
Guard to HEN IV
King of France

William[31]
al. 1577
d. by 1597

Francis Briggs = 1 Mary dau. of 2 = **Thomas** 1 = Anne dau. of William Wyvill of Osgodby
of Old Malton   Sir Marmaduke Wyvill   15 in 1584   al. 1593
of Burton Constable   bur. 6 Feb 1625/6   d. by 1604

Robert
bapt. 12/6/1608
bur. 29/12/1608

Magdalen = Bethell Hunter of Thornton

Mary = 2 Christopher[32] Philipson
Coney St.
m. 1624

William[33]
15 in 1612
d. 1620 in Rome

Elizabeth = Tho. Shirley citizen of London

Margerie = Francis Edmunds of Sussex
bapt. 6 Jan 1606/7
al. 1625

Christopher no. 1 = Frances[34] dau. of Walter Strickland of Boynton
61 in 1665   m. 1626
d. 20/9/1669

Anne = John Foyle of Tisburye Wilts
al. 1625

Thomas[35]
bapt. 14 Mar 1638/9

Christopher[36] no.2 = 2 Susannah 1 = Tho. Vaughan of Whitwell
bapt. 11/4/1636   dau. of Robert Gere
pro.4/12/1711   of Barugh
d. bf. 1708

Frances = John Hayme
bapt. 17/3 1627/8
bur. 2/3/1662/3

Ursula = Will Dove of Appleton
bapt. Dec 1631

Mary
bapt. Mar 1639/40

Robert
bapt. 24/10/1637

Christopher no. 4
born 30/12/1660
bur. 9 Feb 1661/2

Mary Brookes
Hannabell

Arthur Jegon = Milcah
Utter Barister   bapt. 10/3
Lincoln's Inn   1628/9
d. 9/ 1657

Henry = Elizabeth Simpson
bapt. 19/3 1632/3

Francis Wyvill of Ripon = 2 Barbara[37] dau. of Basill Staveley 1 = **Walter**
Great Nephew to Mary   of Ripon Park & Isabell Grant of Pickhill   d.i.f.l.
wife of Thomas Percehay   bapt. 8/12/1636

Elizabeth dau. of Sir William Tancred = **Christopher** no.3[38]
bapt. 23 March 1662/3   of Aldborough 2nd Bart   aged 11 in 1665
d. bf. Christopher   d. bf. 1699

Frances (dau.)
bapt. at Pickhill
10 Feb 1656/7

Barbara = Thomas William Selby[39]
m. bf. 1712
bur. at St Pancras 1755 aged 75

Elizabeth
al. 1705
d. bf. 1712

will also indicates how close she is to this Anne, who is mentioned before her younger daughter Christian by her second husband, William Percehay. Elizabeth's sister Joan's second husband was Henry Bradshawe, Solicitor General then Attorney General to Henry VIII, and Baron of the Exchequer under Edward VI. This accounts for the name of Henry Bradshawe on some of the Percehay documents of the time.

27. The East Riding Crayke/Craike/Creyke/Crake family are also recorded at the Visitations. From Leo Percehay's will it is clear that Isabell and Robert married before 1516.

28. Elizabeth and Richard Smetheley (Smethley, Smythley, Smyth) of Brantingham are also married before 1516, and they produce Anthony. Katherine, his daughter and sole heir, became the second wife of Sir William Ingleby of Ripley (Glover, p283; Illustrated Guide Book of Ripley Castle, p25).

29. Joan and William Ellis produce five sons including Roger, who produces Joan/Jane who marries Robert Saville of Copley, providing the Ellis/Saville connection in YAS MD 92-12. Joan's grandson John, son of Henry, married Mary, daughter of Martin Anne of Frickley who sold some of his extensive properties in Yorkshire to Thomas Spencer, father of Prudence (Percehay). There was also a common Hotham of Scorborough connection.

30. Robert's will of 1625 (NA PROB 11/150/417) gives the origin of the William Cusand in the key document NYCRO 3989/199 of 1655. It also links sister Anne Johnson, Blackhurst Sussex, brother Henry Percehay, niece Anne Foyle, niece Margery Percehay and Midhurst Sussex.

31. Clay vol.2, p448 has this William marrying Elizabeth Crake, daughter of Robert, son of Robert and Isabell (Percehay), making them both great-grandchildren of Leo Percehay.

32. Christopher Philipson's first wife was Elizabeth Wyvill, sister of Mary, who was second wife of Thomas Percehay.

33. Information from *The Yorkshire Gentry from the Reformation to the Civil War* by J.T. Cliffe (1969), p197.

34. Frances was granddaughter of the William Strickland credited with introducing turkeys to England. The family crest still includes a turkey to acknowledge this fact. This family connection explains why the second son of Frances, Christopher no.2, was so close to the Strickland family, as detailed in his will. She was buried 11 January 1659/60.

35. Thomas, Robert and Mary do not live long enough to be included in Dugdale in 1665.

36. This Christopher and his wife Susannah give a silver chalice, engraved with the Percehay coat of arms and crest, to St Michael's church New Malton in 1705. Previously this was incorrectly credited to Christopher no.3. The will of Christopher no.2, written 30 June 1708, confirms his continuing connection with St Michael's. He was appointed Curate of Wintringham in 1657; this was in the 'gift' of his uncle Sir William Strickland at the time.

37. Barbara, baptised at Pickhill 8 December 1636, brings with her lands (or more probably the income from lands) in the Ripon and Pickhill areas. After Walter's death she marries Francis Wyvill of Ripon, son of Sir Marmaduke, and great-nephew of Mary Wyvill who was second wife to the Thomas Percehay above. There is also a Staveley/Spencer connection: Elin, half-sister of Prudence Spencer/Percehay, married Henry Staveley of Ripon.

38. Document NA C5/590/48 in the National Archives detailing Barstow v Percehay in the Court of Chancery, dated 23 October 1705, has clarified a number of issues concerning the last of the Percehay family. Confusion arose mainly because there were three adult (and one infant) Christopher Percehays alive at the same time. Even more information concerning the relationships and problems during this period are given in NA C10/491/137 Jegon v Percehay, and NA C10/139/37 Hayme v Percehay. The records also show that this Christopher was 22 when he married the 13-year-old Elizabeth Tancred, and his mother Barbara had only just passed her 17th birthday when she produced him. At that time thirteen was the legal age of consent, but it is doubtful that Elizabeth was asked about who or when she should marry.

39. Information from *Northern Catholics; The Catholic Recusants of the North Riding of Yorkshire 1558–1790* by Hugh Aveling O.S.B. (1966) [referenced as Aveling N/R], p399.

Chapter 4

Ryton: a 'Deserted' Township of Ryedale

Ryton before the Percehays

Ryton existed as a township in Ryedale well before the arrival of the Percehay family.[1] The settlement (NGR: SE 793 757) stands on a ridge, known as Ryton Rigg, which provided dry ground even during the worst flooding and the wettest weather. A settlement on this high ground, close to a point where two rivers meet, would also have had the benefit of being easier to defend, especially as the vantage point afforded views in every direction. Just where the first settlement was located is not known, although worked flint, not a natural deposit (see Figure 5), has been found in the area of the Percehays' manor house, but there are also signs of settlement along the ridge from this point all the way to the confluence of the River Rye and the Costa (beck) near Howe bridge. Features near this confluence may be ancient, but they may just reflect the presence of the much later settlement called Broomhills,[2] that was sometimes referred to as Sandhills because of the underlying sand. One key element for early settlement was fresh water. The surface watercourses of the Rye and the Costa would have been suitable for only part of the year as they would frequently become discoloured with silt and debris after only moderate rainfall. Consequently, a site with a natural spring or similar would have been preferred, and there is just such a source at the site that became Ryton, close to the location of the later manor house. Today's OS map depicts just a small pond at this location, but the 1st edition OS map of 1850 clearly shows a small watercourse leading from this point. The unusual feature of this pond is that it is located at the top of Ryton Rigg, close to its highest point, but it rarely dries up and should have been enough for the basic needs of the early settlement. Even today it is the main source of water for the cattle in the field. It is possible that there was early settlement at other places along Ryton Rigg, but a similar suitable water source has not yet been identified. The worked flint in this area, with further pieces from the area of *Salescale* and the 'casual' finds of stone implements including two beautiful stone axe-heads (see Figure 5), give reason to believe that there was some habitation in the Ryton area at least as early as the Neolithic, but it is not possible to determine whether this was permanent or just summer camps. An intriguing glimpse of very early settlement a little further up the Costa, approximately two miles from its source at Keld Head in Pickering, was discovered in 1893 and was thought to suggest a Neolithic origin.[3] At that time waterways would have been an important part of the communications network, and rivers in Ryedale need to be viewed as links rather than barriers. This use of waterways would also have made the high ground near the confluence of the Rye and the Costa a very strategic location.

The geology underlying this area, being the bottom of what was once Lake Pickering, has been well documented by the British Geological Survey. Information from their 'Investigation into the underground water supply of Yorkshire' in 1943, along with surveys undertaken in 1876 and 1881 by Fox-Strangways, confirm local knowledge and experience. The lower-lying area of Ryton, from the Costa all the way to the Kirby Misperton to Great Habton road, is covered by a relatively thin layer of productive rich loam, immediately beneath which is a layer of sand or sandy clay on top of blue clay. This clay was the reason for *Brick Pond Moor*, *Brick Kiln Close* and *Brick Kilns* in the area, as well as the Brick and Tile Yard at Golden Square on the opposite side of the Costa at Marishes. These deposits were formed on the bottom of the lake. Under this lake bed is Kimmeridge Clay that has been so compressed it is referred to as black shale (the subject of much discussion in the 21st century). Between the Kimmeridge Clay and the blue clay is a layer of sand and gravel containing the water accessed by all the boreholes in the area; it is probably this water that is being forced to the surface near the old manor house, forming the pond. Unfortunately the key topographical feature of Ryton Rigg does not show up on any geological map and it is almost invisible on modern OS maps, being mostly just *below* the 25m contour, with the surrounding lower-lying land being just *above* the 20m contour. This results in the whole of Ryton being almost devoid of contour lines, and the significance of the ridge of slightly higher ground that is Ryton Rigg has been previously overlooked. The ridge itself seems to be made up predominantly of sand under the overlying loam. This sand gives rise to the names *Sandhills* and the *Foreshores* (areas of sand alongside the River Rye extending to more than one acre to the west of Garforth Hall) and was exploited as a building material in the construction of the new Manor Farm which has a 'Sand Pit' recorded nearby on the 1890 OS map.

This ridge of dry ground running east/west along the north side of the River Rye would have been an obvious course for the earliest tracks taking people along the bottom of the Vale of Pickering, without the need to go up to the higher-level routes that run along the sides of the vale (see Figure 9). Even today there is a line of tracks and paths which follow this ridge all the way from Little Habton in the west, where a footbridge still crosses the River Seven, to the old Broomhills/Sandhills in the east where a footbridge crosses over the Costa to the Marishes. It is along this east/west route that the settlement of Ryton developed, and evidence of this layout is quite obvious on aerial photographs available at NYCRO and in the Cambridge University Collection of Aerial Photography (CUCAP) (Figure 1).[4] However, the Barstow estate plan of 1744 indicates that this original east/west route on top of Ryton Rigg became displaced by the open field system, with the route then running along the northern edge of the open fields adjacent to the Intacks (see *aycfrithewath*). In addition to this east/west route, there would have been a need to cross the Vale of Pickering from north to south, but this will always have been problematic, regardless of the route taken. The marshy condition of the bottom of the vale has probably been grossly overstated in the past, and recent experience with the slowing of the flow of Pickering Beck could indicate that the vale was much drier before wholesale drainage of the uplands into it. There is even a suggestion that at least some rudimentary drainage was attempted in the vale itself as long ago as the Iron Age,[5] but it has to be accepted that for certain periods every year it would have been almost impossible to cross the vale.

The crossing from Ryton towards Malton over the Rye may originally have been just a basic ford, created very simply at a wide, shallow point of the river, and even today there are locations where it would be possible to cross on horse-back. One of the gifts to Malton Priory, estimated to have been made in the 12th or 13th century, is from Helyas the ferryman, so perhaps this was the pedestrian way to cross the river at the time. However, by the time Saxton's map of 1577 was surveyed a bridge already existed, and this is confirmed in the will of 'Rauf Raisinge of New Malton', dated 1 December 1575, when he refers to 'Ryton Bridge end'.[6] A bridge at Ryton is shown on every map after this date. The route to this bridge from either side crosses only a very short stretch of floodplain compared to the crossings at Howe or Newsham, so it is possible that the bridge at Ryton may have been the preferred crossing point of the vale. The entry for *Frerebrigg* in the place-names chapter (see Chapter 5) provides another reason why Howe bridge may have been avoided in the days of the Forest of Pickering.

Having crossed the River Rye, a route north would easily have navigated the Aykeland (Ackland) Beck by a ford as it is such a small watercourse; in fact it was still being crossed by a ford well into the 20th century. Evidence existed within living memory, and is confirmed by earlier maps such as the 1850 edition of the OS, that the route north then headed towards the settlement of Salescale, in the area of today's Costa Manor farm, which was situated on slightly higher ground (see Figures 9 and 10). Evidence of this route continuing northwards remains obvious and can be followed on the 1850 map to where it is shown crossing the Costa by both Tranmer's footbridge and a ford. This is the ancient crossing point referred to much earlier as Frerebrigg (1334) and Lundbrige (1523) (see Chapter 5), with the whole route from Ryton to Pickering via Lundbrige described in detail in the Yorkshire Star Chamber Proceedings, Tailour v Chomley, dated 1523.[7] This route is also shown continuing north, but on the west side of the Costa, as it may well have done for centuries, heading towards Kirby Misperton. The route shown on the 1850 map follows the line laid out in the Enclosure Award of 1703, but it would have been much more direct in earlier times. From Kirby Misperton higher level routes would have given access, via Riseborough, to settlements along the relatively dry east/west route of today's A170. This route north-west from Ryton and Malton had the major advantage of avoiding crossing both the Costa and Pickering becks and may have been yet another reason to cross the Rye at Ryton rather than at Howe. There is even the possibility that this route north from Ryton also crossed the Costa somewhere before it joined Pickering Beck and continued into Pickering via Southgate, which still enters Pickering to the west of Pickering Beck. The name Southgate suggests it was the original route south from Pickering before Malton Road was laid out at a much later date. It is even possible that this is the route described by John Leland in his *Itinerary* of 1538 (folio 73) on his journey from Pickering to Appleton (le Street) heading for Hinderskel (today's Castle Howard). He is obviously aware that 'Costey Water' (the Costa) was relatively small compared to the 'Pickering Brok' (Pickering Beck), a fact he can only have known if he crossed the Costa before it joined Pickering Beck.

How and when the settlements of Ryton and Salescale came into existence, and how they developed is not known. All that can be said with any certainty is that by the time of the Domesday survey of 1086 both settlements existed and each had significant areas of cultivated land, with Ryton having approximately five times more than Salescale. They were on high ground on opposite sides of the Aykeland beck, with Ryton on top of Ryton Rigg and Salescale on ground slightly higher than the surrounding very flat low-lying land near the confluence of the Aykeland beck and the Costa. At the time that Ralph Neville made his gift to Rievaulx Abbey, some time after its foundation in 1132 and before a charter of 1157–58,[8] the area concerned, now thought to be Salescale, was 'held in Rihtuna', suggesting that although it was a separate settlement it was considered to be part of Ryton. The boundary of this gift is clearly defined in a number of charters and is exactly the same area that became the original Lund estate of the Fauconbergs after the Dissolution (as shown on Figure 13 but minus Dicky Ground). The gift also tells us that the tenant was called Aluricus son of Arthur, whose son Gerbodo is also mentioned, as they both had to give their agreement to being effectively evicted. It is significant that Ralph Neville also had to have 'the agreement of Hadewise my wife', demonstrating once again that women were much more significant at this time than previously portrayed. In addition to the cultivated land, with its appurtenances (everything on the land including dwellings, shelters, etc.), the meadow and pasture are included, but no mention is made of trees or forest. This gives an insight into the vegetation that existed in the area. Meadow specifically meant the areas of 'grass' (i.e. mixed types of naturally occurring grass, flowers, etc.) cleared of scrub and set aside to be cut for hay. The word meadow derives 'from the Germanic base of mow',[9] hence the specific association with hay. The areas of meadow may also have been grazed by livestock at certain times to ensure good re-growth, with the benefit of some manure being added naturally. Pasture referred to everywhere that wasn't cultivated or meadow and would have been mainly the natural vegetation that is unhelpfully referred to as 'waste' in so many references to the low-lying area below Pickering. The word pasture comes from late Latin *pastura*, meaning grazing, so it was where the livestock grazed. Anything and everything edible would be grazed – grasses, flowers, tender shoots of shrubs and young trees, and even young growth of holly; the latter was also collected in winter as valuable fodder at a time when so little was available.

Further clues about the actual vegetation growing in these areas of pasture comes from other deeds and charters, such as the dispute between Sir Walter Percehay and William of Habton in 1279–80 when pasture of the moor between Ryton and Habton is mentioned,[10] and in a charter dated 1332–33 which grants the monks of Rievaulx free passage across all the moors of Ryton and Habton. 'Moor' was a general term for what may now be referred to as heath and is known to have included 'broom', 'furres' and 'whynes' (see Chapter 5) which at that time were all generic terms for a number of species that made up the brushwood and scrub. Eventually broom (*planta genista*) and gorse (*ulex europaeus*) became the dominant plants, mainly because of their value as basic fuel and for making brushes, but originally thorn, bramble, heather, elder (burtre/bottry) and holly would have been part of the natural mixture. There can be no doubt that some trees also existed but none is mentioned, and there is nothing to warrant the term 'forest', at least not in its modern meaning. The agreement of 1332–33 was for free passage for the monks, their carts, carriages and animals, so it is unlikely there were lots of trees growing on the moors referred to, otherwise it would have been impractical to use carts and carriages. The Lund estate did have an area referred to as 'stubbings' in 1655,[11] indicating that stubbs (tree stumps) had existed at some time, but this was only a relatively small area and gives no clue as to how many trees there had been. There are other references to trees in the early documents, with oak featuring in a number of names for closes, suggesting it was a fairly common species – perhaps in boundaries – but there is nothing to suggest woodland until two areas were specifically planted in the 16th century (see 'New Forest' and 'Oke Close nowe forest' in Chapter 5). The misleading name of 'Lund Forest', created to glorify the Lund estate by their surveyor in 1796, is also discussed in detail in the place-names chapter.

Thus even before the arrival of the first Percehay, Ryton was a well-established township, strategically located on Ryton Rigg at a cross-roads of key east/west and north/south routes and with a crossing of the River Rye nearby. It also had the major advantage of a secure fresh water supply. Agriculture already existed, with the majority of the dry ground on top of Ryton Rigg and around Salescale being cultivated. While some areas had been cleared of scrub and brushwood for use as meadow to supply hay, there would have been significant areas that had not been completely cleared. These would, however, have been managed to a certain extent to improve the quality of pasture available for livestock and to ensure a good supply of fuel. Trees no doubt existed but perhaps not in significant quantities.

Ryton during the time of the Percehays

When the Percehay family arrived at Ryton, sometime before 1167–68[12] and perhaps much earlier, they took over as Lords of the Manor by knight's service, but they did not own the whole township. Gifts to Rievaulx and Byland Abbeys, and to Malton Priory recorded in their charters clearly show that an open field system existed, with some land in the possession (though not necessarily ownership) of at least 16 other individuals. Byland seems to have received a significant gift from Robert of Gilling and Amice, his wife (yet another wife who needed to give her consent), of two bovates; this was then rented to the Percehays for one silver mark per annum. A bovate was defined as being the area of land that could be cultivated by one ox and plough in a year, but it was not a specific area because the amount varied across the country depending on the nature of the land. Estimates vary from as little as 10 acres to as much as 30 acres and even at that time there was confusion, so to avoid any misunderstanding it was agreed that 'wherever the lord Percehay has 8 selions [strips] in any cultura [block of arable land] of all his fields, 7 are his own land towards the west and the eighth is the Abbot and convent's tenement towards the east'.[13] It is then stated that 'the land of William de Cresacres lies next to them nearest the south', suggesting that this William held a considerable amount of land. Rievaulx Abbey had the whole of Lund (Salescale) by the gift of Ralph Neville and his wife, and at approximately 570 acres it was about one quarter of the whole area of Ryton township (which totalled just over 2324 acres when surveyed in 1850). Malton Priory had had the largest number of gifts, but the total area controlled by them is not specified in their charters. At some point the Percehays and Malton Priory seem to have come to an arrangement to allow all the small areas donated to the Priory to be consolidated into two separate blocks of land. One block is referred to as Brodes or Broates in 1279/80 and coincides with today's Shotton Hall farm, but excluding Red Lilly and the land that is actually in Habton, as both of these were added much later. It is possible that the area that is now Gosling Green farm was also part of the Priory's holdings. The name Broates is appropriate as it is derived from Old Norse 'brot', meaning a small piece of land, so Broates is what resulted when all their small pieces of land were effectively combined into one much more useful, self-contained area. Broates could have been as much as 120 acres. The Priory also had land at the confluence of the Rye and Costa in the area that was later referred to as Broomhills or Sandhills. In the 1842 survey for the Tithe Award the lands of John Newton and William Fox at Broomhills, totalling 66 acres 2 roods and 34 perches, were exempt from the payment of all tithes as they 'were formerly parcel of the possessions of the Priory of Old Malton'.[14] A similar exemption applied to part of Shotton Hall farm. The only other significant landholder mentioned in early documents was a John of Ryton. In the dispute of 1279/80 between William of Habton and Walter Pecehay he is mentioned as a joint owner or tenant of the moors in dispute, but by the time of the Lay Subsidy of 1301 he cannot be identified.

At the time of Domesday Ryton does not seem to be particularly significant but by 1301, when the next detailed information about settlements is available, it is already one of the largest townships in the whole of Ryedale. The Lay Subsidy[15] was a tax on everyone's 'personalty', being all their personal possessions including livestock and agricultural produce, but not homes or land, and was levied at the rate of one fifteenth. By taxing personalty it was possible to take money from most of the population, rather than just landowners, although in this area the minimum tax paid was four pence suggesting that the very poorest (who were virtually slaves in all but name) may have avoided the tax. Even the religious houses had to pay, and were in fact the largest contributors, paying 13% of the total in Ryedale. Consequently the records for this Lay Subsidy, collected at Michaelmas (29 September) 1301, give an insight into the relative size and prosperity of nearly every township at that time. There are some anomalies, such as the omission of Brawby and Salton; at the time they both came under the Prior of Hexham who seems to have avoided most taxes on the grounds that they were constantly rebuilding after raids by the Scots, even here in Ryedale![16] The records also need to be viewed with the usual caution applied to any statistics. It appears that there were no Percehays at Ryton, with Sir Walter failing to return from serving 'against the Scots' the previous year,[17] so at that time Roger of Wrelton is the nominal head of the household. He was husband of Joan Percehay, daughter of Sir Walter, and he was effectively looking after the family's interests until the grandson, confusingly yet another Sir Walter, came of age. The campaign could also have reduced the total population of Ryton as Sir Walter is unlikely to have been the only casualty, but this logic could be applied to most townships in the area as all would have had to provide some soldiers for the Scottish campaign. The basic facts suggest that Ryton, with a total of 36 taxpayers, was the third largest township in Ryedale, at least in terms of the population liable to pay tax, with only Helmsley (37) and New Malton (45) having more taxpayers. This is even more remarkable when it is realised that Lund is not included, being declared separately as part of the Abbot of Rievaulx's liability. However, the people of Ryton do not appear to be particularly prosperous individuals, because when the total tax paid by each township is considered, then Ryton is only the eighth most prosperous. Once again more detailed analysis shows that there are anomalies: Appleton-le-Street only has a higher value because Easthorpe is included in the total; Barton-le-Street had the benefit of a thriving market; Pickering had two rich individuals (Ada Brus and William Malecak) accounting for 25% of their total; and Kirkbymoorside had a very rich resident of the castle, Joan Wake, contributing nearly 50% of their otherwise modest total. However the figures are interpreted, it cannot be denied that Ryton was a very significant township in 1301. So what was so special about Ryton at that time? There can be no doubt that one of the most significant factors was the presence of a prosperous family that had been lords of the manor for well over 100 years, giving stability at a time of constant conflict, especially with raids from the Scots. Their known family connection to William the Lion, King of the Scots, via Joan Vescy (her great-great-grandfather) may have been a significant benefit, giving them a degree of protection against these raids. On the figures available, only seven families paid more tax on their personalty in Ryedale, and most of these were connected to the Percehay family in some way. At that time the economy of the area was almost entirely dependent on agriculture, with all the work being done either by oxen or manual labour, so the relatively well-drained open fields along the top of Ryton Rigg, consisting of light to medium loam, may have been key to making Ryton such a thriving community. Townships at that time were virtually self-sufficient, having their own skilled tradesmen, a situation that continued well into the modern era, so there was little need to travel to the still relatively small market towns in the area; these would expand much later with the advent of the Industrial Revolution and the decline in the predominance of agriculture. Equally, other factors that may have increased the prosperity of the community seem to be missing: there are no records showing that Ryton held a market, and the only references to a mill are in the gifts to St Mary's Priory where a 'milnedich' is mentioned. This suggests a mill probably did exist at some time, presumably a water mill fed by this mill ditch, but one is never mentioned as an asset of the manor. All the known facts point to the prosperity of Ryton in 1301 being the result of favourable conditions for agriculture coupled with a stable environment due to the presence of a respected lord of the manor.

Inevitably taxes in their various forms continued to be levied on a regular basis after 1301. However, it is not until the Hearth Tax returns of 1673[18] that similarly detailed records exist enabling the relative size and prosperity of the townships in Ryedale to be compared, although again the figures need to be viewed with caution. It was a very unpopular tax (not that any have ever been popular) as effectively every household had to pay at least two shillings just because they had a fire, although the very poorest, living on the charity of the townships, were exempt. The tax was doubly unpopular because it was nominally introduced to provide an income for the then restored Charles II and many thought that they had fought (and won) the recent Civil War specifically to get rid of rapacious monarchs, and the very nature of the tax required the collectors to enter every property to confirm the number of hearths declared. As a consequence, every effort was made by some of the richest people to avoid or at least reduce the amount paid, so the figures may not be totally dependable. As ever it was the poor who paid a disproportionate amount. The one fact that is evident from the published figures is that the towns of Pickering (228 taxed properties + 13 exempt), New Malton (202 + 8), Helmsley (93 + 69), Kirby Moorside (103 + 34) and Old Malton (68 + 38) had all seen significant growth in the 372 years since the Lay Subsidy of 1301. The rest of the townships in Ryedale have rather been left behind, although Ryton (34 + 8) is still one of the largest, only Hovingham (57 + 11), Slingsby (52 + 13) and Nunnington (36 + 9) having more dwellings. This does suggest that even towards the end of the Percehay era Ryton was still a substantial township, but like the rest of rural Ryedale there had been little if any growth since 1301 when 36 families paid tax in Ryton. It is also clear just how imposing Christopher Percehay's house must have been in 1673 with its 13 hearths, putting it in the same league as Reginald Graham's hall at Nunnington (12) and the house of Wm Thornton at Newton (19), another township on the banks of the Rye that is now 'lost'. These impressive properties would only have been surpassed by the castle of Lord Fairfax at Gilling (21) and the old Percy castle at Seamer (23).

Ryton after the Percehays

In 1705 Thomas Barstow of the city of York, gentleman, formally petitioned to take control of all the remaining assets of Christopher Percehay of Ryton, esquire, deceased,[19] in settlement of an outstanding debt. This action brought to an end the Percehay family connection with Ryton. As a result, the lordship of the manor of Ryton passed to the Barstow family and the descendants of Thomas technically still retain this title, despite the fact that none of them ever took up residence there. The manor house, approximately 530 acres of land, and the village of Ryton was a business asset rather than home. It should be noted, however, that their absence from Ryton does not seem to have been the major factor in the decline of the township of Ryton, as will be seen later. In fact they continued to be what can only be described as generous landlords right through to the second half of the 20th century. The relationship between the Barstows and their tenants is perhaps best illustrated by a letter from the tenants of South Duffield, another holding where the Barstows were absentee landlords, dated 21 July 1866 and addressed to Thomas Barstow esquire at Garrow Hill in York, the then family home:

Dear Landlord,
We the undersigned tenants of South Duffield, desire through the medium of this note, to thank you sincerely for the very liberal presents you have made us towards replacing the cattle we lost in that severe calamity, the Cattle Plague which has so lessened our stock during the past half year; & further we wish to thank you for the handsome returns so often made to us and our fathers before us in times of agricultural depression. With such a kind Landlord as we have, and our industry assisted by divine providence, we hope soon to be re-established in our former position.
We are Dear Landlord your most obedient servants
Thomas Atkinson
William Wainwright
William Atkinson

Not only does this letter show the recurring problems that are still faced by farmers today, it also shows a tangible mutual respect and understanding. The fact that this letter continues to be held by the Barstow family along with their rent books shows how much that relationship meant and means to them. A book about the Barstow family and their business interests around York, their connections with the Merchant Adventurers, their trading base in the Baltic at Danzig (Gdansk in today's Poland) and the migration of some members of the family around the world, is long overdue.

There were other absentee landlords at the beginning of the 18th century owning much of the rest of Ryton. Thomas Bellasis of Newburgh Priory, 2nd Viscount Fauconberg, and husband of Mary, the daughter of Oliver Cromwell, owned the Lund estate at this time and it continued with that family until 1858.[20] The family's estates totalled more than 20,000 acres so the 620 acres at Ryton were not particularly significant, although again it must be stressed that there is nothing to suggest that this had any detrimental effect on Ryton. The estate survey of around 1683[21] shows that nearly all the land was enclosed, with the exception of part of Lund Moor, and was being farmed by five local tenants. Their final survey of 1849 shows that the remaining moor had been enclosed and a new farmstead added called West Farm.[22] In addition, a row of six cottages, then known as New York Cottages, complete with nearby allotments, had been built to house some of the local labourers. Much confusion has been caused by the sale of the Lund estate in 1858 to a family named Lund. They were also absentee landlords although they did come to live in the area when they built Highfield House in Malton.

Another significant absentee landlord was Thomas Garforth. His mother, Alice, was the daughter and heiress of James Boyes and she inherited a substantial land holding in Ryton. Her husband, John Garforth of the City of York gentleman, purchased adjacent properties so the family owned most of the land in the west of Ryton. This included the whole of what had been the West Field, most if not all of the area around Shotton Hall, and the area in between. The Garforths' main residence was on Micklegate in York, although they did invest some of their wealth in Ryton when they built their country retreat of Garforth Hall. The family were principally merchants, and members of the same Merchant Adventurers company as the Barstow family, so they continued to live most of the time in York. Deeds dated 6 May 1737[23] show that the son of Thomas Garforth was described as 'William Garforth of the City of York esquire' and the properties at Ryton are all rented out, being used purely as collateral. Sadly this William did not leave any direct heirs, despite producing at least seven children,[24] but none of them lived to adulthood and he outlived them all. His inheritance passed to the Reverend Edmund Dring, son of William's sister Mary, who changed his name by Act of Parliament after William's death when he took his mother's name of Garforth. His son, another William, who was no doubt named in honour of his great uncle, was described as being 'of Askham Richard' when he sold all the Ryton properties in 1778,[25] bringing to an end the Garforth family's connections with Ryton.

There have been many other families that have had a long association with Ryton. The Raines family are listed as the main tenants in all the Barstow rent books and may well have been brought in by them shortly after their acquisition of the Percehay estates. The two families would have known each other socially when a Thomas Raynes, son of James Raynes of 'Appleton in the Streete'[26] was Lord Mayor of York in 1688. This connection can be made because at Dugdale's Visitation in 1666 the family of the said James Raynes declared their pedigree and included their coat of arms[27] and it is this coat that is shown on the memorial to Lord Mayor Thomas, alongside those of his wife Mary Conyers, in the parish church of Easingwold. The first mention of the family in the area is for a James Raines who is a schoolmaster at Hovingham in 1618,[28] although they could have been in the area much earlier than this. Letters still exist within the family detailing some of their connections with the maritime trade at Hull, culminating in the migration of John Raines to America in 1822. Descendants of this emigrant family are once again in touch with the Raines families in Ryton, who purchased their properties from the Barstows in the 1970s and are still residents of Manor Farm and Garrow Lodge Farm – the family has now been resident in the village for some 300 years.

The Simpson family also had a long tenure in Ryton. The earliest record known of this family in Ryton is dated Easter 1556,[29] when Roger Sympson acquires '5 messuages with lands in Ryton' from Richard Cholmeley knight and Dame Katherine Scrope, his wife,[30] daughter of Henry, late Earl of Cumberland deceased, and late the wife of John, Lord Scrope. The Sympson family seem to have emanated from Edston[31] and were well-connected minor gentry marrying into the Percehay, Wyvill and Cayley families. By the time of the 1673 Hearth Tax they have built a substantial house, being the second largest in Ryton, on a large site surrounded by a ditch (moat?) that is still evident today. Their land holdings in Ryton were relatively modest, amounting to around 100 acres, and consisted of today's Rye House and associated farm and Bulmer Farm, but they did rent parts of both the Lund and Barstow estates, making them probably the largest farmers in Ryton. By the time of Thomas Simpson the elder of Ryton, farmer, and Thomas Simpson the younger, schoolmaster of York, most if not all their Ryton properties are heavily mortgaged, as indicated by another mortgage taken out on 29 April 1833.[32] Shortly afterwards Edward Rose, of Rose's Brewery in Malton, arrives and builds the villa now known as Rye House, replacing a family that had lived in Ryton for nearly 300 years. Most of the land once held by the Simpson family is now owned by their long-time neighbours, the Raines family. This tendency to remain at Ryton is also reflected by the Woodcock family, who lived here from the early 14th century through to the early 19th century; the Shotton family, who gave Shotton Hall its name and were present for at least 250 years; the Ness family of the New House that later became Ness House and is now Riverdene are recorded in the area for nearly 500 years; and the Hardwick, Hood and Spavin families are all resident at the Hearth Tax of 1673 through to the Census returns in the 19th and 20th centuries.

Ryton – a Deserted Village

Ryton still exists, and in terms of raw numbers even into the 20th century it still appeared to be a large, thriving community according to the 1911 Census returns. However, as early as the Census of 1871 Mr. Richard Brown, the Enumerator, in his 'Description of the Enumeration District' referred to 'the so-called Village of Ryton', suggesting that by then there was so little left of the actual village that he struggled to recognise it as such. So why had the once prosperous township 'disappeared', and when had this occurred? Had John Garforth 'enclosed for dairy pasture farming and destroyed the village'[33] or had the infamous Black Death wreaked its ugly toll as has been previously conjectured? The records clearly show that John Garforth only inherited the West Field of Ryton from his wife Alice Boyes, and this and all the other land he purchased in Ryton were at least a mile from the known site of the village, so he is not to blame. The dreaded Plague no doubt did affect Ryton and may even have accounted for the death of Agnes Percehay in January 1348/9; this was at the time of the first outbreak of the Black Death in the area and it is known to have devastated the monks at Rievaulx in 1348, but later records show that if Ryton was adversely affected, it managed to recover, so neither was this the reason for Ryton's demise. With the availability of so much more information it now seems probable that the answer is much more mundane. The first Census available for the area is dated 1821, although only summary information is given, not specific detail. At this date Ryton has 35 families living in 35 houses, with a total population of 212. This seems to compare favourably with Great Habton (population 136) and Kirby Misperton (170). However, the key difference is that 100% of the families in Ryton are involved in agriculture, whereas it is only 26% in Great Habton and 74% in Kirby Misperton, with the rest of the families in these villages occupied in trade, manufacturing or other crafts. In fact Ryton is the only village in Ryedale that has this total dependency on agriculture, and it is this that ultimately sealed the fate of the village. Ryton covers an area of 2324 acres[34] making it much larger in area than the adjacent Ryedale villages of Kirby Misperton (1791), Little Barugh (610), Great Barugh (1460), Little Habton (472), Great Habton (950), Amotherby (1830), Swinton (1253) or Broughton (866). It is this very large area of relatively good agricultural land that ultimately was the reason for the demise of the village of Ryton.

The civil parish of Ryton is up to three miles from east to west, and two miles from north to south, and the original township sits in the south-east corner of the whole area. This means that both the western and northern boundary are up to two miles distant from the settlement, so at the first opportunity it was almost inevitable that farmsteads would be created away from the township to make day-to-day husbandry more efficient and practical. It is clear from all the records that this process of dispersion did not begin until after the Dissolution. The whole area of Lund is recorded as having only one messuage [dwelling house and its appurtenances] when being valued for Henry VIII (presumably the remnants of Lund Grange).[35] The area originally known as Brotes belonging to Malton Priory, centred on today's Shotton Hall, does have 'two houses or tenements'[36] by 1565, but no other dwelling is documented away from the township before the Dissolution. This is not surprising considering the uncertain and lawless times, emphasised by the murder of Robert Tailor of Ryton in 1523;[37] the prevention of Walter Percehay from exercising his right to dig turves 'by a mob' with 'forces and armes in ryottouse maner' in 1519;[38] and later in August 1533 when William Percehay was set upon by 'Jhon Jackson, chanon and brother of his [the Prior of Malton], havyng a long pykes staffe, Thomas Redehede havyng a playne staffe and a short dagger, Jhon Colson with an yron Forke, a short dagger and a sworde ...'[39] This was clearly not the time to live alone on a remote farmstead. However, as the world became a little more civilised, some tenants were persuaded to create appropriate messuages and tenements with their appurtenances (sheds, barns, cattle shelters etc.) away from the main settlement. By the time of the Dissolution the open field system of agriculture was coming to an end in Ryton. The westernmost part of Ryton Rigg was sold to Sir William Compton in 1522, along with the manor of Swinton,[40] and from that time on it was effectively detached from Ryton, eventually being settled and farmed from Swinton. In 1527[41] the Percehays sold the land that can now be identified as Swan Nest and Abbotts Farm to the Todde family, and in 1533[42] they sold more land in Ryton to Roger Colmeley, now thought to be the whole of Goosecrofts (Rye House farm and Bulmer Farm). However, the most significant event heralding the end of the open field era occurred in 1535 when William Percehay and his wife Elizabeth have to sell the whole of the West Field (West Felde or Oxfelde) in Ryton to Robert Crayke and his wife Isabell, sister of William Percehay.[43] While this open field may have continued to be cultivated as before, it is clear that by the time the descendants of Robert and Isabell come to sell on their asset in 1565,[44] the West Field is now a 'tenemente or ferme called the newhouse' and the corresponding Fine describes it as being a 'Messuage and a cottage with land', confirming this is now a self-contained farm and not part of the township's open field system. The subsequent available documents show that gradually, as blocks of land are sold, a messuage or tenement is added to most of them, so by 1600, the date of the first available parish registers, the whole of Ryton has fragmented into scattered farmsteads. These are shown on Figure 11, which recreates the situation by the end of the Percehay era around 1700. This also means that although Ryton would appear to be a substantial settlement in 1673 when the Hearth Tax is levied, families can be identified that are definitely not living in the village. From the Newburgh Priory estate records[45] it is known that five families (Robert Foster, George Foster, John Atkinson and probably Richard Todd and Richard Wood) are tenants on the Lund estate, and other families can be identified well away from the village. Michael Shotton (Shotton Hall), Thomas Woodcock (White Lilly), Jo Spavin (New House), Jo Harrington (Broom Hills), Robert Slee (also at Lund), Thomas Hewitson (Aykeland Farm), Matthew Leckby (Swan Nest), Thomas Garforth (Garforth Hall), and Thomas Marshall (Lund Grounds, possibly North West Farm) can all be referenced, as well as Longlands Hall which was situated away from the village.

This process of dispersion continues to the point where at the time of the first detailed survey for the Barstow family, in 1744, there are only nine resident families left in the village, although adjacent to this is the large house occupied by the Simpson family. This dispersion to the outlying farmsteads had a particular effect on the village itself. One of the reasons for the total lack of any 'trade, manufacturing or other crafts' in 1821 is that there was no concentration of dwellings remaining requiring the services of a baker, blacksmith, butcher or cobbler. Most of these trades or crafts were carried out at the dispersed farmsteads, or the short journey was made to the relatively convenient facilities in Malton or Old Malton. Even in living memory most farmsteads had some form of forge or smithy, bacon, butter, milk, eggs, and many other items were produced on the farm, and baking was one of the chores carried out in the farmhouse kitchen. Consequently there was little opportunity (or need) for separate trades or crafts to develop as they did in villages that remained as nucleated units, or dispersed at a later date. In some ways it can be argued that Ryton was well ahead of its time, moving away from the constraints and inefficiencies of the old agricultural system of strip farming in open fields to the much more efficient system of individual farmsteads surrounded by all their own land, which was more accessible, easier to work, and consequently more productive. The process of dispersion and the move to this new system of agriculture began as early as 1535 in Ryton, whereas many parts of the country were still struggling to catch up into the 19th century, with an Act of Parliament required as late as 1836 to encourage the enclosure of the remaining open fields in England.[46] As a result of this very early move to the new system of agriculture, Ryton disappeared as a village, leaving only tell-tale undulations (fortunately still undisturbed) in what are now grass fields, with no hint of the long and complex history that caused its ultimate demise.

Notes

1. Township – this was the area of civil government before the advent of the parish in Tudor times
2. Referred to in the parish records from 1600 – see Chapter 5
3. *The Evolution of an English Town, being the story of the ancient town of Pickering in Yorkshire from pre-historic times to 1905*, Gordon Home (1915)
4. CUCAP no. AQH 51 as an example (Figure 1)
5. See *Yorkshire's Forgotten Fenlands* by ecologist and landscape historian Ian Rotherham (2010)
6. YAS/RS 65; Yorkshire Deeds vol.4, p139, no.477
7. YAS/RS 70; Yorkshire Star Chamber Proceedings vol.4, p65
8. YAS/RS Early Yorkshire Charters vol.1, p313, no.402. This description of the area below Pickering controlled by Rievaulx included this gift and has been dated to 1157–58.
9. OED – meadow
10. YAS/RS 69; Yorkshire Deeds vol.5, p72, no.194 dated 1279–80
11. NYCRO mic 3989; ZDV, p199
12. PRS/NS Pipe Roll 14 HEN II (1167–68); p85, Walter Percehay has at least 5 manors from the Nevilles and before 1200 John Percehay is a witness at Kirby Misperton (YAS/RS EYC; vol.1, p475).
13. S/Soc 208; Chartulary of Byland, p318, no.929
14. Ryton Tithe Award – NYCRO mic 1799, p422 et seq.
15. YAS/RS 21; Yorkshire Lay Subsidies, now available online at www.british-history.ac.uk
16. Ministers Accounts 1344, November 4th at Westminster gives an example of their pleas
17. Harl/Soc Knights of Edward I; vol.4 (P–S), p45 – see Chapter 2 for detail
18. NA E179/216/462; Hearth Tax granted 1662. Returns for the North Riding are available in hard copy at NYCRO
19. NA C5/590/48; Chancery pleadings: Barstow v Percehay
20. NYCRO mic 382; D/R Book IM, p162, r 248
21. YAS MS 601; Part of the Terrar of Newburgh's Lordship
22. NYCRO ZDV VI 66; The Property of Sir Geo Wombwell Bart plan of Lund forest (Map)
23. NYCRO mic 260; Deeds Registry book A, p231, record 266
24. York Archive (Explore); Pedigree of Garforth by the late Hugh Murray
25. NYCRO mic 287; D/R Book BM, p236, r364
26. *Dugdale's Visitation of Yorkshire, with additions*, J.W Clay (ed) (1917), Vol.3, p457
27. Azure [Blue] a chevron engrailed between 3 cranes' heads erased Argent [Silver] each holding in the beak an oak branch, leaves Vert [Green], acorns Or [Gold]
28. NYCRO North Riding Quarter Sessions Records vol.2, part 1; p181. Recusants at Hovingham included Mary wife of James Raines schoolmaster.
29. YAJ 73; Yorkshire Fines, 1556 Easter term 2&3 Philip and Mary
30. Note his wife retained her earlier name and title as she was higher up the social hierarchy than her new husband!
31. S/Soc 36; Visitation of Yorkshire by Sir William Dugdale 1665, p124
32. NYCRO mic 348; D/R Book FZ, p286 r292, Thos Simpson to Revd. Richard Brown Scholefield
33. *The Ryedale Story* by John Rushton (nd); published by Ryedale District Council, p114
34. Information from the Ordnance Survey map of 1850
35. S/Soc 83; Chartulary of Rievaulx, p352, Extracts pertinent to Rievaulx from Conventual Leases of Yorkshire Monasteries, no.881 June 6 30 Hen VIII [1538] shows Abbot Rowland has let Lund to William and Mabel Jorden and only includes one messuage.
36. YAS MD 92-7; Indenture of sale from Sir Richard Cholmeley to George Momforte of Cholmeley Moores
37. YAS/RS 70; Yorkshire Star Chamber Proceedings vol.4, p62
38. YAS/RS 45; Yorkshire Star Chamber Proceedings vol.2, p180
39. YAS/RS 45; Yorkshire Star Chamber Proceedings vol.2, p137
40. Y/F 1522; Hilary Term 13 Henry VIII
41. Y/F 1527; Michaelmas Term 19 Henry VIII
42. Y/F 1533; Easter Term 24 Henry VIII
43. YAS MD 92-3; This is the original indenture complete with the signatures of both William and Elizabeth.
44. YAS MD 92-4; Again the original indenture complete with signatures.
45. YAS MD 601 dated to around 1683
46. *English Farming Past and Present* by The Right Honourable Lord Ernle (1927), Longmans Green & Co Ltd

Figure 1: *Aerial view of the site of the deserted village of Ryton looking north (NGR: SE 793 757). (Cambridge University Collection of Aerial Photography ref. CUCAP, AQH 51, 3 December 1966 © copyright reserved)*

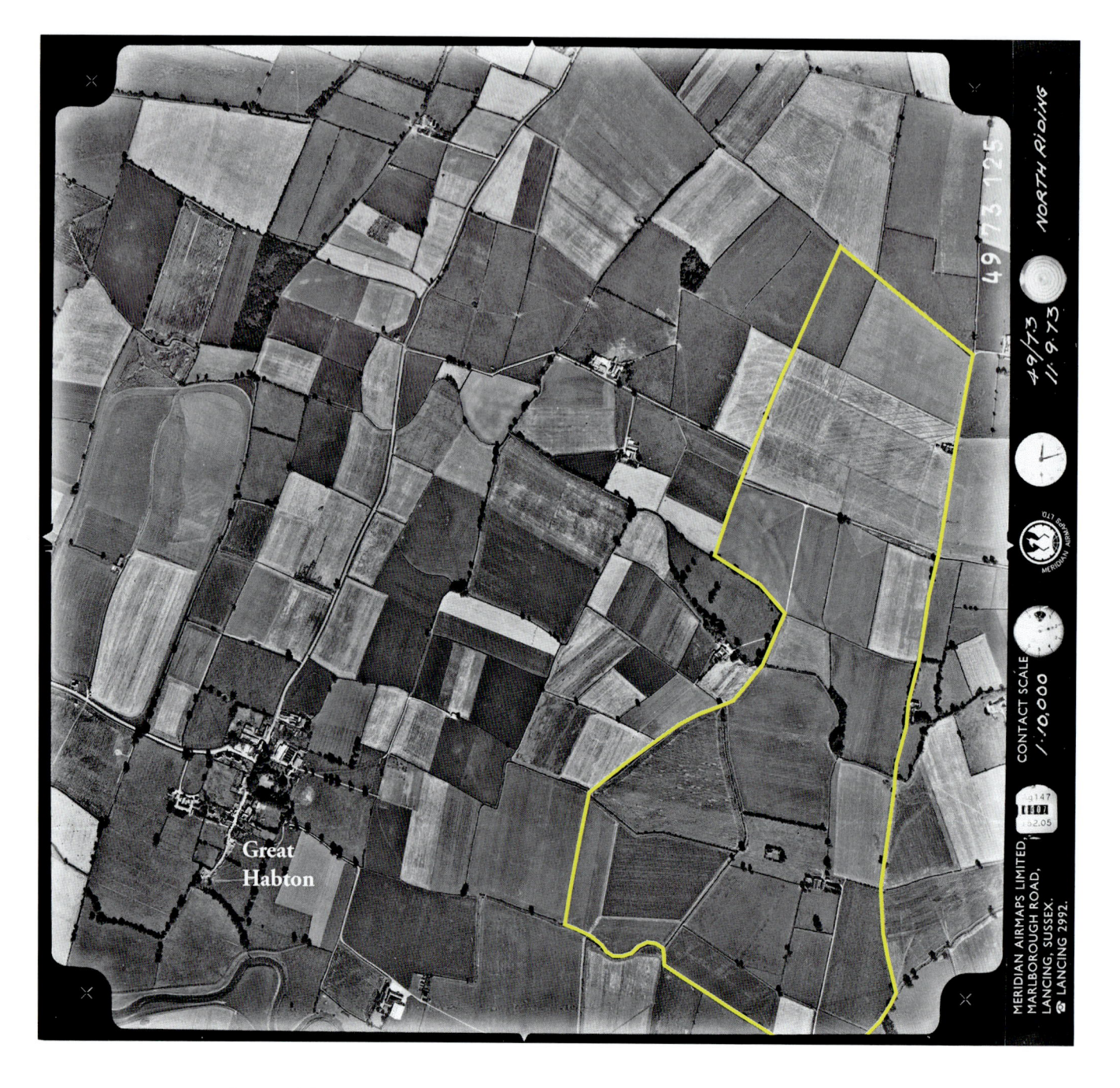

Figure 2: *Aerial view of the western part of Ryton; the settlement at bottom left is Great Habton. Note the old course of the Aykeland Beck. Highlighted area is land distributed in 1604 and re-distributed in 1655. (Meridian Airmaps Ltd ref. 49/73/125 dated 11/9/73; copy held at NYCRO © copyright reserved)*

Figure 3: The chalice – 'The Gifte of Christopher Percehay of New Malton Esq. and Susannah his wife to the Church of St. Michaels 1705'

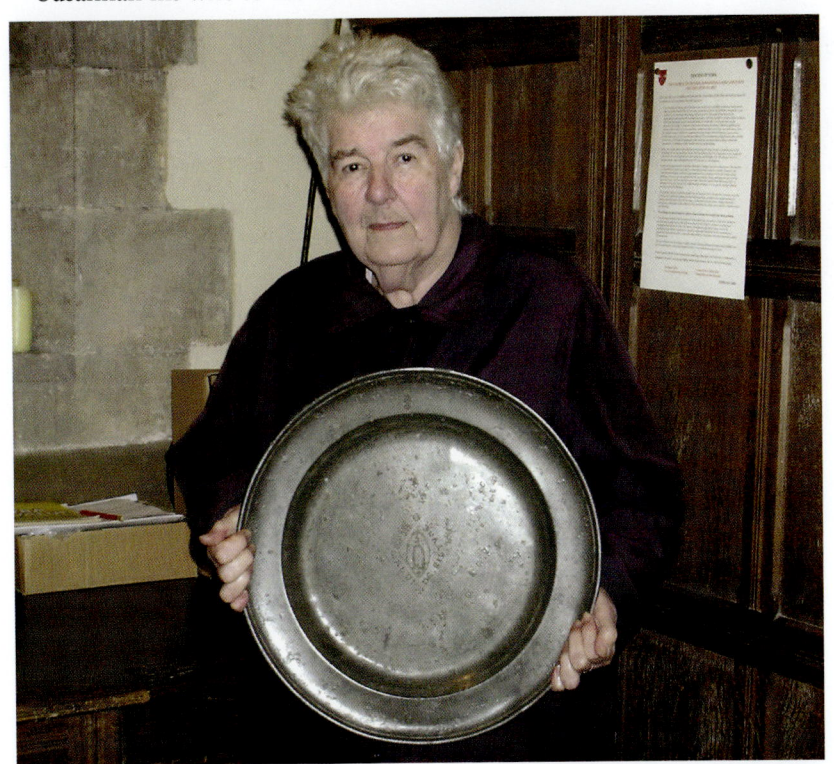

Figure 4: The pewter alms-dish celebrating the Chapel of St Oswald in the Percehay house at Ryton, kindly displayed by Church Warden Edith Collier

Figure 5: Casual prehistoric finds from Ryton

Figure 6: (top) The original deed dated 1356, complete with Sir William Percehay's seal attached, held in the Merchant Adventurers Hall in York;
(below) Seal matrix found at Levisham and the imprint produced by it

45

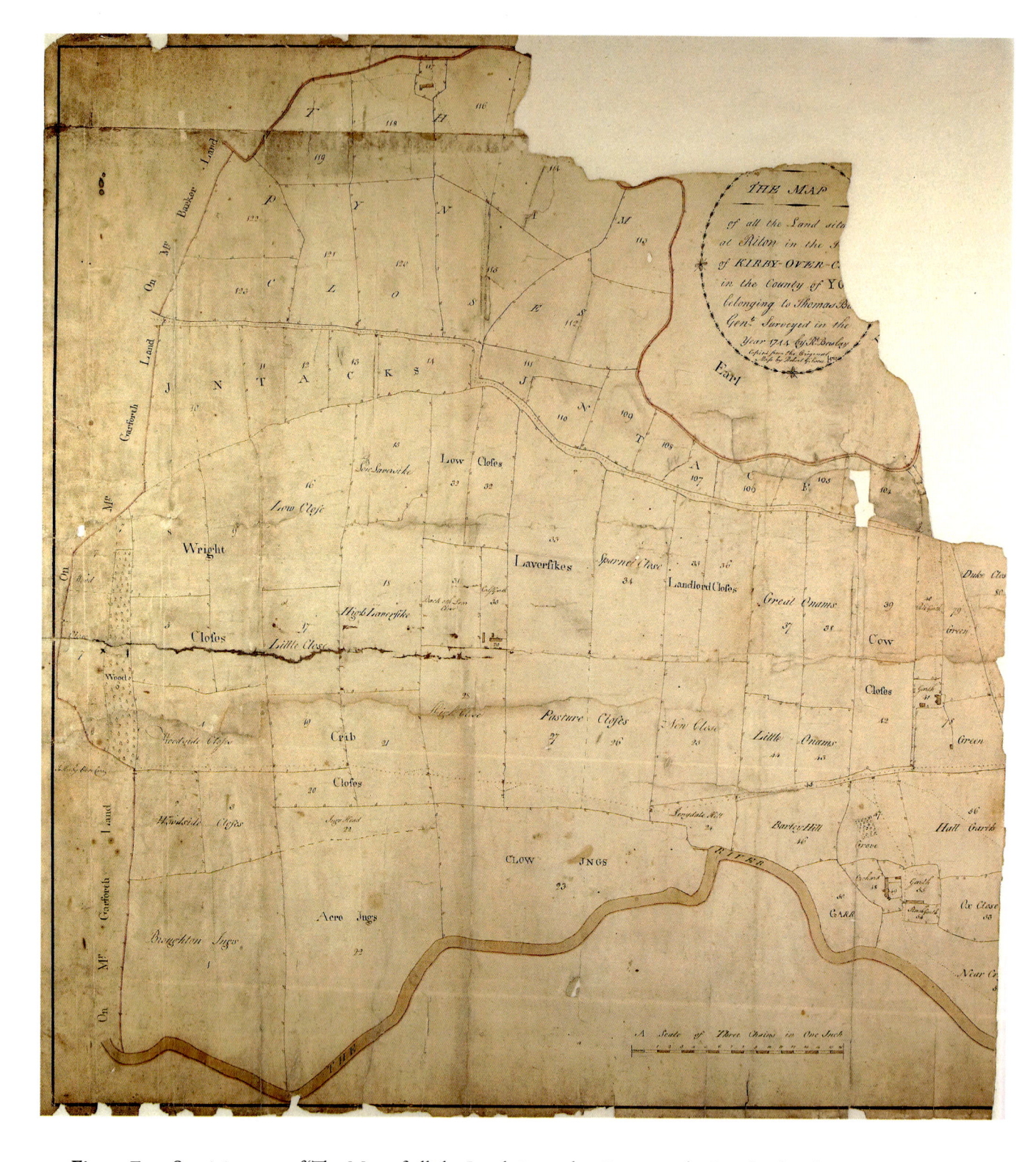

Figure 7: *Surviving part of 'The Map of all the Land situated at Ryton in the Parish of Kirby-Over-Carr in the County of York belonging to Thomas Barstow Gent. Surveyed in the year 1744 by Rt. Bewlay. Copied from the original Map by Robert Gilson 1787' (NYCRO Barstow ref: TD194/1)*

Names of Closes from the Rent Book of Thomas Barstow Gentleman

The numbers correspond to the Map of Ryton Lordship
Surveyed in the year 1744 by Robert Bewlay (see Figure 7)

1) Browton Ings – Meadow
2) Woodside Close – Do
3) Ditto & Do
4) Ditto in two parts – Do
5) Wreet (Wright) Close – Arable
6) The Wood
7) Wood Close in 3 parts-Meadow
8) Wreet Close – Arable
9) Ditto and Ditto
10) Intack in 2 parts – Pasture
11) Intack – Arable
12) Ditto and Ditto
13) Ditto – Meadow
14) Ditto – Arable
15) Low Laversike – Arable
16) Low Close – Meadow
17) Little Close – Ditto
18) High Laversike – Meadow
19) Crib Close – Meadow
20) Ditto and Ditto
21) Crib Close – Arable
22) Acre Ings in 2 parts-Meadow
23) Clow Ings – Pasture
24) Lengdell Hill – Pasture
25) New Close – Pasture
26) Pasture Closes in two Parts
27)   Pasture
28) High Close – Meadow
29) House and Garden
30) Barn Stable & Calf Garth-Past
31) Back'oth Lear Close – Pasture
32) Low Close in 2 parts – Arable
33) Laversike – Meadow
34) Sparnil Close – Meadow
35) Landlord Close – Pasture
36) Ditto – Meadow
37) Great Onams – Pasture
38) Ditto and Ditto
39) Cow Close – Pasture
40) Rye Garth – Arable
41) Thos Dale House Barn
     Fold Yard Lane etc.

42) Cow Close – Pasture
43) Little Onams – Meadow
44) Ditto – Pasture
45) A Lane
46) Barley Hill – Meadow
47) Grove – Pasture
48) Orchard etc.
49) Guy Raines House Courting etc.
50) Carr – Meadow
51) Near Croft – Pasture
52) Far Croft – Do
53) Ox Close – Arable & Meadow
54) Stack Garth
55) A Garth Barn etc.
56) Hall Garth – Pasture
57) Garth – Meadow
58) Thomas Brown House & Garth
59) Robt. Hood Do
60) William Watson Do
61) A Garth
62) A Lane
63) Green – Pasture
64) Smith House and Garth
65) Wid. Harrison House and Garth
66) Ditto Garth
67) Do. And Do.
68) Cowlam Garth – Meadow
69) A Garth – Meadow
70) Old House Garth – Arable
71) Parson Garth
72) Little Close – Pasture
73) Seavey Close – Pasture
74) Luck up Close – Do
75) Croft – Pasture
76) House Orchard etc.
77) Forehills – Pasture
78) Green – Pasture
79) Ditto
80) Duke Close – Pasture
81) Longlands – Pasture
82) Little Do

83) Sellar Close – Pasture
84) Sellar Close – Arable
85) Great Costa Howl – Meadow
86) Long Close – Meadow
87) Little Costa Howl – Do
88) Ox Close – Arable
89) Little Close – Meadow
90) Ox Close – Pasture
91) Paddock Howl
92) Paddock - Pasture
93) Beeld Close Howl
94) Beeld Close - Pasture
95) Orchard
96) Barn & Fore Garth
97) A Garden
98) House & Back Garth
99) Back Garth Howl – Meadow
100) Longlands Howl – Pasture
101) Duke Close Howl – Pasture
102) A Lane
103) Ditto
104) Intack – Meadow
105) Ditto – Pasture
106) Ditto & Ditto
107) Do. & Do.
108) Do – Meadow
109) Do – Arable & Meadow
110) Do – Arable
111) Do & Do
112) Pynam Close – Arable & Meadow
113) Pynam – Pasture
114) Ditto & Ditto
115) Ditto – Arable
116) Do – Pasture
117) House Barn & Garth
118) Pynam – Pasture
119) Do – Meadow
120) Do – Arable
121) Pynam – Arable
122) Do – Meadow
123) Do – Arable
124) A Lane

Figure 8: *Names of Closes from the Rent Book of Thomas Barstow (NYCRO TD 194/2)*

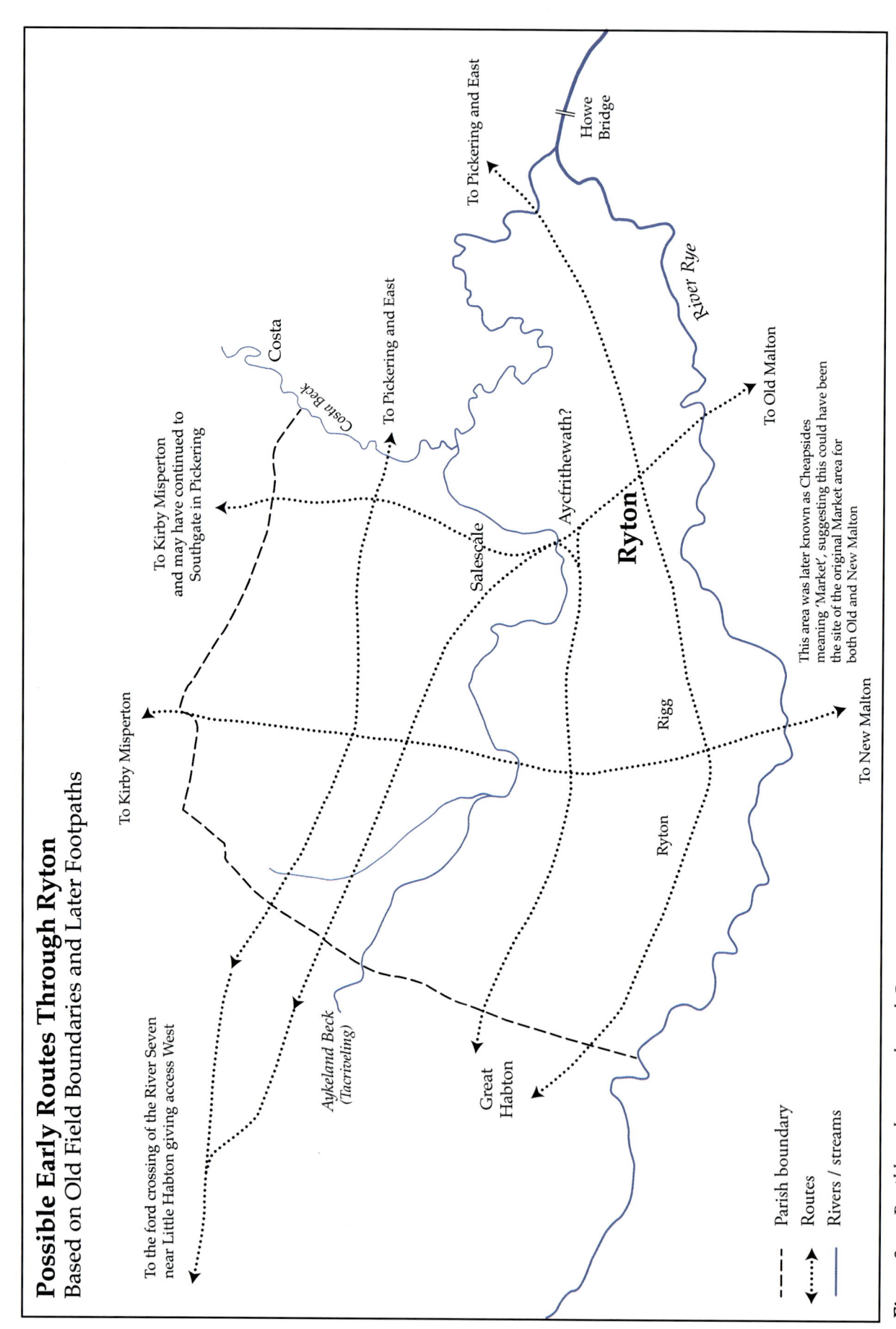

Figure 9: Possible early routes through Ryton

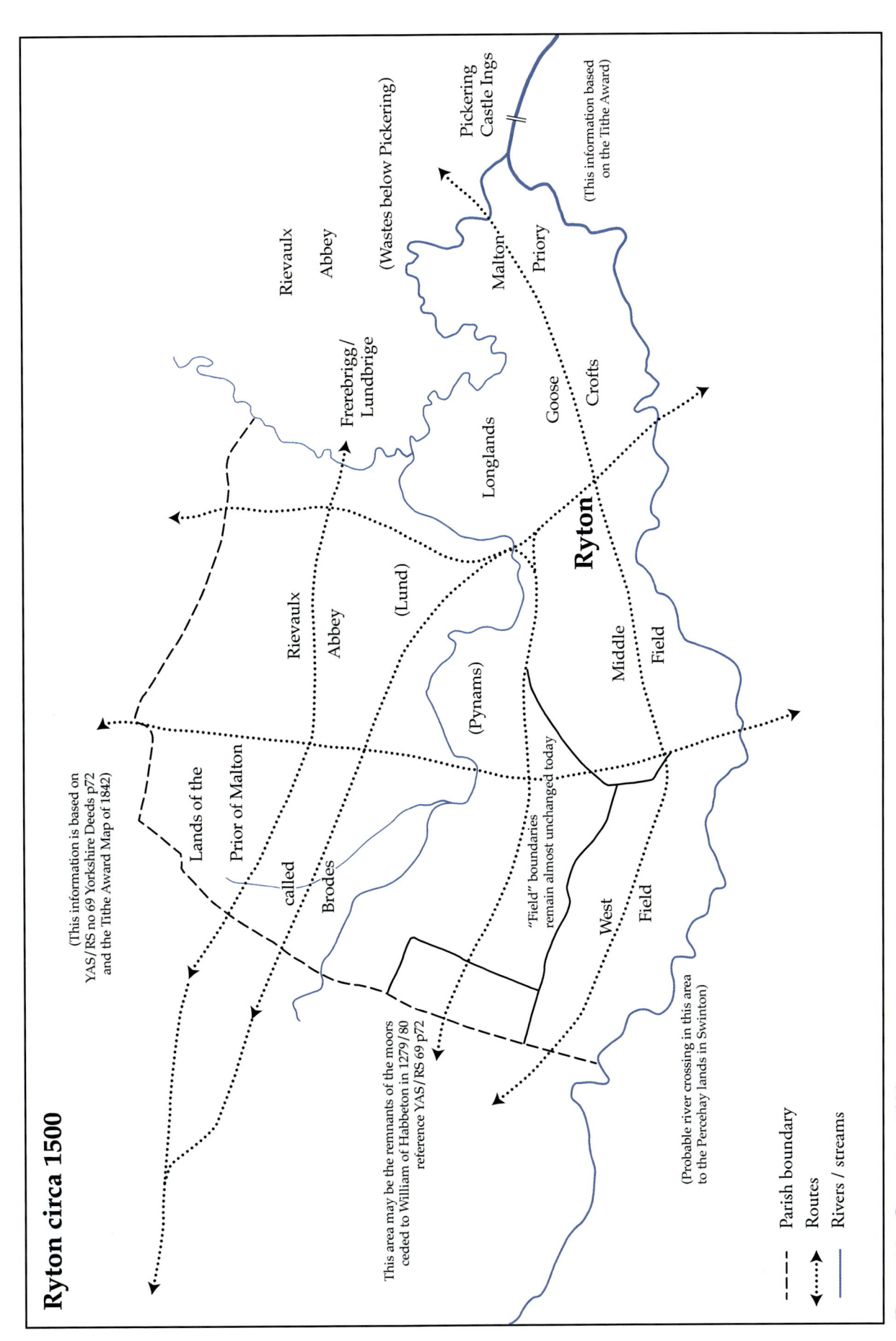

Figure 10: Ryton circa 1500

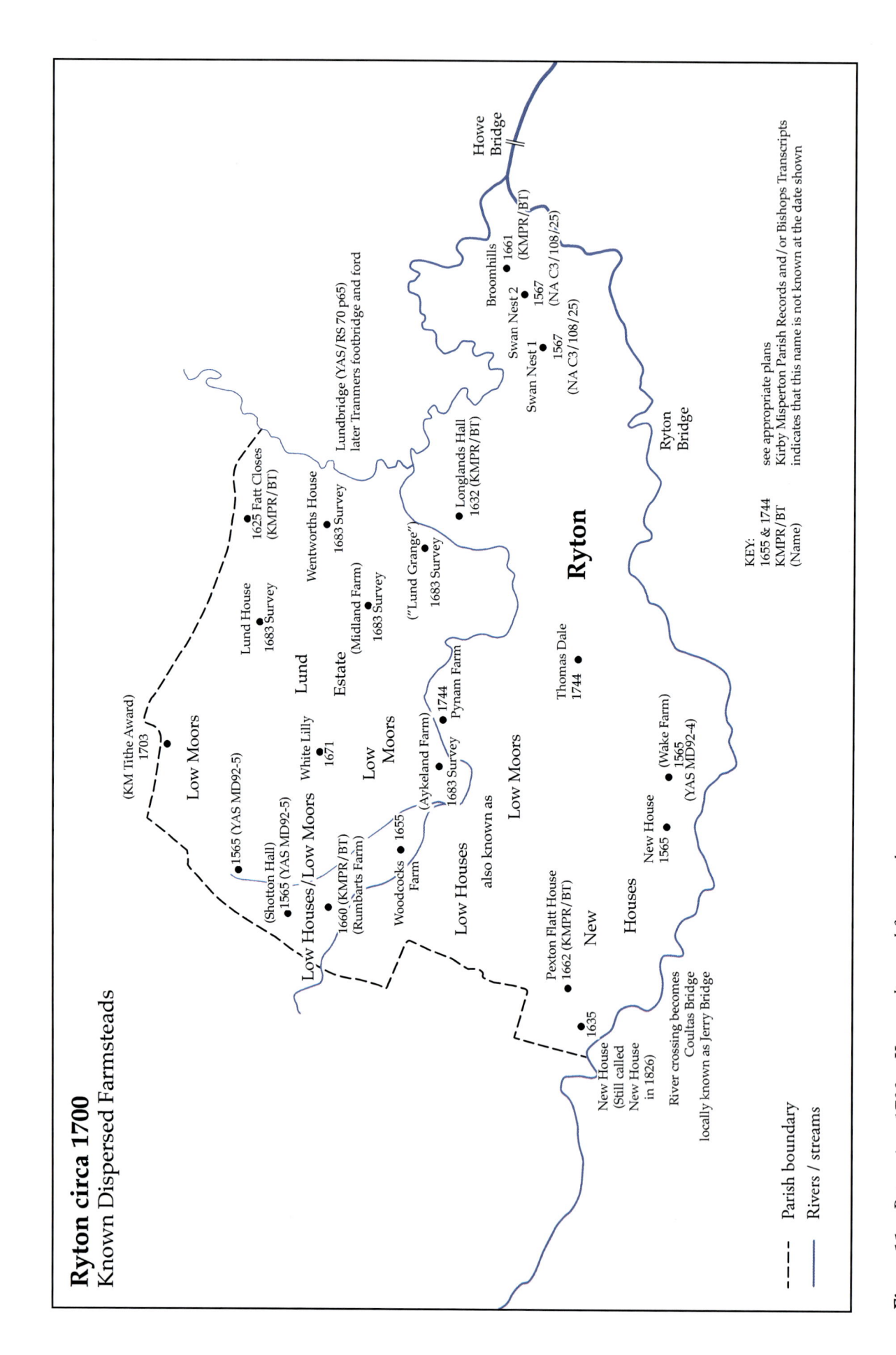

Figure 11: Ryton circa 1700 – Known dispersed farmsteads

1655 Plan 2
New Closes Created in 1655

- Red Lilly Close (1)
- White Lilly Close (2)
- Cowslippe Close (3)
- Primrose Close (3)
- Sage Close (3)
- The Leafield (3)
- Tulapay Close (4)
- Maidenhaire Close (4)
- The Lyons Foote (9)
- Sorrel Close (9)
- Ladyes Bedstrawe Close (4)
- The Adders Tongue (8)
- The Harrow (8)
- The Draggons Close (8)
- The Portculleys (7)
- Wakerobin Close (6)
- The Eyebright Close (6)
- The Oxpasture (5)
- Old Brass Castle (5)
- New Brass Castle (5)

(1) = Katharine Coates
(2) = Elizabeth Garforth
(3) = Alice Garforth
(4) = Judeth Garforth
(5) = Mary Taylor
(6) = Susan Denton
(7) = Martha Beckwith
(8) = Alice Bowes
(9) = Henry Garforth

1655 Plan 1
Names of Closes Prior to Distribution

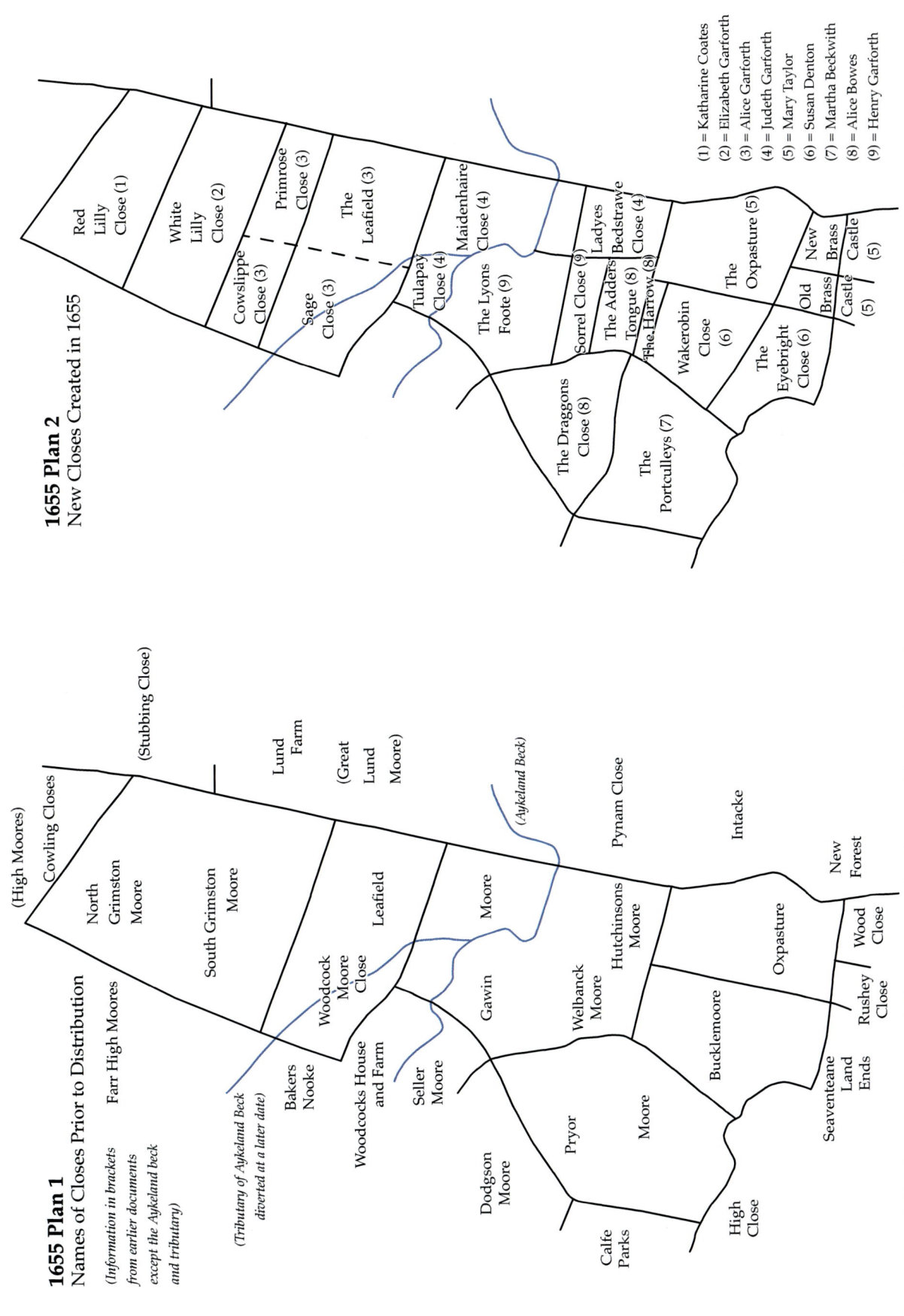

(Information in brackets from earlier documents except the Aykeland beck and tributary)

(Tributary of Aykeland Beck diverted at a later date)

- (High Moores)
- Cowling Closes
- (Stubbing Close)
- Farr High Moores
- North Grimston Moore
- South Grimston Moore
- Lund Farm
- (Great Lund Moore)
- Bakers Nooke
- Woodcock Moore Close
- Leafield
- Woodcocks House and Farm
- Seller Moore
- Gawin Moore
- (Aykeland Beck)
- Pynam Close
- Dodgson Moore
- Pryor Moore
- Welbanck Moore
- Hutchinsons Moore
- Intacke
- Calfe Parks
- High Close
- Bucklemoore
- Oxpasture
- New Forest
- Seventeane Land Ends
- Rushey Close
- Wood Close

Figure 12: 1655 Plan 1 – Names of Closes prior to distribution; Plan 2 – New Closes created in 1655 with new owners

51

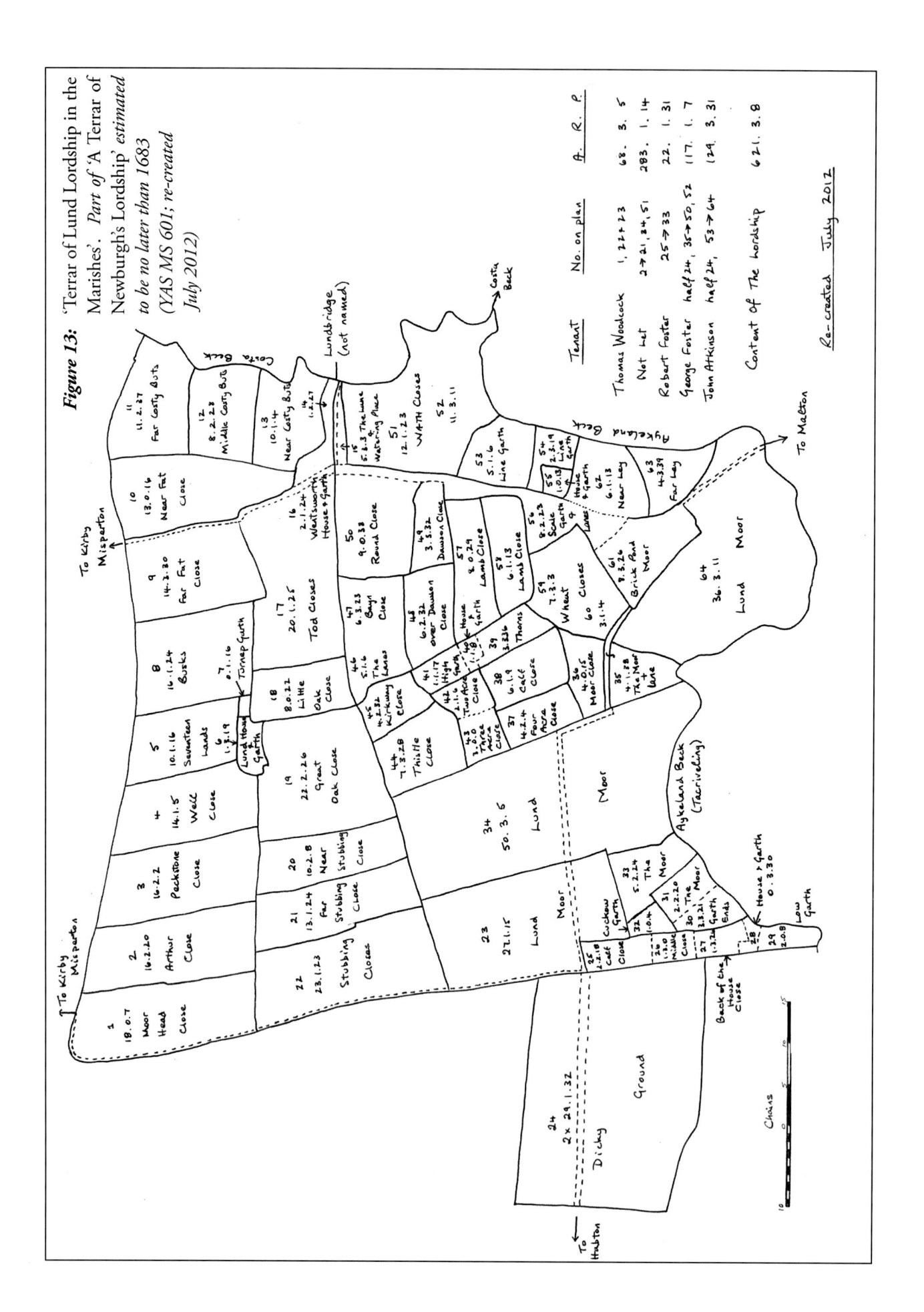

Figure 13: 'Terrar of Lund Lordship in the Marishes'. Part of 'A Terrar of Newburgh's Lordship' estimated to be no later than 1683 (YAS MS 601; re-created July 2012)

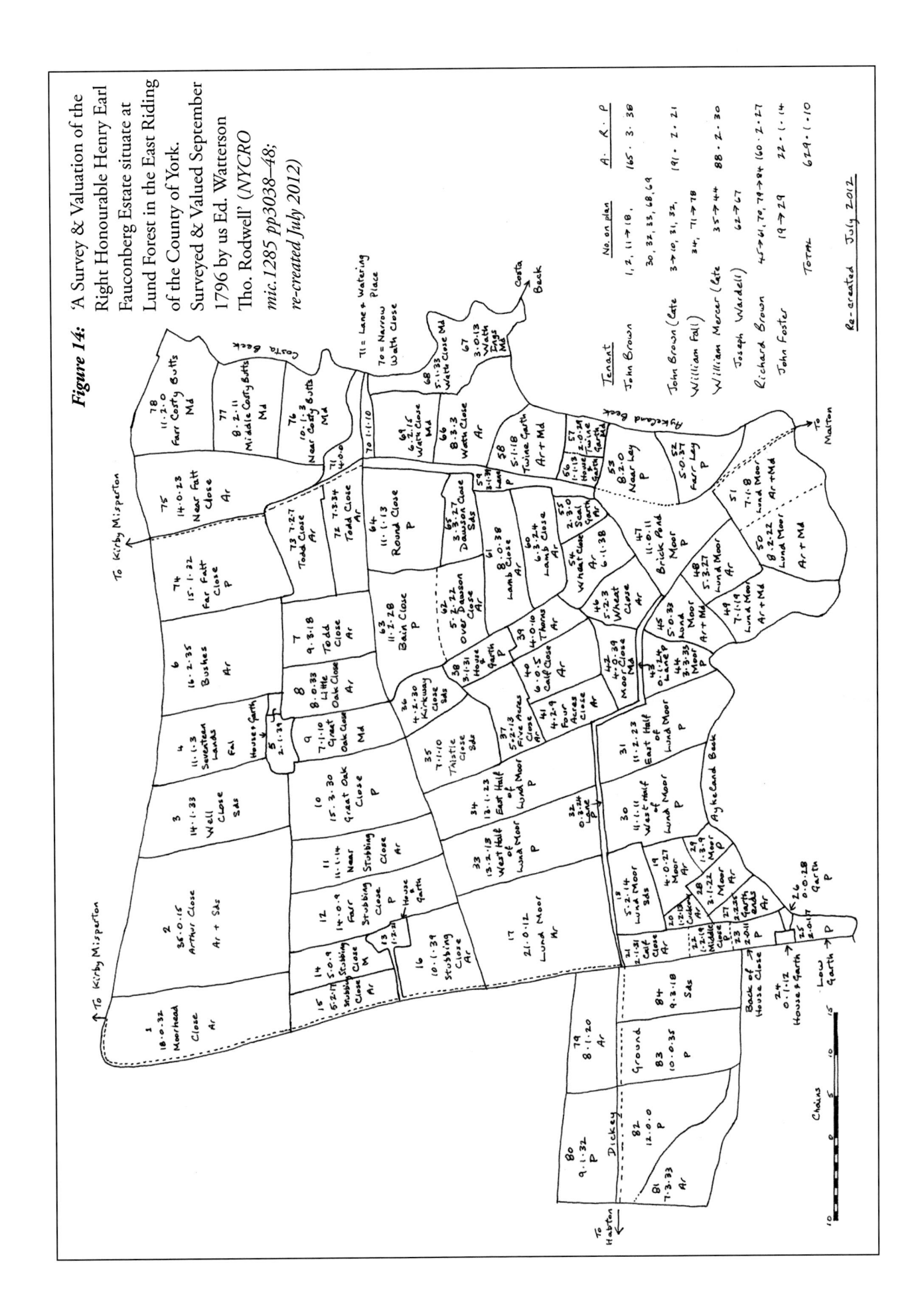

Figure 14: 'A Survey & Valuation of the Right Honourable Henry Earl Fauconberg Estate situate at Lund Forest in the East Riding of the County of York. Surveyed & Valued September 1796 by us Ed. Watterson Tho. Rodwell' (*NYCRO mic.1285 pp3038–48; re-created July 2012*)

Figure 15: 'Plan of Lund Forest in the Township of Ryton and Parish of Kirby Misperton in the North Riding of the County of York the property of Sir Geo. Wombwell Bart. 1849' *(NYCRO ref: ZDV VI 66)*

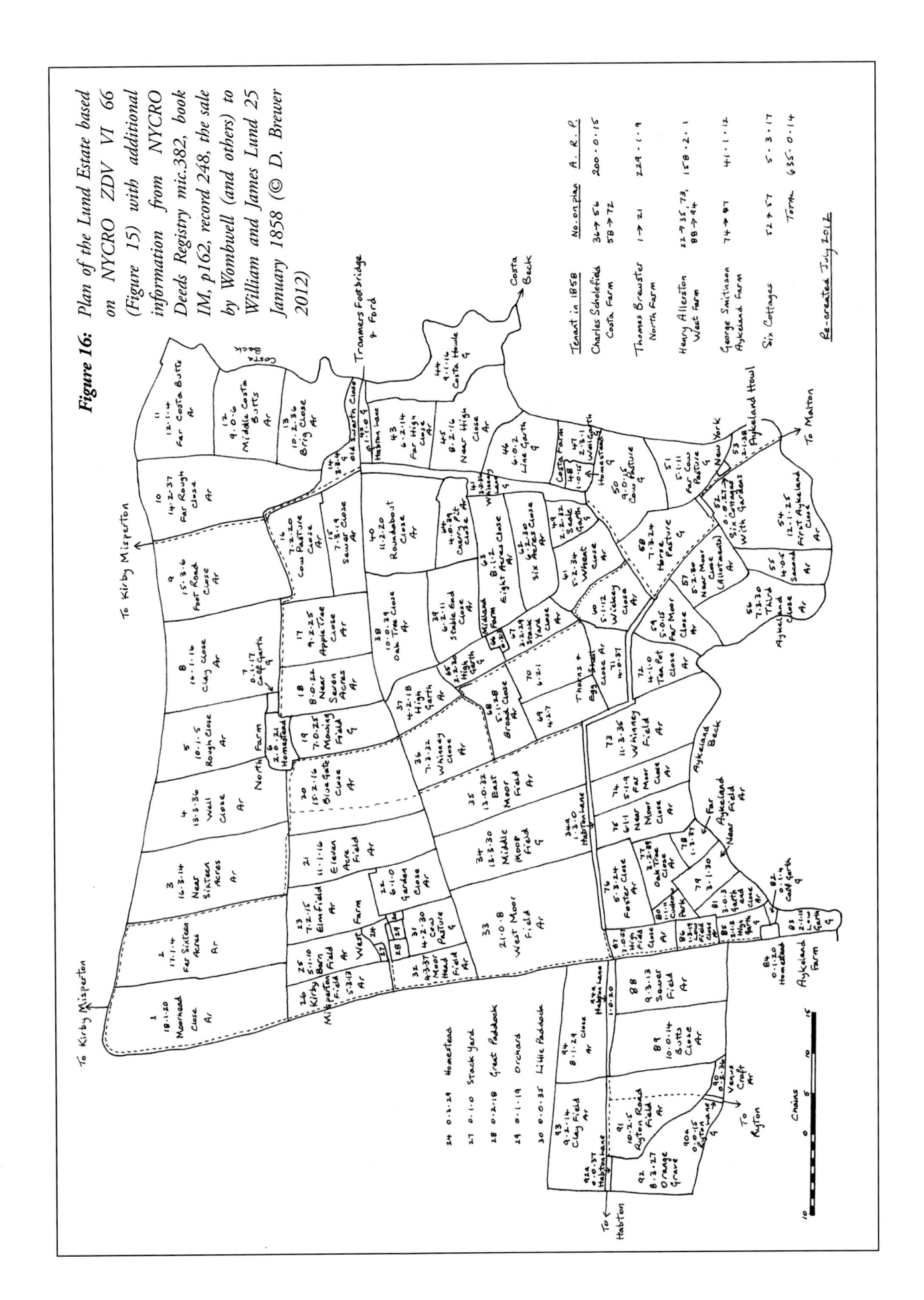

Figure 16: Plan of the Lund Estate based on NYCRO ZDV VI 66 (Figure 15) with additional information from NYCRO Deeds Registry mic.382, book IM, p162, record 248, the sale by Wombwell (and others) to William and James Lund 25 January 1858 (© D. Brewer 2012)

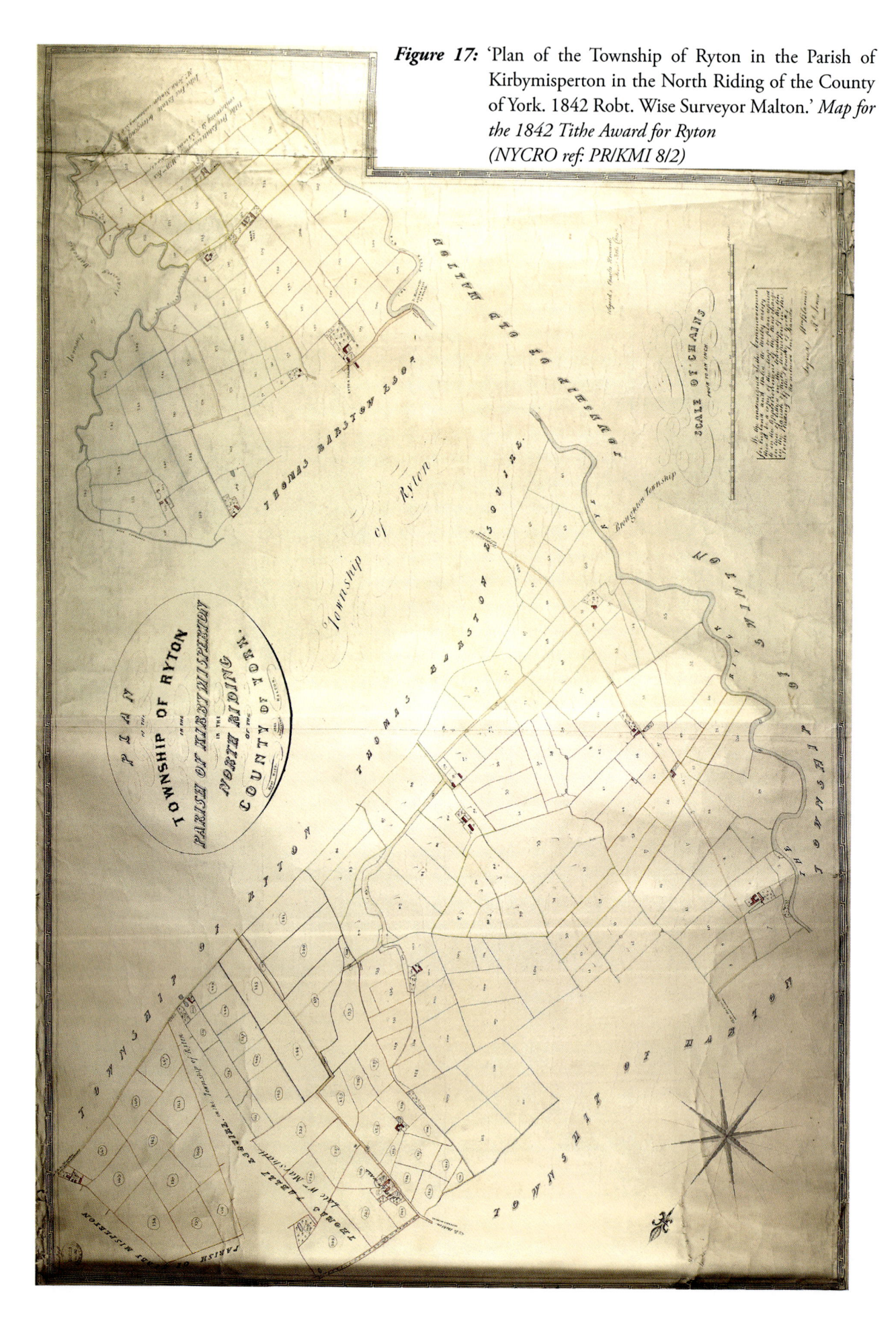

Figure 17: 'Plan of the Township of Ryton in the Parish of Kirbymisperton in the North Riding of the County of York. 1842 Robt. Wise Surveyor Malton.' *Map for the 1842 Tithe Award for Ryton (NYCRO ref: PR/KMI 8/2)*

Names of Closes from the Tithe Award for the Township of Ryton

Numbers correspond to the associated map surveyed 1842

Additional names from contemporary sources

North West Farm (High Farm)
156 Far Corner Field
157 Far Middle Field
158 Ten Acre
159 Middle Field
160 Second Sewer Close
161 Sewer Field
162 Field below Stackyard
163 Stackyard Field
164 Homestead Buildings etc.
165 Sward Close
166 Field below Sward Close
167 First Sewer

Between Messenger & Riverdene
16 Low Field
17 High Field
18 Hill
19 Great Ings
20 Little Ings

North of Park Farm (Low Moor)
128 Low Field
129 Stell Field
130 Snipe
131 Middle Field
132 Little Close
133 Sward Close
134 Orchard

White Lilly
145 Far Field
146 Square Field
147 Middle Field
148 Second Field
149 Front Field
150 House Buildings etc.
151 Paddock
152 Orchard
153 Near Close
154 Long Field
155 Far Little Field

Sparrow Hall / Low Moor Farm
85 West Hill Ground
86 East Hill Ground
87 Middle Do. Do.
88 Low Do. Do.
89 Road
90 Home Field   }
91 Homestead & Garth   } Adders
92 House and Garden   } Tongue
93 Orchard   }
94 Croft   ) The Harrow Close
95 Low Habton Close   }
96 Pond Close   } Draggons
97 Clover Close   } Close
98 Shoulder of Mutton   }
99 High Habton Close

Messenger Farm
21 (No name given)   } Near & Far
22 -   } Ings
23 -   ) The Homestead
24 Garden etc.   )   &
25 House Buildings etc.)   Close
26 (No name given)   Home Close
27 -   West Middle Close
28 -   East Middle Close
29 -   Near Clay Close
30 -   Far Clay Close

Garrow Lodge Cottage
176 Garth   }
177 Clover Close   } Originally
178 House & Orchard   }
179 Barn Field   } four
180 Croft   }
181 High Spencer Close   } Closes

Bulmer Farm
182 Low Spencer Close   } all
183 High Goose Croft   }
184 Middle Goose Croft   } called
185 High Costa Close   }
186 Low Costa Close   } Goose Croft
187 Plantation   }
188 House Buildings etc. } Close
189 Low Goose Croft   }

Rye House
190 Middle Close
191 Do.   Do.
192 Garth End Close
193 Do.   Do.
194 Garden
195 Do.
196 House Yard & Garden
197 Foldyard & Buildings
198 Orchard
199 Low Garth
200 Do.   Do.
201 Short Ends
202 Little Ings
203 Do.   Do.
204 Great Ings
205 Horse Park

Figure 18: *Names of Closes from the Tithe Award for the Township of Ryton of 1842 as detailed in NYCRO mic.1799 pp422–34. Numbers correspond to those in Figure 17. (cont. overleaf)*

Figure 18 (cont.)

Gosling Green (Rumbarts Farm)
113 Bridge Field
114 Oak Tree Field
115 Pond Field
116 Shotten Field
117 Gosling Field
118 High Pasture
119 Orchard Field
120 House Orchard etc.
121 Buildings & Yard
122 Stripe
123 Road
124 Barn Field
125 Bacon Nook
126 Middle Field
127 Jill Field

Park Farm (Glisterpipe)
100 Habton Close
101 Garth
102 Bridge Field
103 East Field
104 Home Field Buildings
105 West Field
106 Stell Field
107 Horse Pasture
108 Brick Kiln Close
109 Plantation Close
110 Ings
111 Far Ings
112 Ten Acres

Garforth Hall (New House)
53 West Ings
54 Ings Head
55 Round Close
56 High Back Close
57 Low Back Close
58 House & Orchard etc.
59 Low Fold
60 High Pasture
61 Weak (Wake) Close Ings
62a Part of Weak Close   } Foreshores
63 Far Little Weak Close
64 Near Do.   Do.
65 Oak Tree Close
66 Low Pasture
69 Near Rushy Close
70 Far   Do.   Do.

Brass Castle
31 North Beckwith Moor
32 West Beckwith Moor
33 Great Do.   Do.
62 Part of Weak (originally Wake) Close
67 Corn Close
68 West Low Pasture
71 Wheat (West) Brass Castle Close
72 Brass Castle Close
73 Road
74 Brass Castle Close
75 Low Ox Moor
76 High Ox Moor
77 East & West Garth
78 Stack Yard
79 House Homestead etc.
80 Near Low Ground Close
81 Middle Do. Do. Do.
82 Far   Do. Do. Do.
83 Road & Waste
84 Whinny Hill

Riverdene (New House / Ness House)
1 Howls
2 Little Howls
3 Great Howls
4 Pickstone Platt   } Peckstone/Pexton Flatt
5 Fore Pasture
6 House Buildings etc.
7 Back Pasture
8 Habton Close
9 Habton Close
10 Horse Close
11 House Close   } This is adjacent to no. 4
12 [Calf] Parks   where there had been a
13 [Calf] Parks   house
14 [Calf] Parks
15 [Calf] Parks

Ryton Grange
34 Brick Kilns   }
35 Six Acre Close   } Wakerobin
36 Poor House Close   } Close
37 Four Acre Close   )Eyebright
38 Stone Horse Close   ) Close
39 Holly Tree Close   } East & West
40 Five Acres   } Seventeen Lands
41 House Garden etc.   } and Near & Far
42 House Close   } Land Ends
43 East Garraby Close   )
44 West Do.   Do.   ) High
45 Fanny Close   )
46 Barn Close   )
47 Well Field   ) Closes
48 Garden & Orchard   )
49 North Richardson Close   } Wyth Gate or
50 South Do.   Do.   }   Wyth Ings
51 Garforth Field
52 Do.   Do.   } West Ings

(cont. overleaf)

58

Figure 18 (cont.)

Sleightholme Farm		*Longlands Farm / Hall*	1744 Plan No.
168 Buildings Yard etc.	} Wilsons	240 Great Costa Howls	85
169 (No name given)	} Closes	241 Little Do. Do.	87
170 -	)	242 Ox Close	88
171 -	) Collectively	243 Long Close	86
172 -	) referred to	244 Seller Close	84 (Sellar Close)
173 -	) as	245 Do. Do.	83
174 -	) Longlands	246 Little Long Lands	82
175 -	)	247 Little Close	89
		248 Ox Close	90
Part of West Farm (Dicky Grounds)		249 Paddock Howl	91
135 (No name given)	Orange Grave	250 Beild Close Howl	93 (Beeld Close)
136 Road	Habton Lane	251 Beild Close	92 + 94
137 (No name given)	Ryton Rd Field	252 Back Garth Howl	99
138 Road	Ryton Lane	253 House Buildings etc.	95 + 96 + 97 + 98
139 (No name given)	Venus Croft	254 Long Lands	81 + 100
140 -	Butts Close		
141 -	Sewer Field	*Swan Nest*	
142 Road & Road Piece	Habton Lane	223 Howl Piece	
143 (No name given)	Solomon Close	224 (No name given)	
144 -	Clay Field	225 -	
		226 -	
Abbotts Farm (Swan Nest)		227 -	
210 Ings	}	228 -	
211 Horse Pasture	} Collectively	229 -	Low Village Close
212 Cow Pasture	}	230 -	Low Pasture Close
213 Stray	} referred to	231 -	Nursery Close
214 House Buildings etc.	}	232 -	Garth End Close
215 Stack Yard	} as	233 -	
216 Orchard	}	234 Orchard	
217 Do.	} Swan Nest	235 Stackyard etc.	
218 Costa Howls	}	236 Orchard	
219 Rabbit Fields	} Closes	237 Paddock	
220 Adjoining Rabbit Field }		238 (No name given)	Low Ings
221 Do. Do. Do. }		239 -	High Ings
222 Costa Howls			
		Part of Rye House	
Shotton Hall Farm (+ another Low Farm)		206 Pennyman Ings	} East & West
255 (No name given)		207 Do. Do.	} Goose Croft
256 -		208 Do. Do.	} Ings
257 -		209 Pennyman Field	East Short Leas
258 -			
259 House Buildings etc.			
260 Orchard			
261 Paddock			
262 (No name given)			
263 Plantation			
264 (No name given)			
265 Plantation			

The above list is set out in the same order as the Award with the tithe for each farm totalled separately, consequently the numbers are not necessarily consecutive. The farmsteads were not named but the land owner and the occupier were given. Not all fields were named, and some additional contemporary or earlier known names have been included.

The Tithe Award did not include details of the areas already paying an agreed fee, or modus, nor the areas deemed exempt having been part of the possessions of a religious house. Consequently the majority of the Barstow estate is not detailed (modus of £8) and neither is the Lund estate as this was previously owned by Rievaulx Abbey. The area at the confluence of the Costa and the River Rye, and part of Shotton Hall farm, were also exempt as they 'were formerly parcel of the possessions of the Priory of Old Malton', although originally the Tithe Commissioners mistakenly recorded this as 'the Abbey of Saint Mary in the City of York'.

Chapter 5

Place-Names of Ryton

Place-names are an invaluable original source of information that can contribute to our understanding of the history of an area. In the case of Ryton, working out the possible origins and meanings of the place-names has cast new light on this local history; aided by publications both in print and online, the history of Ryton can now be viewed from a very different perspective and previous assumptions can be radically reviewed. The term 'New House' was used to describe an area where two new houses had been built in the old West Field at least sixty years before the arrival of the John Garforth who had previously been credited with creating both the new house and the name. Lund probably never had anything resembling a 'forest', whatever that may have meant. The old Monks Bridge referred to as Frerebrigg actually did go over the Costa and not round it, as has been previously suggested in order to place it erroneously at Howe Bridge; and the references to Habton Lane at the farthest point from Habton has resulted in the realisation that it was part of the old east/west route used by the monks from the granges in the area to communicate with the Abbey at Rievaulx. The location of most references can be ascertained with a remarkable degree of certainty and this has been a real advantage when working out possible meanings. The small river named Tacriveling can now be easily identified as the Aykeland Beck; 'Hill Grounds' is located in a very flat, low-lying area and actually refers to the Hill family; and Abbotts Farm refers to a Thomas Abbott rather than one of the many Abbots who have had interests in Ryton. Perhaps the most significant location is that of Scale Garth, situated adjacent to what is now thought to have been the 'lost' settlement of Salescale at Domesday. There are a surprising number of records concerning Ryton – literally hundreds – containing numerous references to local place-names. These include the names of closes (fields), farmsteads, rivers, river-crossings and whole areas. Some, like Goosecroft, have survived for centuries and are noted on many documents. Others, such as Grimston Moor, are mentioned only once and while their name may not have continued in local use, hopefully it will never be forgotten completely.

While many names only survive because of the documents that contain them, others are still in use today. Unfortunately the documents would invariably have been written by specialist scribes, lawyers or land agents who may not have fully understood what the locals were saying, especially bearing in mind the strong local dialect that is common in this area even today. These outsiders also had little, if any, local knowledge, resulting in changes such as the ancient name of a flatt in the West Field called Seventeen Lands becoming Swinton Lands (the handwriting on the previous document contributed to this misunderstanding), that was itself later 'corrected' to Seventeen Acres (which it wasn't), with the result that the name Seventeen Lands was 'lost'. Some of the documents were written well before Samuel Johnson's attempt to standardise spelling in his *Dictionary of the English Language* in 1755, so generally the spelling is phonetic and hence very variable. Account also needs to be taken of the local way of saying words and expressions to understand what was actually meant. It is clear that the team from the Ordnance Survey had tried to improve the standard of English of the locals by 'correcting' some of the words used. They changed the ancient word Intacks and replaced it with Intakes and to this day the OS maps continue to use this word. However, it is not surprising to report that locally the old Intack Lane still runs through the Intacks. One name in particular, Glisterpipe, is thought to be an attempt to belittle both the farmstead it referred to and the intelligence of the local people. The entry for Glisterpipe can leave little doubt that this name was not in everyday use in the area. It is, of course, possible that it was thought-up by a well-educated local who was having a laugh at the expense of either the surveyors for the first OS map or the Census enumerators, as these were the first documents to include this word. Whatever the true origin of this name, it does mean that every new name that suddenly appears needs to be treated with caution. In the case of the Ordnance Survey, a comparison with contemporary local information suggests that New York Cottages became Lund Forest Cottages and Aykeland Beck became Ackland Beck when compared with the Lund survey of 1849 (see Figure 16). A comparison with the Barstow rentals shows that Pynam became Parnham, Intacks became Intakes, and the ancient names of Broughton Ings, Acre Ings and Clow Ings were all lost to a fictitious East Ings that is not even correct geographically, being shown to the west of Ryton. This also resulted in the Ings that were to the east of Ryton being called Ryton Ings, despite the fact that they had been Goosecroft Ings for at least 600 years and were still being referred to as such on the relevant deeds. At around this time the new names of Ryton Grange, Gosling Green, Ness House and Sparrow Hall all appear – names that do not reflect those used on contemporary documents – while the lands of Mr Eddon were re-named Eden Lands. Another institution that seems to have imposed new names onto existing locations and features is Rievaulx Abbey as they seem to be responsible for *Costa, Lund, River Rye,* and possibly *Tacriveling*.

Some of the earliest recorded names are from lists of donations of land in Ryton given to the monastic houses, with the greatest number of individual donations being made, not surprisingly, to the local Priory at (Old) Malton. These were recorded by the Priory as they were received to make sure their ownership was unquestionable. At some later date all these donations were collated and written down in what became Malton Priory Chartulary [Charter]. This means that our knowledge of the original names comes from monks, writing exclusively in Latin, recording what the locals said in their own version of English, perhaps in an accent that was new to them (people came from all over the country to be monks in the northern monasteries), with this all being rewritten later from what by then may have been difficult to read manuscripts. This results in some names having very diverse spellings (e.g. aycfrithewath) and others that cannot be deciphered with any degree of certainty – literally 'lost in translation'. However, despite this, generally the older the reference material the more likely it is that the meaning deduced for a name is credible. It is also perhaps necessary to point out that although the meanings given are educated guesses, based on the substantial amount of information available, some are more reliable than others. In some cases more than one meaning may be interpreted from any one name, and all or none may actually be 'correct'. In the absence of other information, a basic rule seems to be that if in doubt, the name is probably derived from a personal name. Locating the actual person who provided the name then becomes the challenge, and of course it is not always possible.

One other problem that has been encountered is that of 'estate agent's licence', with no offence intended to that honourable profession. It is clear that some of the more grandiose titles, for what may have been relatively humble dwellings, were invented to impress either an absentee owner or a potential buyer. Perhaps one of the more obvious examples was Spring Hall. In 1655 Leafield was part of Alice Garforth's portion from the family distribution (see Figures 2 and 12), and the descriptions suggest it was an area of very average moor without any dwelling. When it was re-sold in 1659 there was a 'howse thereupon lately builded' (see the entry below for full details) but by the time of the sale in 1665 it had become a 'Messuage or Mancion howse lately erected commonly called Spring Hall'. The real substance of this dwelling is perhaps indicated by the fact that it seems to have disappeared by 1683. It may be significant that from 1659 to 1665, all the owners were 'Gentlemen' with addresses at the Inns of Court in London who were unlikely ever to have seen their property at Ryton, since it was purely an investment, and were even less likely to have built themselves a mansion there. The description of the estate of The Right Honourable Henry Earl Fauconberg in 1796 as Lund Forest also seems to have more to do with impressing an employer than with any presence of trees or a history of Royal hunting.

The use of a particular place-name also depends on the perspective of the people involved. To the Rector of Kirby Misperton completing the parish register, it would not be unreasonable to think of most of Ryton as 'low', resulting in the frequent use of Low Moors, Low Houses and Low Grounds to describe parts of Ryton. However, in Ryton, an area that could arguably be said to have nothing that could be described as 'high', the terms Low and High seem occasionally to be used to mean South and North, with the result that Thomas Woodcock in his will of 1752 left a farmstead he called 'High Farm' (today's North West Farm), despite the fact that it was situated at one of the lowest parts of Ryton and was at the time described as Low Moors by the Rector. To Thomas Woodcock the farmstead was situated to the north of his land, and was the most northerly in the whole of Ryton, so it was not unreasonable for him to refer to it as High Farm. A look at the many maps and plans confirms that invariably the 'high' close was always situated to the north of the farmstead and had nothing to do with the relative height above the surrounding area.

While all opinions and comments are the author's, it would not have been possible to produce this chapter without the considerable knowledge and research that has gone before and has been condensed into the *English Place-Name Elements; Addenda and Corrigenda* published by the English Place-Name Society, School of English Studies, at the University of Nottingham. Sincere thanks are specifically expressed to Dr. Paul Cavill of this organisation for encouraging the initial interest in place-names, and for his advice and guidance while compiling this list of possible meanings and interpretations of these fascinating names.

To avoid tedious repetition key documents are referred to as follows:

OS = Ordnance Survey (with appropriate date)
1086 = Domesday
C12/13 = Malton Priory Chartulary; Original in the British Library, copy available at the Borthwick Institute on microfilm MF(E)44 BM Cotton MS Claudius DXI f.102/3
1535 = YAS MD92-3 (see Appendix 1)
1565 = YAS MD92-6 (see Appendix 1)
1572 = Cause Papers, C.P.G.1628 ; 1572, Ellerker vs Woodcock re tithes
1604 = The distribution of the Percehay lands (YAS MD92-16) (see Appendix 1)
1655 = The distribution of the Garforth lands (NYCRO mic3989 p199) – Figure 12
1683 = Lund survey, undated but estimated as no later than this date (YAS MS601) – Figure 13
1744 = Barstow survey of 1744 (NYCRO – TD 194/1) – Figure 7
1796 = Lund survey of 1796 (NYCRO mic1285 p3038) – Figure 14
1841, 1851, 1861 etc = Census returns
1842 = Tithe Award for Ryton; map NYCRO PR/KMI 8/2 + mic1799 p422 – Figure 17
1849 = Lund survey map of 1849 (ZDV VI 66) + Sale of 1858 (mic382 Bk IM, p162, r248) – Figure 16
1850/1890/1910 = Survey dates of OS maps of the area
KMBT = Kirby Misperton Bishop's Transcripts, B.I., mic494 (Kirby Misperton)
Parish Registers = NYCRO Kirby Misperton Parish Registers, and the 'Green Book'

Abbreviations used:

pn	personal name
ME	Middle English
ODan	Old Danish
OE	Old English
OED	Oxford English Dictionary
OFr	Old French
ON	Old Norse
OScand	Old Scandinavian

Aichefritlh, aycfrithewath, haythefrihtwatgate C12/13
There are a number of references to gifts of land in the Malton Chartulary that probably refer to the same area, although at first glance they appear to be different. The gifts are: 'at the road to the ford of aichefritlh', 'at [or nearby] the ford of Ethfrid', 'at haycefrithewath', 'at the farthest part of the way called eikfrithwathgate', 'as far as haythefrihtwatgate towards habeton', 'on the west part of aycfrithewath'. In context the key elements seem to be:

ON akr = wild undeveloped land. This original sense is the most likely of a number of possibilities (see *Aykmoore Closse*); OE frith = protected, secure, refuge; ON vath = a ford; ON gata = a road, a way, a path.

At the time of the Chartulary there may have been a number of fords in the Ryton area, but at least one would have crossed what later became known as *Aykeland Beck*, so it is reasonable to think that the ford referred to in every name variation would have crossed this beck. From this the wild area referred to would have been to the north of the open fields of the village, and to the south of the beck. In that case the road would have followed the same route (or similar) as the track from Ryton to Habton shown on the Barstow 1744 estate plan (see Figure 7), with this route continuing into the 20th century,[1] and the footpath along Intack Lane follows the same route today. The reference to Habton is also covered by this assumption. From all the name elements and their context, the reference is to 'a route through undeveloped land, that at some point crossed the Aykeland Beck, with either the route or the ford (or even both) deemed as safe'. The ford over Aykeland Beck may well be that shown on the plan of 1744, John Ogilby's survey of 1675, and the OS maps from 1850 to 1910, eventually being replaced by the road bridge that exists today.

Abbotts Farm OS 1910: Note the double 't' spelling – this is because this farm, originally one of the two called *Swan Nest*, did not have the name of Abbotts Farm until after the tenancy of Mr Thomas Abbott in 1861. Not surprisingly it had been assumed that the name was from Malton Priory who had owned land in the area, and may even have owned the land that became Abbotts Farm, but clearly the name is from Thomas.

Ackland Farm OS 1850: This name first appears on the 1850 OS map. This does not seem to have been the name in use locally as the name *Aykeland Farm* was still in use by the owners into the 20th century.[2] Ackland seems to have been the interpretation of Aykeland by the OS surveyors, who appear to have had their own agenda in this area.

Acomore Wood 1534:[3] ON akr = wild undeveloped land + moor + wood. The variation in spelling of the first element is not surprising as it would have sounded just the same as 'ayke'.

(Two) Acre Close no. 42 1683: OE aecer = a plot of cultivated land, developing into the measure of land area + *close*. In the Lund survey of 1683 there were 64 closes, and only three were referred to by area: Two Acre Close (2a 1r 6p), Three Acre Close (3a 0r 0p), and Four Acre Close (4a 2r 4p). By the survey of 1796 the first two had been made into one larger close called Five Acre Close, though ironically in the survey of 1849 this was then given the name of Broad Close. This was a notable exception to the trend of moving from names to acreage; in this survey six other closes lost their earlier names, being referred to only by their acreage. Sadly this was an irreversible trend with the result that few fields are now known by a name.

Acre Ings no. 22 1744: ON akr = wild undeveloped land + ME ing/ynge = meadow near a water course and subject to inundation. The use of the element *akr* based on the sense of wild, undeveloped land had been very common in this area (see *aichefritlh, aykmoore closse, aykeland beck*). However, the use of the word *acre* to describe the type of land, as in this context, right up to the 19th century is quite surprising, as by then the more usual understanding of acre as a measure of area was in common use (see *Two Acre Close*). It is even more surprising considering Acre Ings covered an area of over 23 acres!

Adder's Tonge Close 1655: *Ophioglossum vulgatum*, common name Adder's Tongue, is a small, now scarce, fern of old grassland. It may well have been growing in this close when this new name was given at the distribution of 1655, and could explain why the name remained in use until at least 1805. By 1842 a farmstead had been built on it and the name had consequently changed to Home Field.

Allotments no. 57 1849 (name in use until 1960s): At some time between the surveys of 1796 and 1849 a terrace of six workers cottages with gardens were built on the edge of the Lund estate with the name of *New York*. In addition to the gardens, each cottage had outhouses so pigs could be kept (a very common practice in this area which persisted at these cottages into the 1960s) and each had an allotment of approximately one acre in this nearby field, referred to as Allotments, enabling the residents to be almost self-sufficient. The Census returns refer to these as 'Poor Houses' but they remained the property of the Lund estate, suggesting that it was the Fauconberg family who built them for the benefit of their workers on the farms of the Lund estate.

Aykeland Beck 1849: ON akr = wild undeveloped land + ON land = tract of land of considerable extent + beck = a stream. The 'aykeland' that the beck runs through extends from the boundary with Habton right through to the Costa. Unfortunately the name of the beck does not seem to have been written down before 1849, but it fits in with the crossing of this beck called *aikefrithwath* in the 12/13th century. The earliest written name for this beck was *Tacriveling* but that name does not seem to have survived beyond the 13th century and because of its Latin origins is unlikely to have been created by the locals. Aykeland Farm, Aykeland Field, Aykeland Close and Aykeland Howl were all first recorded in 1849 but the names had probably been in use for a long time before; all survived into the 20th century.

Aykmoore Closse 1604: ON akr = wild undeveloped land + moor + close. This area was described as moor, *whynnes* and pasture, with no mention of trees or woods. From this description the whole area seems to have been unreclaimed land in a near-native state, with the boundaries of the closes suggesting that the whole of this area was initially only divided into two very large closes, being part of the original Aykeland.

Baker's Nooke pre-1655: Probably *pn* + ME noke = land in a secluded corner (which this certainly was). By 1842 (no. 125) it had become Bacon Nook. This probably reflects the fact that by then the Baker family were long-gone, and the shape of the field is very reminiscent of the hind quarter of a pig.

Barren/Barrow/Burrow Nook: This is the local name for *North West Farm*, although none of the variations has been seen in print. The deeds can be traced back to 1752 and there is nothing to suggest why the local name is one of the above. A logical explanation could be given for each variation, but it remains a mystery why this alternative name is used locally but not recorded.

Barstow House Originally a semi-detached council house built in the early 1950s on a corner of one of Barstow's fields with the name reflecting their connection to the area.

Bayn Close no. 47 1683: Bayn could just mean difficult or causing distress (as in 'the bane of my life') indicating land that is difficult to work, which it is. However, it could also indicate that Common Fleabane (*pulicaria dysenterica*) grew there as this plant grows in meadows, on the sides of ditches, and prefers clay or wet soils, all of which apply in this location. Fleabane gets its name from the belief that the strange scent given off by the leaves would keep away fleas and 'bunches were hung in rooms or dried and burned as a fumigant'.[4] As with a number of old traditions there could well have been some truth in this belief as we now extract pyrethrum from a close relative of this species for use as an insecticide.

Beeld Close nos 93 & 94 1744: ME Beild & dialect bield = a refuge, a place of shelter. The boundaries of the closes in 1744 suggest that Beeld Close originally included the adjacent close where the house was built, so perhaps the shelter later became the farmstead, with the whole then being separated from the original Beeld Close.

Beckwith Moor 1737:[5] *Portculleys* was given to Martha Beckwith and her husband in 1655 but it was known as Beckwith Moor by 1737, a name it retained in documents until at least 1842 and it was preserved orally into the mid-20th century.

Brass Castle (Old and New) 1655: This was one of the new names given at the Garforth distribution in 1655. The use of the prefixes 'old' and 'new' suggest that the name was in use before, but the documentation says clearly that both closes were divided out of a larger close previously called Oxpasture. This is one of the few new names to survive to the present day, although today's Brass Castle Farm is at the opposite end of the Oxpasture close. The migration seems to have occurred because Brass Castle was the name eventually used for most of the original Oxpasture. The OS maps are not consistent in the naming of this farm; Brass Castle in 1850, Low Moor Farm in 1890, Brass Castle in 1950, and Low Farm in 1986. Brass Castle is much more memorable and likely to survive.

Brick Pond Moor no. 61 1683: The underlying clay is just below the surface of most of the low-lying area of Ryton. It is not known if the clay was made into bricks/tiles on site or taken elsewhere, but Brick Kiln Close (no. 108) and Brick Kilns (no. 34) in 1842 leave little doubt that some manufacturing took place at these locations.

Brig Close no. 13 1849: ON bryggja, OE brycg & dialect brig = bridge or causeway. This is in the area now believed to have been the ancient crossing of the Costa (see *Frerebrigg*). Brig and brigg are still in use today in the north of England with both these meanings, and both would be appropriate here. *Tranmer's Footbridge* crosses the Costa at this point on the first OS map of 1850 and an adjacent ford is also shown.

Brodes 1279/80:[6] ON brot = a small piece of land. This is also quoted in other references to Malton Priory as Broades and Broats, and is always referred to in the plural, suggesting a number of pieces of land. In the reference quoted, 'the land of the Prior of Malton called Brodes' is now thought to lie in the area of today's *Shotton Hall*. The location is deduced from the reference to *Tacriveling* and its acquisition after the Dissolution by Roger Cholmeley, when it became *Cholmeley Moors*. These moors are identifiable when Sir Richard Cholmeley sold on this block of land to George Mountford in 1565,[7] although it is not possible to say when they came into the possession of the Shotton family. The deeds at both YAS and NYCRO allow this land to be followed from 1743 to the present day, where it is all the land of Shotton Hall within the boundary of Ryton.

Broom Hills / Broomhills 1601[8] onwards: Broom was, until very recently, a common plant in the area, and Broom Hills is one of the highest points of *Ryton Rigg* situated at the confluence of the Costa and the River Rye. In the 1842 Tithe Award this area was exempted from tithes as the lands were 'formerly parcel of the possessions of the Priory of Old Malton'. By the early 1600s there were at least four families registering births from Broomhills and it seems to have been effectively a separate settlement. As late as the OS map of 1890 there appear to be two homesteads in the area. It is occasionally referred to as *Sandhills* due to the underlying sand. The OE Brom originally referred collectively to any coarse shrubs and bushes, but it eventually became used only for *planta genista*, the common broom.

Brother's Ditch C12/13: The context shows that by the time of the donation by Alexander of Ryton to Malton Priory, the monks already had land in the area and had given their name to one of the ditches. They may, or may not, have created it themselves. The location appears to have been towards the confluence of the Costa and the Rye. It is not thought to be the *Monks Ditch*, as that was associated with the monks of Rievaulx and in a very different, easily identified location.

Bucklemoore pre-1655: It could just be a *pn* but a Mr Buckle cannot be connected to the area. However, according to the key document concerning the distribution of 1655 this close was one of three purchased from Sir William and Robert Belt before 1655. Someone with a sense of humour could easily have named this close after them (belt…buckle?).

Bulmer Farm 1861: *pn* Thomas Bulmer was resident at the 1861 Census. This had been part of *Goose Crofts*, with the farmstead built between 1769 and 1842.

Busks no. 8 1683: ON buskr = bush, shrub, that becomes ME busk. This explains why the name of this close at the survey of 1796 was 'Bushes'. By 1849 the bushes would probably have been removed and the type of land was noted as it had become Clay Close.

(Costy) Buts/Butts no. 11 1683: *Costa* + ME butte = a strip of land abutting a boundary. In 1683 there were three closes, all adjacent to the boundary marked by the Costa called Far, Middle and Near Costy Buts, indicating their geographic relationship to the nearest farm named as *Wentsworths House and Garth*. In 1547 the local name for the Costa was Costey.[9]

Byuretre & Burtre C12/13: ME burtre = Elder. Still locally called 'bottry bush', the common elder was always surrounded by myth and superstition which continue today. It is highly scented (wood, roots and leaves as well as the flowers) and was used to keep flies away from cattle and horses, but it was also associated with witches and the devil. It is still considered unlucky to take the wood indoors and burn it, although having a bottry bush near the house was supposed to ward off witches, which may account for why none has been seen in this area for such a long time!

Calfe Parks pre-1655: Calf + ME park = an enclosed area of land. Park does have hunting connotations, especially royal hunting, but there is no evidence for that here. The fields in the area were all 'Parks' by 1842.

Carr no. 50 1744: ON kjarr = a bog, marsh or fen. Despite the fact the parish is Kirby Misperton alias Kirby-over-Carr, suggesting the low-lying areas would be referred to as carr, this is the only occurrence of this name in Ryton.

Casteldich C12/13: OE/OFr castel = castle + OE dic = a ditch. At first glance the meaning of this word, that occurs twice in the Malton Chartulary, is fairly obvious. However, there are no other references to anything resembling a castle in any other document, although the presence of Siward (see *Siwardeus*), the Earl of Northumbria, could be significant; further information is required before any conclusions are drawn. The word castle may mean camp, or fort, or just an easily defended area. Ryton Rigg would have been an obvious location for any of these, and the high ground at the confluence of the Costa and the Rye would be easy to defend, with a ditch being defensive rather than for drainage. Another possible explanation is that this refers to a ditch that drained towards *Castle Ings* at the other side of the Costa, near its confluence with the Rye.

Castle Ings C14: The Ings to the north of the Costa and the River Rye, with the River Derwent to the east. This was originally called eduimersch (many different spellings) and was retained by Henry I for his own use from a grant to the monks of Rievaulx (see *Frerebrigg*). It was administered from Pickering Castle and was clearly identified in 1651 in 'A Survey of the Honor of Pickering with the Rights Members and Appurtenances thereunto belonging'.[10] The Demeasne Lands in Lease included 'All those several parcels of Meadow Ground almost encompassed with the Rivers Darwent and Rye belonging to the said Castle and known by the Severall Names of Edusmarsh als Edusmersh otherwise called How Ings or Castle Ings'. It is also known that William Stuttes was 'keeper of Castle Ings and the Derwent' in 1322.[11]

Cherry Pit Close no. 64 1849: According to the OED, Cherry-pit was a children's game that consisted of throwing cherry stones into a small pit or hole. Pit might also have referred to the cherry stone. Interestingly, there is a variety of plum still grown in this area with small fruit, little more than the size of a cherry, with roundish stones. No doubt these could have been used to play the game instead of cherry stones.

Cholmeley Mores 1565:[12] Area of moor named after Sir Roger Cholmeley of Rokeby (Roxby) near Thornton Dale. It had been 'the land of the Prior of Malton called Brodes' and at the Dissolution it was acquired by Robert Holgate along with the 'site of the late Priory of Malton'.[13] At some time Sir Roger acquired this block of land, and when he sold it on in 1565 it was described as having two houses, thought to be the later *Shotton Hall* and *Low Moors Farm*, and had four closes occupied by Thomas and Rarfe Nesse (see *Ness House*) and Thomas Clerk. The name Cholmeley Moors survived until the 1655 distribution when it was called Farr High Moors (note the 'high' meaning north again). The Cholmeleys and the Percehays were near neighbours and had a relationship that could best be described as variable, ranging from pursuing each other in the courts, to hunting and socialising with each other.

Closse 1535[14] became **Close**: ME clos(e) = an enclosure. This is what today would be termed a field but that is a much later progression of *Felde*. Although the first record of close in this area is 1535 the term was probably in use much earlier. It was an enclosed area of land, but not to be confused with those created by later enclosure awards. This use of the word close was retained through to the 20th century.

Clough/Clow Ing no. 23 1744: OE clus(e) & dialect clew = a dam or a sluice. This is a very simple mechanical device placed over the end of a ditch where it flows into a river. It stops flood-water from the river flowing back into the ditch and inundating the area. Today, locally it is called a Clew, which could well be the pronunciation indicated by both spellings. For clough think of through, and for clow think of cow (pronounced coo locally). The latter also explains why Cuckoo Garth was originally *Cuckow Garth*. There is still a clew across the ditch in this ing today.

Coat Green Close 1703:[15] OE cot = a hut, a shelter + OE greon = gravelly or sandy ground. This close is actually in Kirby Misperton but has been attached to what is now North West Farm since at least 1703. It is at a point where the land rises from the bottom of what had been Lake Pickering, the underlying sand and gravel reflecting the shore-line.

Common Pasture C12/13: This was the open, uncultivated area where the people who worked the cultivated land were entitled to pasture their stock. There was a formula for agreeing the level of use of common pasture based on the amount of land a person tenanted. This formula was mentioned in the Cause Papers as a question, but sadly no answer survives so the formula is not known. In Ryton, ownership of the Common Pasture remained with the Lord of the Manor.

The Costa: Mediaeval Latin costa = side and OFr coste =

side or border. The earliest reference is in 1157/8 when the boundary of the Rievaulx possessions in the 'Wastes below Pickering'[16] were given in detail including references to the Costa. (NB: even today it is known locally as the Costa, not Costa beck.) By this time Rievaulx had acquired both their gift from Henry I (actually on his death in 1135 but granted earlier) and the area later called *Lund* from Ralph Neville. The Neville gift has not been dated, but it was after that of the king as one of the signatories was the first Abbot of Rufford Abbey, created in 1148. During the period when the monks held only the king's gift, the whole of their boundary on the west side was the existing stream that almost certainly would have had a local name. However, the monks had good reason to try to make it their stream, since that gave them rights to the fish in it (very valuable at that time as meat was only allowed on certain days), so by calling it something that related it specifically to them endowed an assumed ownership. Hence the name meaning their 'side boundary' (to the west) and of course, it would have been written in Latin – Costa. In October 1334[17] the Abbot had to defend his right to fish in the Costa, which he claimed his predecessors had done from ancient time, so it was a principle worth establishing at an early stage. This was not the only local name changed by the monks to suit their own objectives – see also *Salescale, Lund, and River Rye*.

Costa Farm no. 48 1849: The farm near the Costa. This name was retained through to 1904,[18] but at the time of the Lund estate sale in 1950 it was Costa Manor Farm, the name it retains today. The change of name is thought to have been to differentiate it from the farm directly across the Costa in Marishes. That had been called Nook House in 1850, but had changed to Costa Farm by 1890. This was still causing confusion in the 1960s and by then a very long detour would have to be made if you got it wrong, as the crossing at Tranmer's Bridge was pedestrian only! Costa Farm was probably the site of the grange for Rievaulx Abbey and the lost settlement of *Salescale*.

Courting no. 49 1744: OFr/ME court = a space enclosed by walls. In this case it was the range of farm buildings attached to the Manor House forming what would be termed the fold yard today.

Cowlam Garth no. 68 1744: This is a small garth adjacent to the old village settlement. Although the village disappeared, the area it once occupied was still referred to as Cowlam into the 20th century. Unfortunately the site of the village and Cowlam Garth are on the missing part of the 1744 plan so the exact locations and layout are not known. However, the general area is known, and one explanation of Cowlam could be OE cule = a hollow, a hole + OE lam = clay, making Cowlam the remains of a clay-pit, of which there are many in the area (see *Brick Pond Moor*). It could also explain some of the unusual features near the site of the village.

Croft C12/13: OE croft = a small enclosed field. Usually a croft would be in the vicinity of a house and worked by the individual, but it is not the house itself. This was the case with the area still shown as The Crofts adjacent to, and south of the settlement. However, *Goosecrofts* was a large area to the east of the village, so it may originally have been made up of many individual crofts.

Cuckow Garth no. 32 1683: Still called Cuckoo Field.

Dicky Ground no. 24 1683: This was the block of land given to Alice Garforth in 1655 that was bought by Sir Rowland Bellasise in 1665 to add to his family's adjacent estate of Lund. By the time of the first known survey of the Lund estate in 1683 the names assigned in 1655 of Cowslip, Primrose, Sage and Leafield had all been replaced by this one name. It had been thought, not unreasonably, that Dicky was a derogatory term used to indicate a very poor, wet area of land, but it is no worse than some other land in this area, all of which was originally moor. It is also extremely unlikely that a surveyor would say anything uncomplimentary about his master's possessions, whatever he may have thought. The meaning behind the term Dicky becomes obvious when looking at a plan of the Lund estate: imagine a horse-drawn carriage of the day with a platform at the rear for the driver to stand on, with the occupants enclosed to the front (see Figure 13). The course of the Aykeland Beck is even in the shape of a wheel-arch. The name for the platform was a 'Dicky', a term used in early motor-cars for what we now call the boot. This block of land was later subdivided, with new names used for each separate close, but the whole area was still known as Dicky Grounds and that is the name for the lane that crosses it today.

Dodgson Moor pre-1655: *pn* + moor. The first person known of that name was Alanus Dodgeson who was recorded in the Poll Tax returns of 1377. Despite being referred to as Hodgson Moor in 1790, the name Dodgson was still in use on deeds in 1838.

Duke Close nos 80 & 101 1744: *pn* May be from Martyn Duke who was one of the witnesses to the will of Leonard Percehay dated 10 February 1593/4.

Eden Lands 1850: This block of land was owned by a William Eddon who died in 1831. This is yet another example of a surveyor not really understanding what the locals were trying to say.

Eyebright Close 1655: Common eyebright (*euphrasia nemorosa*) is an annual flower that would have been common on this type of moorland habitat. Needless to say, with a name like this, it was used as an eye treatment.

Felde, West Felde, Myddylfelde, 1535:[19] OE feld = open country. In this original sense a feld (now of course called field) was the area cleared for arable farming. In Ryton this open area seems to have been divided, although not necessarily with any physical boundaries, into West Felde, Myddylfelde, *Landgelandes* and *Goosecrofts*. When the West Felde was sold off by the Percehays in 1535, to a sister and brother-in-law, it was described as being all one close. This implies there were no divisions, but there would have been separate 'flatts' each containing numerous 'lands'. By 1606[20] the area had been physically divided into 'diverse closes' but the whole was still referred to as West Feilde, and this term was still in use in 1622.[21] This may have been the last time that the word 'fielde' was used in this original sense. The word 'felde', however, is preserved in South Africa where veld (veldt) still refers to unenclosed country or open pasture.

Field 1842: This is actually the first record of field being used in the sense that we understand today, where it means an enclosed area of land. The term may well have been in use for many years before 1842, but the Fauconbergs did not record it at all in their survey of the Lund estate in 1796, and the Barstow (ex-Percehay) estate had no 'fields' as late as 1821. A thorough search of the deeds held at NYCRO concerning Ryton up to 1838 did not produce one reference to a 'field', although not all enclosures were named. However, by the time of the survey of 1842 for the Tithe Award, 'field' was a commonly used term, although still well outnumbered by the term 'close'.

Flatt 1663:[22] ON flat = a piece of flat level ground. In Ryton the term was used to refer to a division of the open field (see *Felde*) with the flatt being sub-divided into strips (a much later term) called lands (e.g. *Pexton Flatt*). The area still known as 'The Flats' in Old Malton has the same origin.

Focmar C12/13: OE focga = tall, rough grass + marish. A wet area with rough grass, similar to what is now called Yorkshire Fog.

Foot Road Close no. 9 1849: By this date the ancient route that passed to the side of this close from Kirby Misperton to Malton was only a foot road rather than a carriage road.

Forge Farm 1851: *pn* from Thomas Forge, but of course there may still have been a forge there.

Foreshore 1778:[23] This was a sandy bank of the River Rye near Garforth Hall extending to over one acre, indicating the existence of the underlying sand that formed *Ryton Rigg*.

Frerebrigg 1334:[24] OFr & ME frere = a brother, a friar + ME brigge = a bridge. This has been variously translated as the friars/brothers/monks bridge. It only appears in the Duchy of Lancaster Records, in 'Matters relating to the Forest presented at Pickering before Richard de Willoughby, Robert de Hungerford and John Hambury, Monday 6th Oct 1334'.[25] In this the jury present to the three justices that the Abbot of Rievaulx is bound to repair Frerebrigg, which is in such poor repair that people travelling from Pickering to Malton, on foot or horseback, are unable to use the bridge and have to divert about 1.5 miles to the next nearest bridge. This diversion results in 'annoying the Lord's deer and treading down their pasturage'. It had always been assumed that Frerebrigg was the bridge at Howe, where a relatively modern bridge carries the A169, but to fit with this assumption the translation of the original Latin has had to be creative to say the least. The result is the phrase 'a bridge called Friar Bridge beyond the Costa'. Bridges invariably go 'over' not beyond, and the original word 'ultra' could just as easily have been translated as over (or above). However, the bridge at Howe does not go over the Costa, it goes over the River Rye just after its confluence with the Costa.

There is further information in the same hearing (pp 4–5) that also casts doubt on the bridge being the one at Howe. This time the jury are trying to force the Prior of the Hospital of St John and the Prioress of Yedingham to repair and maintain the bridge at Pul, which is also within Pickering Forest. This confirms two important principles: firstly that the repair and maintenance of the road is the responsibility of the person holding the tenure of the land that the road crosses; and secondly that the responsibility for the repair and maintenance of the bridge rests with the person holding the tenure of the land at each side of the bridge. In that particular case it was the Prior who held the land at both sides of the bridge, so he had the responsibility to look after it. In view of this ruling, if Frerebrigg really was located at Howe, then the Abbot of Rievaulx would only have been responsible for half of the cost of the maintenance, the other half falling to the tenant at the Malton side of the bridge.

There is also serious doubt about whether the Abbot was even responsible for the road leading up to Howe bridge. The area to the north of the Costa and the Rye up to the confluence with the Derwent was shown on the 1850 OS map as 'Pickering (detached)', meaning it came under the parish of Pickering but was physically separated from it. It also had the name *'Castle Ings'* and covered an extensive area of just over 300 acres. The reason for both these names again dates back to the time of Pickering Forest, which was administered from Pickering Castle on behalf of the Crown. Castle Ings was described as demesne meadow,[26] meaning it was not let out but kept for the use of the Lord; in this case it was mainly used to supply hay for the stables at Pickering Castle. The annual account of John de Kilvington for the year 29 September 1325 to 30 September 1326 even details the 'yearly wages of the warrener [in this case a game-keeper rather than just responsible for rabbits] keeping Castle Ings and the Derwent which is the outer march of the forest',[27] indicating that the Castle was very protective of its meadow and game rights at Castle Ings, with one person specifically responsible for them. This all ties in with the fact that Henry I did not grant everything in the 'wastes below Pickering' to Rievaulx. His original gift is referred to a number of times in the Early Yorkshire Charters, with most giving a description of the boundary of the Abbot's possessions (this has been invaluable in confirming the location of *Tacriveling*) but within that boundary the King retained possession of the meadow of 'Edivemersc'.[28] This name had been lost, but can now be positively identified as Castle Ings.[29] The presence of this meadow belonging to Pickering Castle also explains why anyone straying from the main routes would be encroaching on the Lord's possession as they approached the real Howe bridge, which was one of the complaints of the jury. In view of the location of Castle Ings adjacent to Howe bridge, it would have been the responsibility of the Castle, not the Abbot, to repair the road leading to the bridge and more importantly, it would be the Castle's responsibility to repair the bridge, or at least half of it.

If Frerebrigg was not Howe bridge, then where was it? On the assumption that it actually did go over the Costa, then it would presumably be approximately 1.5 miles upstream from Howe bridge. The actual distance would not have been measured precisely, and the 'statute mile' was not fixed until 1592,[30] but at approximately that distance there is one very obvious candidate for this location. On the OS map of 1850 there was a crossing of the Costa then-named Tranmer's Footbridge, alongside which a 'Ford' was marked. This point coincides with *Habton Lane* (no. 42) on the Lund estate plan of 1849 (see Figure 14). Previous plans drawn up for the estate in both 1683 (Figure 13) and 1796 (Figure 14) confirm it as 'Lane and Watering Place' with *Wath Closes* adjacent (OScand vath = ford). This crossing point of the Costa was clearly referred to even earlier in the case of Alice Tailour v Roger Chomley in 1523 in the Court of Star Chamber,[31] when it was called *Lundbrige*. The original complaint of the jury in 1334 described the bridge as one for people on horseback and on foot, so even at that time there was probably a ford nearby for use by carts, carriages and larger numbers of livestock. If Frerebrigg was this crossing point of the Costa, it explains why the Abbot readily accepted his responsibility for it, as he tenanted the land on both sides of the Costa at this point, and it was in his interests to maintain it. The item on Habton Lane explains why a crossing of the Costa from the Rievaulx granges of Kekmarrish, Newstead and Loftmarrish was so important, and how the link was made back to Rievaulx.

One other item concerning this crossing point of the Costa raises even more questions. In 1695 a new edition of Camden's *Britannia* was published. It included an updated map of the North Riding attributed to Robert Morden[32] and was the first to include roads (from the John Ogilby survey of 1675). A copy of this edition is available at NYCRO and it shows the roads from York to Malton, Malton to Scarborough, and Malton to Pickering. The latter route is clearly shown crossing the River Rye at Ryton and then the Costa (in the area now thought to be the site of Frerebrigg), before heading north to Pickering. This raises the possibility that even up to 1675 the preferred route from Pickering to Malton was indeed over Frerebrigg, with the bridge at Howe being only secondary. This situation is also hinted at by the early Saxton maps which show a bridge at Ryton but not at Howe, although it must be remembered that very few bridges were shown on these early maps even if, as is the case with Howe, one was known to exist. It may be that the King's meadow near the bridge at Howe, and the real concerns of the Foresters for both the deer and the hay for the castle, were the reasons that people were not encouraged to use Howe bridge, with the result that Frerebrigg became the key crossing point on the route from Pickering to Malton.

Furres 1572:[33] OED furze = gorse. This became furze, although in numerous references in the Cause Papers it is invariably furres, furrs or furs, and the context of the documents perhaps gives the reason for the name. Furres (gorse, *ulex europaeus*) had long been used for fuel because when it is dead it burns with an intense heat, even if it is not dry. It also had the distinct advantage of being a very common plant growing wild in the area and it was free, unlike wood that was effectively owned by the Lord of the Manor. It was such a staple fuel for the community that it was harvested in large quantities. 'Ten waine loades of whynes or furres'[34] were the subject of a court case brought by the local rector who wanted his 10%! This extensive use as a fuel may account for the name as OE fyr = fire. Also, both whynes and furres are always plural, suggesting they were generic terms for a number of species that made up the brushwood such as thorn, gorse, broom, bramble, even heather and holly, and the areas were not entirely scrub, since part of this case was about loads of hay taken from the furres.

Garforth Hall 1778:[35] John Garforth, a Gentleman of York, married Alice Boyes, the daughter and heir of James Boyes who died in 1623. James had acquired some lands in Ryton and these went to Alice.[36] There has been much confusion concerning this inheritance caused by the name of the area that included the old West Field of Ryton being given the general title of *'New House'*. The Percehays sold West Felde as a single close in 1535. By the time of the next sale, in 1565, there were two dwellings, one of which was called the 'new house'. However, probably because there were two new houses, the whole area became known as 'New House' or 'New Houses' from that time. While John Garforth probably did build himself another new house, he retained his house in York as his main residence and was 'late of the City of York' in 1655, despite the fact that his wife and children were of 'Newhouse in the county of York'. John's new house was clearly substantial, being the third largest in Ryton in terms of fire-places in the 1673 Hearth Tax, when it had six hearths, compared to Thomas Simpson's (later Rye House) with eight, and Christopher Percehay's Manor House with thirteen (one of the largest in the whole of Ryedale on that basis). However, the 'New House' was only described as a 'messuage, farmhouse or tenement' in 1737[37] but when it was finally sold in 1778 by William Garforth, then of Askham Richard, it was called Garforth Hall for the first time.

Garrow Lodge Farm: This is not named as such until the Barstow rentals of 1932, but it may have been called this from the time it was built in the 19th century. The name comes from the Barstow family home at Garrow Hill in York, near what is now the University. In fact the recent extension of the University is on what had been Barstow lands.

Garth: ON garthr = a yard or enclosure associated with a dwelling, developing into the word garden. The Lund survey of 1683 shows every dwelling as 'house and garth', as does the survey of 1796, but by the survey of 1849 the word 'homestead' is used instead, although some of the adjacent enclosures still use the word garth in their names, indicating their proximity to the house. By the time of the Barstow survey of 1744 the term 'house and garth' remained in use, but no. 29 was Isaac Halliday's 'house and garden', which seems to be the first use of the new word 'garden' in Ryton.

Gawin Moore pre-1655: Gawen Moor by 1737 but lost by 1842. Gawen/Gawin was a name frequently used by the Woodcock family and they gave their name to this moor and the adjacent *Woodcocke Moore Close*. This moor was renamed in 1655, having been divided into three closes: Tulapay, Lyon's Foot and Maidenhaire, but these new names do not seem to have been adopted by the locals.

Glisterpipe 1850: This is the name given to a farm on the first OS map of 1850. The farmstead existed (lately erected) in March 1752,[38] by which time it consisted of *Dodgson* and *Peters* Moors. There were then 20 further changes of ownership and/or tenant up to April 1838[39] when Robert Spanton became the owner, as he seems to be in 1850. In all these documents the farmstead was referred to simply as a messuage or tenement with Dodgson Moor and Peters Moor. Nowhere is there any reference to Glisterpipe, and perhaps it becomes clear why no-one with any connection to this farm would have called it Glisterpipe, when the meaning of the word is known. A search for this word on the OED website directs the enquiry to 'clyster [noun], a medicine injected into the rectum, to empty or close the bowels, to afford nutrition, etc; an injection, enema; sometimes a suppository.' An alternative spelling is given as glister, and the pipe or syringe used to administer the glister was a glister-pipe. This method of administering both medicine and nutrition to patients had been common in much earlier times, but the expression is unlikely to have been known to either owners or farm workers in 1850, and if it had been, then the name Glisterpipe would certainly not have been used for this farm. The use of such an obscure, derogatory, and downright rude word has raised suspicions that names that appear for the first time on the OS map of 1850 may not be original or even genuine. The name survived on government documents, but on the 1910 OS edition the name had (fortunately) been replaced with *Park Farm*, the name it retains today.

Gosecroft C12/13: OE gos = goose + *croft*. This was a large area covering either half of one of the three open village fields, or it was a separate field in a four field system. The name in various forms (Goose Croft Closes, Goose Croft Ings, plus high, middle, low, east and west Goosecroft) persisted right through to the Tithe Award survey of 1842, and may even still be referenced on existing deeds. It is usually written in the plural, suggesting that it was an area made up of many separate crofts.

Gosling Green Farm 1850: The adjacent field was named Gosling Field in 1842, but the farm was not named. It had been known as *Rumbarts Farm*.

Grimston Moore pre-1655: *pn* but as yet not identified. The distribution of 1655 is the only reference so far found for the name Grimston. This had been part of *Aykmoore Closse* in 1604.

Grove no. 47 1744: This pasture was named after the grove of trees situated within it. The 1744 plan indicates that trees still existed, growing in a rectangular plot, and this can still be identified in this field. The plot itself is defined by a ditch creating a raised platform, and is most likely to have been a method of separating what had been an orchard from the rest of the close to stop animals spoiling the fruit.[40] By 1744 the adjacent but separate no. 48 is listed as orchard, indicating that a new orchard had replaced the original one that probably existed as early as 1534, with the close then being referred to as *Orcherde Ende meadowe* (see below).

Green nos 63, 78 & 79 1744: By the time of the 1744 survey there were two areas shown as 'Green'. No. 63 was the open pasture near the centre of the village, and nos 78/79 were a continuation of this, with a track heading towards Lund. The grazing of these greens was owned by the Lord of the Manor, and allocated to particular tenants. It is not clear how these tenants would have prevented their stock from grazing these greens when they were being taken (slowly) to other fields.

Habton Closes 1761 (had been Hapton Closes in 1750): These were part of *New House* lands and were next to Habton (nos 8 & 9 1842, Figure 17). Habton Close, and Low and High Habton Closes in 1842 (nos 100, 99 & 95, Figure 17) were along the side of the old route from Ryton to Habton that ran to the north of the West and Middle Fields (see *Aichefritlh*).

Habton Lane no. 42 1849: This was at a crossing point of the Costa about as far away from Habton as it was possible to get in Ryton, so why 'Habton' lane? This was 'The Lane and Watering Place' in both the 1683 and 1796 Lund estate surveys, with *Wath Closes* adjacent, suggesting the existence of a ford somewhere in this area. The 1850 OS map shows Tranmer's Footbridge at this point with a ford next to it, so this was still an active crossing point at that time. The current Definitive Rights of Way Map in Northallerton shows this crossing as a public right of way and a footbridge still exists today. So, it was a lane, probably dating back some centuries, but why the lane to Habton? It is all about perspective: from the Pickering/Marishes side of the Costa the lane does indeed head west in the direction of Habton, although by 1850 little of it remained. Also, this is now thought to be the location of the original Friars Bridge (see *Frerebrigg*) of 1334 and *Lundbrige* of 1523, and it was the monks of Rievaulx that needed this route west to move produce from their granges at Kekmarrish, Newstead, Loftmarrish and Lund back to their abbey at Rievaulx. The route west across Lund (see Figure 10) followed the bank of a ditch, possibly created by the monks themselves, with the spoil from the ditch making a relatively dry path. This route continued heading west in an almost straight line towards the ancient crossing of the River Seven near Little Habton (hence Habton Lane), a route that can still be followed via field boundaries on maps of today, although it is much more obvious on the 1850 OS map which included the word 'path' along most of its length. Once across the river there would have been a relatively safe route back to Rievaulx as it was almost exclusively over land tenanted by the monks. The monks had even gone to the trouble of ensuring their right to free passage across the moors of Ryton and Habton for themselves, carts, carriages and their animals,[41] creating immutable and secure passage from their easternmost granges all the way to the River Seven.

Chapter 5: Place-Names of Ryton

Habton Lane nos 34a, 92a & 94a 1849: This lane does not actually connect with the above Habton Lane until it is nearly at Little Habton, because it originates from a different location. It *may* be part of an ancient route from Salescale to the river-crossing at Little Habton, and part of it seems to form the boundary between the new closes set out in 1655, so it may have existed before that date. Enclosures from the moor abruptly changing the direction of the route make it difficult to be precise about its original course.

Haumidding, haumitting, hothmitting, hostmitting C12/13: These were all gifts of land to Malton Priory, with haumidding and haumitting confirmed as the same gift, so it is not unreasonable to suggest that the similar spelling of the other two gifts could have been for the same area. In that case the 'mitt' or 'midd' could be from OE mythe = confluence of two rivers, meaning the Costa and the River Rye. The ridge of high(er) ground called Ryton Rigg runs right up to this confluence and this could account for both 'hau' from ON haugr = hill, and 'hoth/host' from OE ost/oster = hillock. Taken together these elements give 'the ings near the high(er) ground where the rivers meet'. Perhaps coincidentally, as the donations to Malton Priory were given piecemeal and distributed across Ryton, at some point their possessions were consolidated into two compact holdings, with one at the confluence of the Costa and the Rye.

High Barn 1890: This barn was part of the farmstead shown as *Midland Farm* in 1849, but by the time of the sale in 1858 the farmhouse was not mentioned, and even as early as the 1850 OS map only the barn was shown. The name of the barn may reflect the fact that it was two storeys high, but by 1890 it was part of the adjacent field called High Garth since 1683 (no. 41), so perhaps it was High Barn because it was in High Garth – again the garth had been to the north of the farmstead.

Hill(s) Ground(s) 1773:[42] *pn* The Hill family owned adjacent property in 1755 and they may well have owned this, but the records do not go back that far. This low-lying area of land is not hilly.

Howe Bridge pre-1175:[43] This name had a number of spellings: Howe, Hou, Houm and even Holme, giving two similar definitions. Howe from OScand haugr = hill, mound or barrow, and Holme from OScand holmr = dry ground in marsh. Both apply to the settlement site known as Howe, and it was near this point that a bridge was built over the River Rye just after it is joined by the Costa. The bridge is known to exist before 1175 from the references in the Rievaulx Chartulary.

Howl (various) 1744: ME howl = a hollow or low place. In this area it is difficult to distinguish between Howl and *Ing* as both are still in use and describe the low-lying meadow adjacent to the water-courses and subject to flooding. With one exception, Howl is used for areas near the Costa and the Aykeland Beck, while Ing is used for areas near the River Rye. More confusion arises with *Houlendinge*, which incorporates both names. The word Howl was obviously misunderstood by visiting surveyors and agents who have used the words Hold and even Knowl.

Houlendinge C12/13: At first glance this seems to be tautology as *Howl* and *Ing* mean the same thing. However, if Howl referred to meadow near the Costa and Ing to that near the Rye, then the area called Houlendinge could be where the two meet. As this was a gift to Malton Priory, and as they did have land in this area, then this indeed could be the meadow where the two rivers meet.

Hutchinsons Moore pre-1655: Nicholas Hutchinson was tenant here in 1604, and his name was used again in 1655, allowing the location to be deduced.

Ing (various): This noun is still in common use in this area, but for some reason it does not feature in most Oxford-centric dictionaries (or spell-checkers!). Ings are meadows near a water-course that are subject to seasonal inundation, and as there are a number of water-courses surrounding Ryton, there are a number of Ings. Some of these are dealt with under their specific names e.g. *Acre Ings*.

Intack pre-1655: ON intack = a piece of land taken in or enclosed. The Intacks were 'taken in' from the undeveloped land for cultivation. They lie to the north of what was the Middle Field of Ryton. The team from the OS obviously tried to 'improve' the English of the locals by recording the Intacks as the Intakes, an interpretation that exists today, but the locals persist in referring to the Intacks, thus preserving the origins of the name.

Jerry Bridge: This bridge over the River Rye between Ryton and Swinton has only been named once in documents, on the first OS map of 1850, when it was named 'Coultas Bridge (wooden)', although it was shown but not named on

73

the Tithe map of 1842. Locally, both in Swinton and Ryton, it has always been referred to as Jerry Bridge. It is possible that there had been a river-crossing somewhere in this area going back centuries. As the Percehay family of Ryton also held the greater part of the manor of Swinton from at least 1328 to 1521,[44] a river-crossing between these two manors would have been almost inevitable. It had been thought that the name of the bridge may have come from the term 'jerry-built', indicating something badly built using poor-quality materials from the association with the walls of Jericho that fell down at the sound of trumpets. This may have been because for most of the 20th century it had been ruinous. However, the deeds register at NYCRO probably has the real answer – as long ago as 1605 the part of Ryton between what became known as *Messenger* and *Ness House* was owned by Chas and Ursula Atkinson, along with part of the manor of Swinton.[45] This part of Ryton continued to be associated with Swinton and at the Tithe Award in 1842 it was owned by the Cayley family, along with Swinton. The Cayley tenant in 1808[46] was a Jeremiah Coultas, so perhaps it was this person who (re)built the bridge and both the names – Jerry and Coultas – can be traced back to him.

Kirkway Close no. 45 1683: This was adjacent to a track leading to Kirby Misperton. The track is still shown as a footpath today.

Kyrkeby Mysperton alias Kyrkeby Overkers 1523:[47] OScand kirkju-by = village with a church. The Mysperton may be from the OE mispeler = a medlar tree + OE tun = an enclosure or a farmstead, giving the farmstead where medlars were grown. At Domesday 'Mispeton' was a separate settlement. The Overkers refers to the position of Kirby above the carrs, from ON kjarr and ME ker = wet ground especially where brushwood grows (see *Furres* and *Whynes*).

Land(s) C12/13: ON land = a strip of arable land (in an open field). The word 'strip' in this context is a relatively recent use of the word, with OED crediting A.D. Hall as late as 1913 with the first use of the expression 'strip farming' relating to the open field system.[48] In this area the word used was 'land' and it survives in the place-name Longlands. A number of 'lands' made up a *Flatt*.

Land endes 1572:[49] The ends of the *Lands* were used to turn the plough teams and so covered a large area that also provided good hay. It was hay from these land ends of the open fields that was part of the dispute about tithe payments in 1572.

The Lane and Watering Place no. 15 1683: This leads down to the crossing of the Costa at today's *Tranmer's Footbridge* at the point where both *Frerebrigg* and *Lundbrige* are now thought to have been. This lane heads west from the Costa, crossing the north/south carriage route from Kirby Misperton to Ryton after 250m, and after a further 750m it crosses the Kirby Misperton to Ryton (foot) route in the close called *The Lanes*.

The Lanes no. 46 1683: This is at the junction of the old east/west route from the granges in the area back to Rievaulx, and the north/south (foot) route from Kirby Misperton to Ryton.

Langelands C12/13: OE lang = long + ON land = a strip of arable land (see *Land*). This name has survived almost unchanged for some 800 years. Originally Langelands and *Gosecrofts* seem to have been part of the open field system of the village, although no record remains of how that operated. After these long lands had been enclosed, the name continued with the 'longlands' in the Barstow surveys for some of the closes at what is now Longlands Hall, and with the 'Long Closes' at Sleightholme Farm.

Longlands Hall: This farmstead occupies the northern part of the old open field called Langelands that was originally part of the Percehay possessions, but it seems to have been sold off to clear some serious debt around 1530, although the sale has not yet been identified. In August 1625[50] Thomas Lord Fauconberg sold one Mansion House, land and grounds in Ryton, to George Chambers, who was noted in the Bishop's Transcripts of 1632 as being 'of longe lands'. The description needs to be related to the standards of the day – think of a good farmhouse rather than Nunnington Hall. This 'Mansion House commonly called Langlands' was then bought back by Christopher Percehay senior some time before 1662[51] and it remained part of the estate that eventually defaulted to the Barstows. In their survey of 1786, 'Robert Halliday farmstead is well situated for an out House farm and consists of a very anchant bud strong Dwelling house...' gives the impression of a very old but well-built and still serviceable farmhouse. It is not known how much of the original remains.

Laversike no. 33 1744: OFr laver = to wash + ON sik = a ditch. This could have been the ditch used to wash the sheep to clean off any dirt or debris before they were clipped. This washing had to take place some days before clipping as the

Chapter 5: Place-Names of Ryton

fleeces needed to be dry. A similar sheep-wash was shown on the 1890 OS map at Kirby Misperton, and local knowledge confirms that this practice continued into the 1950s when the stream running through Hovingham was dammed near the railway station and the local farmers brought their sheep to be washed.

Laytegest, Lattegest C12/13: Perhaps from ON hlatha & dialect laithe = a store-house, a barn.

Leafield pre-1655: OE laes = pasture, meadowland + field. In the Percehay distribution of 1604 all the land was described as open moor, and one of the areas set out from that moor became Leafield. This may have been the first use of the word 'field' to mean an enclosed area of land, but in this case the term field is still thought to be from the old sense of open country because of the continued use of the word 'close' in this area to mean enclosure even up to the 19th century.

Lengdell Hill no. 24 1744: This is a relatively high point on Ryton Rigg, at the end of a natural valley, so the hill at the end of a long valley.

Ley (Near and Far) nos 62 & 63 1683: Today the word ley is used to indicate a field put down to grass for a limited period. However, in this case the same names were used again in the 1796 survey, so the grass had become permanent. In fact the grass survived right through to the late 1950s when the ridge and furrow was levelled and the fields became arable again. Perhaps some time before 1683, when the fields were being cultivated (hence the ridge and furrow), it was decided to turn them into pasture temporarily but this became permanent and the names were retained.

Line Garth nos 53 & 54 1683: Probably named after the variety of linaria (*linum usitatissimum*) that was grown to produce flax, locally known as lin(e). The plant grows to about one metre high and produces long fibres that are made into linen, canvas, twine and even writing paper. The fibres are extracted by pulling the plants up by the roots and soaking the whole plant, including roots, for a few days in water to dissolve the vegetable matter, a process known as retting. These garths are adjacent to the Aykeland Beck which would have been an easy source of water, and there are still signs of retting ponds in these garths.

Low Houses: The name given to an area of scattered farmsteads in the north-west part of Ryton, later called *Low Moors*.

Low Moors: This term was used for all the low-lying land below Kirby Misperton to the south and east, running from below the Barughs, through the north of Ryton and all the way round to the east of Kirby Misperton. The first use of this name does not appear until 1711, when Jane Waind was 'of Ryton Low Moors' (thought to be today's North West Farm) in the parish register. Before 1711 the same source usually referred to this area in Ryton as *Low Houses*. Unfortunately in 1771 Thomas Jeffrey's map, supposedly based on a new and accurate survey, named a separate area as Low Moors but he erroneously located it on top of Ryton Rigg, towards Habton (see detail in *Wake Farm*). From the parish register it appears that more than ten farmsteads were referred to as being in Low Moors, including North West Farm; a farm north of Shotton Hall (now lost); Shotton Hall; Gosling Green; a farm north of Park Farm (now lost); Park Farm; and Brass Castle. In addition, in his survey notes of 1796, Edward Watterson refers to the Lund estate as 'Lund Forest otherwise Low Moors'.

Lund 1176–79: ON lundr = a grove or small wood, also a sacred grove, one offering sanctuary. Lund could be so-named for both these reasons. The whole area was given by Ralph Neville to the monks of Rievaulx some time before 1157–58 but it was not named, except that it was held in Ryton (Rihtuna). The boundary of the land given was confirmed in detail in a number of early charters, including that of c. 1176–79 by Henry II[52] confirming all the monks' possessions in the waste below Pickering and this named the area in Ryton as Lund for the first time. The original gift was for one carucate (approx 120 acres) of arable land with all meadow and pasture appertaining to it. Note that no mention was made of any forest or wood. However, the much later name of *Stubbing Closes* suggests that before 1683 there had been at least some trees, and these may have been the grove that gave rise to the name Lund. In the circumstances, it is perhaps more likely that the monks tried to choose a name that emphasised their ownership and the fact that, being part of their monastic lands, the area was indeed one that offered sanctuary, hence Lund. At the Dissolution, when Sir Roger Cholmeley purchased Lund from the king it was described as 'the Manor and Grange in the Marish called Lund'.[53] However, Lund never was a separate manor in the feudal sense, and the Tithe dispute of 1572[54] shows that it came under the manor of Ryton, although during the time it was owned by the monks they did not recognise any other feudal lord. In 1599 Lund was sold on to Sir William Belassis (later Fauconberg) of Newbroughe (now Newburgh Priory) and that family held it until 1858 when it was bought by the Lund family,[55] who were manufacturers from Keighley. The purchase of the Lund estate by a family called Lund has been the cause of much confusion. That family eventually sold the estate after the death of the last survivor in 1950, so the area called Lund had had only four (five if Henry VIII is included) owners over a span of 800 years.

Lund House(s)/Lund Grounds: Both these terms seem to have been the general reference to any farmstead or house in the whole area called Lund. The first reference was in the Cause Papers of 1572,[56] where the dispute was about whether the Abbot of Rievaulx had ever paid tithes in this area and, although specific closes were detailed, the whole area was referred to as 'the Grange or Lunde Howse'. The use of the singular 'house' throughout may mean that at that time there really was just one large farmstead – the remains of the grange of Rievaulx. However, by 1636 there were a number of houses, as indicated by the references to Lund Houses, and the number of different family names shown in these houses in the parish register. By the survey of 1683 there were at least five farmsteads in Lund. Lund Grounds appears as a reference name from 1634 and entries for Richard Todd in the parish registers of 1661 and 1662 suggest that the term Lund Grounds, Lund Houses and Lund were all interchangeable.

Lund Forrest 1796: This is another name that has caused much confusion. As stated in the entry for *Lund*, there is absolutely nothing to indicate that this area was heavily forested, in fact quite the contrary. 'Forest' was a specific term used to mean woodland belonging to the King and devoted to hunting, very much as Pickering Forest was supposed to be, but that status was never confirmed on Lund. The family from Newburgh (Belassis – Fauconberg – Wombwell) commissioned three surveys of their possessions at Lund over their 250-year ownership. The surveyors gave their resulting plans suitably impressive titles. The first, around 1683, was titled 'Terrar of Lund Lordship in the Marishes'. In this case Lordship was a complimentary title as Lund came under the Lordship of Ryton, although by then the family really were Lords, being Viscounts Fauconberg. This survey showed that the whole of the area had been enclosed some time before, and the three closes called *Stubbing Closes* did indicate that at least a relatively small area had originally had some trees growing there. The survey of 1796 by Ed. Watterson and Tho. Rodwell had the grand title 'A Survey and Valuation of the Right Honourable Henry Earl Fauconberg Estate situate at Lund Forrest in the East Riding of the County of York'. Apart from the glaring error of placing Lund in the East Riding (there is a Lund in the East Riding near Beverley which has frequently been confused with the one at Ryton),[57] this is the first-ever mention of Lund 'Forest'. At the time there were clearly few, if any, trees as Watterson's notes attached to the survey refers to 'Lund Forest otherwise Low Moors' and he describes the land of the estate as being 'of a moorish quality' and either 'grass' or 'under plough' with no mention of trees at all. The term Lund Forest seems to be a grandiose, complimentary title meant to impress; clearly it did, as the name endures.

Lund Moor pre-1655: The whole of the meadow and pasture given to the monks by Ralph Neville in addition to the arable carucate may well have been predominantly what was later referred to as moor; initially Lund Moor may have covered up to 450 acres. In the documents concerning the distribution of 1655 this area was referred to as 'Great Lund Moore', and by the survey of 1683 enclosures had reduced it to three areas totalling just 115 acres. By 1796 it had all effectively been reclaimed and subdivided into eleven closes, and by the survey of 1849 the name Lund as a prefix to any field or close had been lost forever. Today, what had been Lund Moor has been worked into good-quality arable land and little remains to indicate its origins as a moor.

Lundbrige 1523:[58] The descriptions in the case of the murder of Robert Tailour, during a raid by Roger Cholmeley's men into Ryton to distrain cattle to pay a disputed debt due to the Foresters of Pickering, clearly located the bridge called Lundbrige at the crossing of the Costa later known as *Tranmer's Footbridge*. It also fits in with the location of *Frerebrigg*. It was described as being situated a mile from Ryton, with the Marish moor at the other side of the Costa, and a mile further on across the Marish moor towards Pickering Castle there was Pickering Carr. All these descriptions coincide with the location of today's Tranmer's Footbridge.

Marish: Variations of this name were recorded at Domesday for settlements in the area of what we now call Marishes, but it has also been used as a generic term for parts of Ryton. OE merisc, and OFr/ME mareis refer to marsh or watery land. In 1544 when Henry VIII sold Lund to Sir Roger Cholmeley it was described as the grange in the 'maresse' called Lunde. Subsequently some reference was made in the parish registers to people being 'of the Marrishe' who may have been from Ryton, but there was a time when part of today's Marishes came under Kirby Misperton, so it is not possible to be sure. At the distribution of 1655 some of the original closes were described as being 'of marish grounds or pasture', but they are then referred to as moor. In this area marish, moor and carr all implied poorly drained, undeveloped land growing rough pasture and scrub; once it was properly farmed and ditches dug its nature changed, but the names did not.

Messenger Farm 1891: There was a farmstead at this location in 1818[59] and it may even have been there as early as 1767, but the reference is unclear. The name may have one of two meanings, but sadly the people who could confirm which one are no longer with us. It may go back to the days of the telegraph when this was a dropping-off point for the messages, or it may have been where the local paper, then called *The Messenger*, was dropped off for local distribution, a system that still exists, the local papers now being delivered to an address in Habton.

Midailes (next Costa) C12/13: The 'mid' may come from OE myde = confluence of two rivers with the 'next Costa' indicating that this gift was next to the Costa, not the Rye.

Midland Farm no. 66 1849: George Foster had this farmstead in 1683 but it was not named. Geographically it was near the middle of the Lund estate, hence the name. By the sale of 1858 it had been amalgamated with Costa Farm, and in the 20th century all that remained was one building called the *High Barn*; the existence of Midland Farm had almost been forgotten.

Milnedich/Milnedig C12/13: OE myln = a mill + OE dic = a ditch. These references are the only indication of a mill in Ryton. From the date, and the fact that it was the mill ditch, it may be assumed that there was a water-mill fed by this ditch, rather than a windmill that just happened to have a ditch nearby. Unfortunately it has not yet been possible to locate the site of the mill.

Monks Ditch 1157–58:[60] This was referred to in the confirmation of the possessions of Rievaulx Abbey in the area, where the boundary was described in detail. The Monks Ditch ran north/south connecting *Tacriveling* (*Aykeland Beck*) with the ditch that separated Ryton and Kirby Misperton. The ditch still exists, although it has been partly piped-

in, and it has the unusual feature of having so little natural fall in either direction that it can actually drain to either the north or the south depending on the levels in the two water-courses.

Moor (more, moore) 1279–80: This term was used extensively in this area, but so were *waste*, *marish*, carr, and heath, with very little to differentiate any of them. In Yorkshire today, say 'moors' and everyone would think of Ilkley Moor or the North York Moors, both of which are higher ground covered with heather and bracken. However, in the case of Ryton at least, moor originally referred to the lowest-lying area, poorly drained and virtually untouched by human hand. Another similar low-lying area was Marston Moor; both these areas of 'moor' are now very productive arable land. The area of Ryton covered by moor was to the north of Ryton Rigg, running all the way to the boundary with Kirby Misperton. The vegetation was variously described as moor (suggesting that anyone reading the word would know what was meant), *furres* and *whynnes*, and it is clear from the context that all three words referred to non-specific brushwood or scrub. Eventually gorse and broom do seem to have become dominant plants, probably because they were the most useful, and the other scrub plants were eventually eliminated, leaving rough grass. The grass was used for both pasture and hay, and the areas of furres and whynnes were managed for use mainly as fuel. The first known use of the word 'moor' was in the dispute between Sir Walter Percehay of Ryton and William of Habton in 1279–80 where the moor involved clearly provided good pasture.[61]

Ness House 1850: The Ness family had been in the locality as early as 1377 when Robertus de Nesse was one of the three residents nominated to collect the Poll Tax for Habton. The Ness family inherited what was then called *New House* sometime between August 1772[62] and December 1796,[63] when Arthur Ness was described as the grandson of James Spavin. The Spavin ownership of New House went back to 1737[64] at least, but the family were in Ryton at the 1673 Hearth Tax. The name Ness House was in use into the 1960s, but by the sale of 1967 the 'modern' name of Riverdene Farm had been adopted.

New Forest pre-1565: When the West Felde of Ryton was sold in 1535 the area to the east was referred to as Myddyllfelde (Middle Field), suggesting that both were still part of the open fields of Ryton. By 1565 the area to the east was referred to as 'a close called the newforest', clearly indicating that in the intervening period the new forest had been planted in that part of the old Middle Field. This area of trees persisted into the 20th century and is clearly indicated on the Barstow estate plan of 1744. The term 'forest' was perhaps a little flattering for something covering ten acres at most, and by 1744 it had reduced down to three acres of wood. In the 19th century at least six dwellings were built within the southern part of this wood and the settlement was called *Wood End*.

New House 1565:[65] In August 1535[66] one of the open fields of Ryton, called the West *Felde*, was sold by William and Elizabeth Percehay to Robert Crayke and his wife Isabell, nee Percehay, William's sister. It was described as one close, and no mention was made of any dwelling. The boundaries of this large area were clearly defined and have been adhered to almost unchanged through to the present day. By the time of the next sale, in 1565, the descendants of the Craykes described the whole as their 'ferme called the newhouse', and the 'Fine' registering the transaction had it as a 'Messuage and a cottage with lands in Ryton'. By 1605[67] the two messuages and closes were called Newhouse Grounds. Confusingly the whole area, including the land further west previously sold to Sir William Compton in 1522,[68] became known as 'Newhouse/New Houses' and in the parish registers no distinction was made between these areas. The name New House was given to the dwelling built on the West Field which eventually became Garforth Hall (a name in use by 1778) but it was also the name given to a house built on the Compton property.[69] The name New House was still in use on the deeds for this property in 1826,[70] but it became first Ness House, then Riverdene.

New York: Between the Lund estate surveys of 1796 and 1849 a terrace of six cottages was built, named New York on the 1849 plan, and they seem to have been in existence at the 1841 Census. The name New York did not make it onto the 1850 OS map, where they were shown as Lund Forest Cottages, although the Census of 1891 had them as York Cottages, so perhaps the locals kept the name New York. The Census returns refer to these cottages as 'poor' cottages, but there is nothing to indicate that they were ever owned (or controlled) by anyone other than the Lund estate. In the sale details of 1858 the six cottages had associated large *allotments* in a nearby field, and these were still being cultivated by the householders into the 1960s.

North West Farm 1904: This farm does not have this name until after its acquisition by the Lund family to add to their estate. Geographically the name fits with its location on this estate, and also complements the names of North Farm and West Farm, also parts of the same estate. A farmstead existed at this location in 1703, when John Waynd lived there, and he was awarded land adjacent in Coate Green in the Kirby Misperton Enclosure Award. This accounts for the two fields still belonging this farm, named Pick-moor Close and Coat Green by 1752, which are in Kirby Misperton. Ironically, for a farm that is situated in the area referred to as *Low Moors*, it has also been called High Farm (see Introduction above).

Oak Close (Little and Great) nos 18 & 19 1683: Of all the trees growing in this area the oak gave its name to the most closes, indicating that it was not only native, but also widespread.

Oliver Lane 1850: Another name first encountered on the OS map of 1850. In 1841 William Oliver (senior and junior) lived at *Rumbarts Farm*, and as this lane passes that farm, they are probably the source of this name.

Oke Close (nowe forest) 1535:[71] The context suggests that this was oak close, and the 'now forest' implies that there may originally have been only one oak tree, more being added later to produce a forest, which in this case would have been a small wood.

Okke more close 1535: In the same document as Oke Close, but the different spelling and a later reference to part of it as Oxpasture suggests that the 'okke' was trying to convey 'Ox'.

Onams (Great and Little) nos 37/38 & 43/44 1744: on, upon + OE nam = a piece of land (see *Pynams*)

Orange Grave no. 92 1849: Later references change this to orange grove, but the first known use is definitely Orange Grave. At some point between the surveys of 1796 and 1849, the tributary of the Aykeland Beck that ran through Dicky Grounds seems to have been diverted. This is most obvious on aerial photographs.[72] Perhaps when the new channel was being dug something resembling a grave, filled with slightly different coloured soil, was uncovered. A farmstead existed in this area in 1655, and in October 1661 a George Holmes of the Low Houses (this area) was buried in his own garden,[73] so it is actually possible that it was his real grave that gave rise to this obscure name.

Orcherde Ende meadowe 1534:[74] This is the first reference to an orchard as a separate area to grow fruit trees, although they would have been a common feature of this area. The Barstow survey of 1744 specifically referenced three orchards (nos 48, 76 & 95) and at the same time an orchard existed at what is now *Sleightholme Farm*. This meadow may be the *Grove* mentioned earlier.

Ormestoftes C12/13: *pn* Ormr + late OE toft = a building plot, a curtilage, a messuage. *Toft* is taken to imply habitation of some description, and Orm was a name well known in this area.[75] However, at Domesday Ryton belonged to the principal manor of Kirby Moorside; part of this manor was held by a person named Ormr, probably Ormr, son of Gamall[76] who rebuilt Gregory's Minster at Kirkdale. In addition, it is believed that this was the same Ormr who had married Aethelthryth, whose sister Aelfflaed had married Siward, the Earl of Northumbria,[77] making the presence in Ryton of both Ormestoftes and *Siwardeus* even more intriguing. The context in which Ormestoftes is referred to could even imply a small, separate settlement.

Oxfelde Close 1535: This was another name for the West Field. Oxen were the primary draught animal and gave their name to a number of Ox-closes/moor/pasture. They were in use in Yorkshire well into the 20th century.

Paddock Howl nos 91 & 92 1744: ME paddock = a frog + ME howl = a low place. This remote, low-lying meadow bordered the Aykeland Beck and the Costa. Living memory confirms that before the water-courses were completely re-engineered in the 1950s, the Aykeland Beck at this point was a major breeding place for toads and frogs. It still is, but not quite so dramatically as the natural pools no longer exist. The opposite side of the Costa is shown as Toad Hole on OS maps.

The Paddock 1789 (no. 199 1842): This is the more modern meaning of the word paddock, as a small enclosure, usually pasture, adjoining or near a house or stable, as this location is.

Park Farm 1910: There are two possible reasons for this name. The farmstead was near the area of land that had been referred to as the Parks, although the farm was actually made up of *Dodgson* and *Peters* moors. A barn had been erected by 1738 and a farmstead by 1751. Equally, the Parke family in the area may also have given their name to this farm. Richard was involved at Garforth Hall in 1778, and Matthew at Rumbarts Farm in 1836, although a direct connection has not yet been made. This farm briefly had the ignominy of being called *Glisterpipe*.

Parnham Farm see *Pynam Closes*.

Peters Moor 1750:[78] The eponymous Peter has not yet been identified. This part of Park Farm retained its name until 1838, but by the Tithe Award of 1842 the individual closes that it had been divided into were named separately.

Pexton Closse 1572, **Peckstone Close** no. 3 1683. See *Pexton Flatt*.

Pexton Flatt 1663 (no. 4 1842): This was a *Flatt* in the old West Field with the name surviving after the area was divided into closes. First mentioned in 1663, it was recorded in the parish registers (1658–72) as Righton-Flatt Houses but the same entry, for the burial of Jane Harrison, was Pexton Flatt House in the Bishop's Transcripts. The location was later confirmed on the deeds registry relating to *New House* (Ness House) in 1750 when House Close was the name of the adjacent close, but by then no house existed on either plot. Later deeds gave the names Peckstone Flatt (1818), Pickstone Flatt (1825), and on the map of 1842 (no. 4) it was referred to as Pickstone Platt [sic]. Although Pexton Flatt and *Pexton Close* are more than a mile apart, it is possible that both were named because of the number of stones that had to be cleared from them in an area where there were relatively few naturally occurring stones. Unfortunately, having been cleared of stones that would no doubt have been put to good use elsewhere, there is little left to confirm this theory.

Philadelphia Cottages 1851: In 1851 these were relatively new cottages built on the Barstow estate. The large Barstow family (13 children survived into adulthood) had dispersed around the world, with considerable numbers in New Zealand and America. The name probably recognised the location of one of the relatives (see also *Garrow Lodge Farm* and *Redington House*).

Pond Close/Pond Field nos 96 & 115 1842: Ponds were a useful, even necessary, water source for livestock, but for some reason they were usually ignored by cartographers and there are no early place-names indicating their existence. Every farm would have had at least one pond.

Poor House Close no. 36 1842: There had been a messuage in this area in 1778 but it had gone by 1842. The term 'Poor House' is usually taken to mean it was controlled by the 'Overseers of the Poor', but this connection has not been made. The Census returns of 1851 refer only to the cottages at *New York* on the Lund estate as being 'Poor Cottages', but these seem to have been under the control of that estate.

Prior More 1565: This was part of the *Okke More Close* that was recorded in 1535 as being in the tenure of the Prior of Malton, hence the name, and was recorded as Pryor Moore before the distribution of 1655.

Pynam Closes pre-1655: OE pie = an insect or ME pie = a magpie + OE nam = piece of land. Being near the Aykeland Beck there would have been many insects, and magpies are very common. A farmstead was shown in the area by 1744 but not named. Because of the low-lying nature of the area the Barstow accounts referred to it as Low Farm, a name it had as late as April 1969. The surveyors of 1850 'corrected' the spelling to Parnham, a name that was eventually adopted.

Redbeck Lyes or Close 1572: OE hreod = reed + beck. This was also described as 'Ryton Towne Inges'. It is not possible to locate this area precisely, although by 1572 it is known that the Ings associated with the West Field had already been sold, so it was most likely somewhere near the River Rye towards the south or east of the township. Could this have been *Rutebech* originally?

Redington House 1950: Originally a semi-detached council house built on a corner of one of Barstow's fields. The name reflected their then address at Redington Road in London.

The Rig/Rigg (Ryton Rigg) C12/13: OE hrycg = a ridge, a long narrow hill; also ON hryggr and dialect rig = a ridge. This is today's Ryton Rigg, although the settlements of Great and Little Habton also lie on this ridge of higher ground. It is the presence of this Rigg that made the area habitable in the distant past. Unfortunately this ridge of land does not show up on modern OS maps as most of it is just below the 25m contour, and the low-lying ground surrounding it is just above the 20m contour. This may not seem much of a difference, but it was more than enough to keep the Rigg well above even the worst flooding, and it also drained naturally because of its height and the underlying sand (see *Foreshore* and *Sandhills*). The Rigg extends from the confluence of the Rye and the Costa in the east to the foot of Great Barugh Hill in the west, a distance of some five miles. The significance of this Rigg seems to have previously been overlooked as it is not particularly obvious, either on a map or on the ground. However, stand on top of the Rigg on a clear day and the distant views show how strategically important it would have been. The security of the position is even more impressive during a serious flood. There can be little doubt that the presence of this Rigg was not only the reason for Ryton's name, it was the very reason for its existence.

Rochenvald C12/13: OE rocc = a rock + ME fald = a fold. A fold for animals built of stone.

Roskefwath C12/13: ON hross = a horse + OE ceaf = chaff (debris) + OScand wath = a ford. This could be a ford across one of the water-courses that was best crossed on horseback rather than foot. As with most fords it would be slightly shallower at the crossing point, causing a build-up of debris when the water ran lower than normal.

Rumbarts Farm 1768:[79] The Rumbart family were in this part of Ryton, and probably on this farm, in 1660, when William and his wife Elizabeth are mentioned in the parish register. The name was retained through to the deeds of 1836, but was replaced on the OS map of 1850 by the new name of *Gosling Green*.

Rushey Close pre-1655 (nos 69 & 70 1842): This field still has patches of soft rush (*Juncus effusus*) indicating the poor drainage. Rushes were very useful and an additional source of income, as they could be made into rush-lights; these would have been more common than candles in this area. The dried pith was soaked in grease/fat/wax (whatever was available) producing something resembling the wick of a candle; placed in special holders, they would burn for up to an hour depending on their length.

Rutebech/Rutesbec C12/13: OE Rudig = ruddy, red + beck. Some of the drainage ditches in the area still show signs of rust contamination, presumably from natural iron deposits.

River Rye (Rie) 1131: There are no records of this river name before the arrival of the first monks at Rievaulx around 1131. In fact the first known reference is in the original foundation charter of Walter Espec, granting land to the

Abbey of 'Rievalle', suggesting that the monks had already chosen the name for their community. In Mediaeval Latin, the language of the monks, rivus = brook or stream and vallis = valley, or situated in a valley, and Rivallis is sometimes the word used.[80] From this the naming by the monks of the river as the Rie is not surprising, and by the time the foundation charter is written down 'ten years – and it might easily be eleven or twelve years - subsequent'[81] the name has already come into general use. The monks had a desire to imply possession of the stream (and its contents) that ran to the side of their lands, and what better way than to name it after the abbey (see *Costa* above). If this interpretation of the origin of the name Rie is correct, then it reinforces the explanation given for the name Ryton below, but it does mean that the name of the lost Domesday manor of Ricalf (Riccal) near Helmsley requires explanation. Ricalf sat on a long narrow ridge of land formed between the valleys of the two rivers, now called the Rye and the Riccal. This ridge of land is dominated by the much larger ridge of land to the south that runs parallel to it, now called Caulkleys Bank. Consequently Ricalf could be so named from the Old English words ric = a narrow strip and calf = calf, or a small thing nearer a larger one (e.g. the Calf of Man), describing both its shape and its location adjacent to a much larger but similar ridge. The name Rievalle was changed at a later date to Rievaulx to conform to a French style of spelling.[82]

Rye Garth no. 40 1744: This was distant from the River Rye, so it probably refers to the cereal crop (rather than the grass) as it was listed as arable. Rye was used to make (black) bread and as animal feed, while the long tough straw was used for thatching and to make hats and paper.

Rye House: This was Rye House Farm on the first OS map, but eventually the house became detached from the farm. Adjacent and to the east, a much earlier moated site was also shown. The whole of this area, along with part of the *Goosecrofts*, was probably one of the purchases by Sir Roger Cholmeley from the Percehays in 1533,[83] and when his son Sir Richard sold it on to Roger Sympson in 1556[84] it was described as '5 messuages with land in Ryton', so it included part of the village. One of the Simpson family created what must have been an impressive house complete with moat, and the 1673 Hearth Tax shows it was second only to the Percehays' in terms of numbers of fireplaces (8 and 13 respectively). That house may still have been standing in 1789[85] as it was described as a 'Capital Messuage' (a term usually indicating a manor house, although it wasn't) in the deeds registry, but by 1828 it was only a 'messuage or dwelling house'. The Simpsons retained an interest until 1834[86] when Edward Rose (of Rose's Brewery in Malton) became the owner.

Ryton: 1086 R.tun (1N 60M) and Ritone (23N 21B) at Domesday / 1148–58 Rihtuna[87] / 1159 Rictuna & Rictona[88] / 1160 Rictuna[89] / 1170 Rictuna[90] / 1189 Rictona[91] / 1199–1216 (Temp John) Rigeton[92] / 1252 Rictona[93] / 1272–73 Rygtona.[94]

It has always been assumed that Ryton was so-named because it was the 'tun' (OE for Settlement) by the side of the River Rye, although the river itself does not seem to have a name recorded before the arrival of the monks at Rievaulx in 1131. However, when some early references to Ryton are collated chronologically, as shown, it is clear that the name Ryton has a different origin. One of the Domesday references records it as 'R.tun'. In Domesday, because of the size of the task of recording so much information, abbreviations are used extensively, and as the full stop takes up just as much space as the letter 'i', it is reasonable to think that more than one letter is indicated. After Domesday the name of Ryton is recorded with at least two letters between the 'R' and the 't', with variations on Rihton, Ricton and Rigton. Once it is realised that Ryton actually stands on a ridge of land that was, and still is called the *Rigg* (see above), a name derived from the Old English 'hrycg' meaning a ridge or a long narrow hill, it then seems likely that Ryton was so-named because it is the 'tun' on the ridge, explaining both Ricton and Rigton.

Ryton Bridge: The very first modern map of the county by Christopher Saxton, dated 1577, clearly shows a bridge at Ryton. More surprisingly, it does not show one at Howe or Newsham, although they probably existed. The presence of the bridge is also confirmed in the will of Raufe Raisinge of New Malton dated 1 December 1575 when he referred to his 'close called Batt Inge lying at Ryton Bridge end'.[95] There would have been some form of river-crossing to Ryton from earliest times but the date, or indeed location, of the first bridge is not known.

Ryton Grange 1850: This assumed name seems to have confused many. The location is near the centre of the old West Field and no messuages are mentioned in the sale of 1535. There was still no farmstead when it was acquired by Joseph Wardale in 1778,[96] but one is shown on the Tithe

Award map of 1842. There is no connection with any of the religious houses, being owned by the Percehay family until the sale of 1535.

Salescale: 1086: OE sale = willow + ON skal = a bowl, a hollow. Salescale was a settlement that existed at Domesday and was listed in what is known as the summary rather than in the Domesday Book proper. The entry has been translated as 'The King, in Salescale, 6 bovates' and comes in the section listing landholders in Maneshow (later Ryedale) Wapentake between the King's holdings in Habton and his holdings in Ryton.[97] It is probably this position of the entry that explains why later notes suggest that Salescale was 'lost in Ryton township'.[98] No other information can be found giving reference to Salescale, and there are no local stories about this lost settlement or its possible location. However, a chance discovery of an area referred to as '*Scale Garth and Lanes*'[99] (no. 56, Figure 13) in a survey carried out around 1680[100] for the then owners of the Lund estate in Ryton, the Belasise (Fauconberg) family from Newburgh Priory, may provide the missing clue required to work out the location of Salescale. The survey was very detailed, giving the name and area of every one of their 65 fields, which covered 621 acres, and it included the names of the four tenants, with one of the farms shown as 'not let'. Unfortunately no corresponding map has survived, but the Lund estate was surveyed again in 1796 (no map) and 1849. Fortunately there is a map to go with this 1849 survey[101] and a Scale Garth is clearly shown (no. 49, Figure 16) adjacent to Costa Farm (now Costa Manor Farm), enabling the whole area originally referred to as Scale Garth and Lanes to be identified. There is one very particular feature within this area that is key to confirming the location of the original Salescale. To the north of the existing farmstead is a pond that at first glance looks like any other farm pond, but on closer inspection the depression forming the pond has a very regular rectangular shape, measuring approximately 150ft x 100ft (46m x 31m). This is far too large to have been dug out manually just to make a pond. The pond itself is also on slightly higher ground than the surrounding land, suggesting that it is fed by a natural spring, confirmed by the fact that it rarely dries out completely. It is not possible, without archaeological excavation, to determine what was removed from this site or when it was done, or even if it is just a natural depression, although that seems unlikely. However, if this feature existed when the area was given its name, then the use of the word 'scale' from the Old Norse word 'skal', meaning a bowl or hollow, would be understandable. Add to this the Old English word for willow – 'sale', a tree known for growing near water and still very common in the immediate vicinity – then the name Salescale, meaning 'the bowl-shaped depression or hollow where willows grow', would have been particularly appropriate.

So if this really is the location of Salescale, why did it disappear without any known references after Domesday? This whole area is now know as Lund and is extremely well documented. It was given by Ralph Neville to 'God and the Church of the Blessed Mary of Rievaulx'[102] shortly after the formation of Rievaulx Abbey[103] (in 1131) but the area is not named. The name Lund does not appear until well after the monks have arrived[104] and was probably an attempt to emphasise their ownership, using the name of Lund in the sense of a sacred area, one offering sanctuary (from Old Norse Lundr). The monks also seem to have tried to re-name the area known as 'the wastes below Pickering' granted to them by Henry I, referring to the various 'marishes' collectively as Theokemarescum.[105] These were known at Domesday as Odulfesmare, Aschilesmares, Chiluesmares and Maxudesmares, and all are also now referred to as 'lost'. Their choice of the made-up word of Theokemarescum seems to be an attempt to imply the area was 'God's marishes', but the word was not generally adopted and the original phrase 'the wastes below Pickering' continued to be used. The monks also seem to have been responsible for the name of the river *Costa* (from mediaeval Latin meaning 'side') when it ran along the side of their original possessions in the marishes. Once the monks had been given an area they were quite ruthless in evicting all existing tenants and even the local churches complained about their tactics. In 1284 Archbishop Peckham objected to the foundation of another Cistercian monastery because 'wherever they set their feet they destroy villages, take away tithes and detract from the authority of the bishops'.[106] At the time of Neville's grant it is clear that there was active agriculture, with one carucate (= 8 bovates, approx 120 acres) of arable land plus the associated meadow (mainly for hay) and pasture (grazing) being rented at the time by someone called Aluricus, who was probably head of either an extended family or a community. The fact that Aluricus and his son Gerbodo both signed the deed of transfer from Neville to Rievaulx Abbey suggests that in this case their departure may have been amicable. Extensive ridge and furrow around the location of Scale Garth confirms that some form of open-field system was already in operation. The monks would not have begun this, and by the time of the Dissolution the open-field system in Ryton had already been abandoned, so it is extremely unlikely that it would have been reintroduced. Looking at the Lund estate plan of 1849 (Figure 15), the curvy field boundaries centred around Scale Garth give an idea of the extent of the original open-field system and contrast with the much later enclosures to the north and west. Perhaps by coincidence the arable area indicated by these old field boundaries is in the order of 100 to 140 acres, depending on the fields included. More significant is the fact that the farmstead now adjacent to Scale Garth sits on a site that is slightly above the surrounding very flat, low-lying ground. In addition, the farmstead is built mainly of stone and there are substantial stone foundations adjacent, suggesting this was the site of Rievaulx Abbey's Lund Grange. This does not necessarily make it the site of Salescale, but the 'lanes' (note the plural) referred to in the original Lund survey did still converge on this area. The main lane was the remnants of the old north/south route linking Pickering and Malton via the 'monk's bridge' (*Frerebrigg*) over the Costa, the ford across Aykeland Beck (the original *Aycfrithewath*?) and on to Ryton and the crossing of the River Rye (see Figure 9). In addition, a route went north-west to Kirby Misperton and as late as the OS map of 1950 a footpath followed most of this route – today the associated public right of way is slightly to the south, following later field boundaries. The actual road south from Kirby Misperton to Malton that linked with this lane was redirected by the Kirby Misperton Enclosure Award of 1703 to meet the Pickering to Malton road near the crossing of the Costa known as Lund Bridge (*Lundbrige/Frerebrigg*). Finally, recent field-walking has discovered an unusual amount of flint in the vicinity of Scale Garth and Lanes, suggesting that this could have been a settlement site for millennia. The information now available suggests Salescale was located on the slightly higher ground near Scale Garth, and may even be underneath the foundations of both Costa Manor farm and the earlier Lund Grange.

Sand Hills 1831:[107] Great and Little Sand Hills were two closes on the area known for centuries as *Broomhills*, but after this date it was occasionally known as Sand Hills. The reference to sand comes from the sand that underlies the whole of the *Rigg*. This was such a good source of sand that a pit near the site of the Old Manor on the 1890 OS map seems to have been used to provide building sand for the construction of the new Manor Farm in 1821.

Scale Garth and Lanes no. 56 1683: ON skal = a bowl, a hollow + garth (see *Salescale*) with the associated lanes that converged on this area

Seavey Close no. 73 1744: ON sef = a sedge, a rush, surviving as dialect 'seeaves' (rushes).[108]

Seaventeane Land Ends pre-1655: This is the earliest reference to Seventeen Lands, meaning the *flatt* in the open field (the West Field in this case) that contained seventeen *lands*; this close was made up from the *Land Ends* at the end of that flatt. Multiple references leave no doubt about the location, or that of the adjacent, separate close called Seventeen Lands, that was first referenced in 1737. In 1778 East and West Seventeen Lands and Near and Far Land Ends were also referenced in the same document, but by the survey of 1842 the names were lost.

Sevescip/Sewelscip/Sculescip C12/13: OE swelh = a pit, a whirlpool + OE scip = a sheep. This could have been where the sheep were washed to clean their fleeces (see *Laversike*).

Sewer Field no. 88 1849: Originally sewer meant a drainage ditch rather than anything to do with sanitation. All fields with this name are next to ditches.

Shotton Hall no. 59 1842: The first member of the Shotton family known in this area was Roger Shotton. He was Prior of the Gilbertine Priory at Old Malton from *c.* 1495 to 1517. The location of the Grange of Malton Priory called *Brodes* is known quite specifically, placing it in the same area as today's Shotton Hall. How the Shotton family came to own this land is not known, but as Shotton was not a common name, it is unlikely to just be coincidence. In 1603 the Kirby Misperton Bishop's Transcripts record 'Aprill 16 Susann Shotton daughter of Leonard of Ryton was baptised'. At that time the Shotton family may well have lived at what became Shotton Hall. The parish register records are quite sporadic, but they do include Michael Shotton (of Ryton baptised 6 October 1639) and Edward Shotton (married Jane Carrick 30 November 1669) indicating a continuity in the area. By the time of the more complete deeds registry, the farm now known as Shotton Hall was referred to in February 1747 as Low Moor Farm (probably no. 265 1842), Red Lilly Closes, and 'the Messuages lands and tenements which were the estate and inheritance of Michael Shotton late of Ryton deceased'. By March 1842 the whole 'are now known as Shotten or Shortten Hall Farm',[109] which explains some of the (mis)spellings on later maps and documents.

Siwardeus/Sywardehus/Suwardehus C12/13: *pn* Siward + ON hus = a house. A Siward was Earl of Northumbria from

83

around 1040 to his death in 1055. Little seems to be known about this Siward, and most of it is second-hand. Despite already being dead, he was shown as one of the three people who held Malton before the Conquest, so he had land across the River Rye from Ryton. At the moment there is nothing conclusive to connect this particular Siward with Ryton, although the presence in Ryton of *Ormestoftes* (see above) and 'Siward's House' is quite intriguing.[110] Siward's status would explain why his name persisted in the area, especially if he really did have a house in Ryton. His presence is one of the few things that could also explain the existence of a castle (see *Casteldich*) and the Percehay coat of arms.

Sleightholme Farm: *pn* The name seems to be from William Sleightholme of Fadmoor, yeoman, who bought this farm, including a newly erected messuage, in April 1806.[111] He did not stay very long, selling on to John Newton in June 1815,[112] but his name survives.

Sparrow Hall 1850: This farmstead was built in the close called Adder's Tongue in 1655 and adjacent to a close named 'the Harrow', so perhaps that accounts for the name of 1850.

Spring Hall 1665:[113] Alice Garforth acquired Leafield as part of her settlement on 14 September 1655; six days later she sold it, but no mention was made of any dwelling.[114] By the time it was re-sold in August 1659,[115] Leafield had a 'house thereupon lately builded' that was still there in March 1662, but by July 1665 it had become 'Messuage or Mancion howse lately erected commonly called Springhall'. However grand, or otherwise, Spring Hall may have been, it did not make it on to the survey of 1683. The name is not surprising as there are still a number of springs in the area, although there is now no sign of one in the Leafield itself. The fanciful description of a mansion house probably reflects the fact that none of the parties concerned would ever have seen this remote part of the world and it was a real case of 'buyer beware'.

Stack Garth no. 54 1744: This garth, adjacent to the Manor House, was where the stacks of hay and corn would have been over-wintered. One of the necessary requirements was that this had to be permanently dry ground, and this was, being on the highest ground and sitting on a deep stratum of sand just below the surface.

Stapel C12/13: OE stapol = a post, a pillar and often used as a marker for a meeting place or a boundary, or to indicate the location of a ford, with the latter being quite appropriate in Ryton.

Stell Field 1842: OED stell = an open ditch or brook. There were two stell fields, one (no. 106) contained the source of an unnamed ditch, the other (no. 129) bordered the Aykeland Beck.

Strudightyn Martyn pre-1290: Joan Percehay, nee Vesci, gave 'the whole of her Manor of Strudightyn Martyn in County Forfar in Scotland' to her son and heir Walter. This information comes from 'The Ordinary of Mr Thos Jenyn's book of arms' dated around 1400[116] and it is also quoted in the Visitations of both Glover (1584/5) and Foster (1612). The inheritance came from Joan's great-grandmother Margaret, an illegitimate daughter of William the Lion, King of Scotland. Scottish sources suggest that the location is the modern Strathmartin, shown as Kirkton of Strathmartine on today's OS road maps, on the outskirts of Dundee. These possessions in Scotland were probably lost under the treaty signed between Robert the Bruce and Edward III in 1328 and while an attempt was made to regain these lands by the disinherited nobility from England in 1332,[117] no more is heard of these Percehay possessions in Scotland, so it can only be assumed that the venture failed.

Stubbing Close pre-1655: OE stubbing = a place where trees have been cleared leaving the stubbs (tree-stumps). In the Lund survey of 1683 there were three adjacent Stubbing Closes. Two were named showing their positions relative to the farmstead at today's North Farm. However, by the survey of 1796 a new farmstead, today's West Farm, had been built and these closes were then part of that farm, but the names were retained, with the result that Farr Stubbing Close was next to the farmstead and Near Stubbing Close was further away. The situation was rectified at the next survey of 1849 by when all the Stubbing Closes had been renamed, and all references to these original trees had disappeared.

Sugeholme C12/13: OE sugge = a sparrow, a bird + ON holmr = water-meadow. Perhaps the meadow preferred by the sparrows or the birds. Sugge eventually became 'spuggie', the local dialect name for sparrow.

Swan Nest: This name first appeared in 1558 when it was Swanne Nest or Swanne Close, and it was already in two parts.[118] By the time of the will of Thomas Woodcock in

Chapter 5: Place-Names of Ryton

1752[119] it was two separate farms, both confusingly called Swan Nest, with both names surviving through to the Tithe Award of 1842. The farmstead nearest the village of Ryton became known as *Abbotts Farm* after Thomas Abbott lived there, with the other retaining the name Swan Nest, although that farmstead was eventually abandoned in the 20th century. The name Swan Nest indicates the presence of swans, and the area is adjacent to the land owned by the Prior of Malton, who would have been one of the few people allowed to kill and eat swans, so perhaps the name indicates that he bred swans in this area. Swans can still be seen on the Costa near the old farmsteads.

Old Swarth Garth no. 14 1849: OE swaeth = a track, a pathway. This leads to the river-crossing now thought to be the location of *Frerebrigg*.

Synekeker/secneker C12/13: OE sik = a small stream + OE hnecca = a neck of land + ME ker = wet ground. This again relates to the confluence of the Costa and the River Rye.

Tacriveling 1157/8: OE taecels = a boundary + ME riveling = a rivulet. This is the stream, beck, small river, or 'rivulet' that divided the lands of Rievaulx and Ryton. The detailed description in the charter by Henry II confirming the earlier grant of Henry I to the monks of Rievaulx of 'the whole of his waste and pasture below Pickering' that included the boundary '…ascending Rye where Costa falls into it, ascending Costa to Tacriveling and by it to the monks' ditch as it runs around Lund and flows into Costa …'[120] leaves no doubt that Tacriveling was what became known as Aykeland Beck. Tacriveling had been mentioned in the same context in other charters relating to this grant,[121] and it is identifiable again in 1279/80[122] in a dispute between Sir Walter Percehay and William de Habbeton. Surprisingly, no other references can be found naming this stream until 1849 when it was named Aykeland Beck, although in 1311 the Register of Archbishop Greenfield[123] shows that Joan Percehaye was granted a licence to hear divine service in her oratory of Ryton partly due to the problems caused by the flooding of this (un-named) stream. The name could also have been in use much earlier, as this is now thought to have been the boundary between Ryton and the 'lost' Domesday vill of *Salescale*, although as the name seems to arrive with the monks, perhaps this was another name they introduced.

Teapot Close no. 72 1849: One of the few names to survive, perhaps because of its novelty. It doesn't take too much imagination to see the shape implied by the name.

Thistle Close no. 44 1683: Thistle is a very difficult weed to eradicate, with special hoes, only two inches wide, being used to hoe between the rows of corn to try to control it. As the name persisted to 1796, it suggests the battle was never ending. In fact thistles were a real problem weed, especially in corn, right up to the introduction of herbicides in the second half of last century.

Tod Closes no. 17 1683: pn Richard Todd was a tenant on the Lund estate in 1658. The family name occurred in 1523[124] when Thomas and Christopher Todd were some of the men named as servants to Roger Cholmeley in the case of the murder of Robert Tailour. This may put them in the area of Lund at that time. In 1527 Thomas, Simon, John, Silvester and William Todde purchased what later became known as the two *Swan Nest* farms from the Percehay family.[125] At that time the adjacent landowner to the east was Malton Priory, and the Prior at that time was a William Todde.

Toft C12/13: ODan, late OE toft = a building plot, a curtilage, a messuage. The name implies habitation of some description.

Tranmer's Footbridge 1850: The Tranmer family owned land on the Marishes side of the Costa at this point. This is the location now believed to be the ancient river-crossing of *Frerebrigg* and *Lundbrige*. Some of the Tranmer descendants now live in Lancashire.

Turnep Garth no. 7 1683: This date is well before the agricultural revolution, caused in part by the adoption of crop rotation pioneered by Lord 'Turnip' Townshend (1674–1738). Turnips are thought to have been introduced from Holland as early as 1550 and were invaluable as fresh food for animals in winter when grass was dormant. Turnips will survive a long time in the ground, and in a good (mild) winter would have seen the stock through to March/April when the grass would have begun to grow. However, the very small size of this garth, little more than a quarter of an acre, suggests that Turnep Garth was actually used as an area to store the turnips, grown elsewhere on the farm, in a similar way to the hay and corn that were stored on the *Stack Garth*. The customary way to store root crops (potatoes, mangolds, turnips and swedes) in this area was to 'pie' them. This involved piling the roots into a large heap on a dry, well-drained area, covering them with an insulating and waterproof thatch of either straw or dry reeds, and then covering the sides of the pie with earth. The final covering of earth provided more insulation, and prevented the straw/reeds from blowing away even in the fiercest winter storms. The very top of the pie was not covered in soil as this allowed the whole structure to breathe. As may be obvious, this method is still in use and is described from first-hand experience, although today potatoes especially are much more likely to be stored in purpose-built sheds, complete with full climate control and forced ventilation.

Wake Farm 1737: becomes **Weak Closes** nos 61–63 1842; OE waed = a ford. The transition from waed to wake to weak can be explained by the local accent. A number of tracks and paths converge on the river in this area (see Figures 9 and 10). Old field boundaries between the Rye at this point and heading north all the way to Kirby Misperton are almost continuous, with tracks and paths following most of this line today. To the south of the river Cheapsides Road heads in this direction from Malton, and a track from Broughton heads towards this area past Hazel House. It would appear from information in a 'Terrier' sent by Leonard Conyers, the incumbent of Kirby Misperton, to the bishop, some time around 1700, that at the time there was a bridge in this location that he referred to as Broughton bridge.[126] Jeffrey's map of the area dated 1771 may also show the river crossing at this point, but there are so many local errors on this map that it cannot be considered reliable.[127] No trace of either the ford or the bridge can be seen on the 1842 Tithe map, or any subsequent map.

Wath Closes nos 51 & 52 1683: OScand vath, OE waed = the ford. Adjacent to the Costa in the area where *Frerebrigg* is now thought to have been. That bridge was only for foot traffic, so there was probably a ford next to it for carts. A ford was shown at this point in 1850, and *Tranmer's Footbridge* still exists at this location.

Wath Hill 1850: This is north of the Costa, just before its confluence with the Rye. There is still a crossing of the Costa at this point, with a footbridge carrying a pedestrian right of way. Topography suggests that this may have been a crossing from an ancient route along the top of Ryton Rigg (see Figure 9), and its use has continued because the land on the Ryton side of the Costa has belonged to the farm on the Marishes side since at least 1831[128] and probably back to the Dissolution.

Well Close no. 4 1683: The underlying impervious clay always made it easy to find a supply of water and farmers still remember the locations of a number of wells.

Wentsworth House and Garth no. 16 1683: The surveyor of this plan probably misheard Mr Wentworth's name. There does not seem to be a tenant in this house in 1683, and as no house was there in 1796, perhaps Mr Wentworth was the last person to live at this remote location. In the days of Rievaulx Abbey's ownership it would have made sense to have a house here to keep an eye on the north/south and east/west traffic and especially their crossing of the Costa. A Mr William Wentworth was a tenant on the adjacent Barstow estate in 1744.

West Farm no. 24 1849: This farmstead on the Lund estate was built between 1683 and 1796 and its name on the 1849 plan reflected its relative position on that estate.

White Lilly Close 1655: This name of one of the closes from the Garforth distribution was adopted for the name of the farm built upon it. A farmstead may have been erected as early as 1671, and there is certainly one by the time of Thomas Woodcock's will dated 1752. A full set of deeds for this property are on file at NYCRO, and research has now connected this land back to the original ownership of the Percehays who had it as part of their Ryton Lordship until 1604.

Whynes 1572: ME whin = gorse. There are many references to whins (various spellings) and *Furres* in the documents relating to Ryton, and it seems likely that both originally referred to areas of brushwood, rough scrub, and grass, rather than a specific species. It would also explain the OE wynn, meaning pasture, because it is clear from this specific case that the area referred to was quite productive, despite being called whynes and furres, with the loads of hay taken from the area being part of the dispute.

Woodcocke Moore Close pre-1655: *pn* This was named after the family, not the bird. Andrew de Wodecoke was in this area in 1300[129] but did not register anywhere in the 1302 Lay Subsidy, perhaps because he was too poor. In 1655 the location of Woodcock's House and farm was given, and a Gawen or Gawin Woodcock also seems to have given his name to the adjacent *Gawin Moor*. The family can be followed through various records down to the last known male in the area, John, who was deceased by April 1805,[130] but he was survived by his niece Mary Woodcock who had married a John Dowker of Salton.[131]

Wood End 1841: On the 1744 Barstow plan the remnant of the Percehays' *New Forest* was shown as no. 6, covering just three acres. This was still shown as 'wood' when new contracts were agreed with their tenant, Guy Raines, in May 1821. However, by the Census of 1841 there were six dwellings listed named Woodend, and the OS map of 1850 confirmed them as being in the south end of the wood, complete with a well. They were all still noted in 1871, but by the 1891 Census only one dwelling was listed as Woodend; this was almost certainly Bees Cottage which was separate from Woodend. So, in the space of around 60 years a settlement was created in the wood, with an average of 20 people living there, but by 1891 the only evidence of their existence on the OS map was the remaining well and some tracks through the wood. The dwellings may have been very basic, although the bricks covering the earth floors were still being found into the 1930s.

Wyth Gate Ings 1737 (nos 21, 22, 49 & 50 1842): ODan with = a willow + ON gata = a path, a road + Ings. There may have been an ancient river-crossing in this area between the Percehay manors of Swinton and Ryton, that was eventually bridged (see *Jerry Bridge*). The road leading away from the original crossing may be the reason for this name. The ancient field boundaries between numbers 20 and 21 on the 1842 plan indicate the meeting of the old West Field and the lands sold to Sir Wm Compton in 1522 and may well indicate the line of the old Wyth Gate. When closes nos 16 to 20 were all farmed from the Swinton side of the river this road would have allowed access to all their fields in Ryton. Part of that road can still be seen on the 1842 map (Figure 17).

Notes

1. Interviews with Mr E Richardson confirm that this was his way to school in the 1920s.
2. NYCRO Deeds Registry; vol.155, p416, r155
3. YAS/RS 45; Yorkshire Star Chamber Proceedings, vol. 2, p137 Percehay vs Prior of Malton
4. *Flora Britannica*, Richard Mabey (1996), p364
5. NYCRO mic 260; D/R Book A, p231, r 266
6. YAS/RS 69; Yorkshire Deeds vol.5, p72
7. YAS MD92-5
8. KMBT for 1601
9. S/Soc 91; Yorkshire Chantry Surveys vol.1 (for Henry VIII), p128, no.146
10. NRRY/NS vol.1, p67
11. NRRY/NS vol.4, p205
12. YAS MD 92-7
13. YAS/RS 48; Suppression of Monasteries. Grant dated 26 June 1540
14. YAS MD92-3
15. Kirby Misperton Tithe Award, part of the Inclosure Award 1703. www.kirbymisperton.org.uk/inclosure
16. YAS/RS EYC vol.1, p131, no.402
17. NRRY/NS vol. 3, p8
18. NYCRO D/R vol.155, p416, r155
19. YAS MD92-3
20. YAS MD92-18
21. YAS MD92-28
22. KMBT for 1663
23. NYCRO mic287; D/R Book BM p236, r364
24. NRRY/NS vol. 3, pp2–3
25. NRRY/NS vol. 3, pp 2–3
26. NRRY/NS vol. 3, pxxix
27. NRRY/NS vol. 4, p227
28. YAS/RS EYC vol. I, p315, no.406
29. NRRY/NS vol.1, p67
30. See OED – mile
31. YAS/RS 70; Yorkshire Star Chamber Proceedings, p65
32. YAS/RS 86; *Maps of Yorkshire*, Harold Whitaker (ed) (1933), p42
33. Cause Papers C.P.G.1628; 1572 Ellerker vs Woodcocke re tithe
34. Cause Papers C.P.H.5227; 1685 Leonard Conyers vs Gavin Woodcock re tithe
35. NYCRO mic 287; D/R Book BM, p236, r364
36. See all MD92
37. NYCRO mic 260; D/R Book A, p231, r266
38. NYCRO mic 269; D/R Book T, p438, r592
39. NYCRO mic 357; D/R Book GP, p100, r119
40. Information kindly supplied by Alastair Oswald, Department of Archaeology, University of York.
41. S/Soc 83; Rievaulx Chartulary, p289
42. NYCRO mic 283; D/R Book BC, p241, r390
43. S/Soc 83; Rievaulx Chartulary, p139
44. See Victoria County History and many other references
45. YAS/RS 53; Yorkshire Fines 1605–12: 1605 – 3 James I Michaelmas term Atkinson & Ascough to Chas. & Ursula Atkinson
46. NYCRO mic 310; D/R Book DF, p563, r637
47. YAS MD92-2
48. *A Pilgrimage of British Farming*, A.D. Hall (1913), p103
49. Cause Papers C.P.G.1628; 1572 Ellerker vs Woodcocke re tithe
50. NYCRO mic 3989; ZDV – Fauconberg (Belasyse) of Newburgh Priory Archive at NYCRO, p177
51. NA C10/139/37 Chancery pleadings, Christopher Hayme vs Christopher Percehay
52. YAS/RS EYC vol.1, p315, no.406
53. NYCRO mic 3989; ZDV, p160
54. Cause Papers C.P.G.1628; 1572 Elleker vs Woodcocke re tithe
55. NYCRO mic 382; D/R Book IM, p162, r248

56. Cause Papers C.P.G.1628; 1572 Elleker vs Woodcocke re tithe
57. *The Place-names of the North Riding of Yorkshire* (A.H. Smith (1979) English Place-Name Society vol.V, p76) quotes 'Richard de Breaus had enclosed his wood at Lund' as convincing evidence of the forest at Lund but this land owner is not connected to the Lund near Ryton and it is the wrong Lund.
58. YAS/RS 70; Yorkshire Star Chamber Proceedings, p65 Tailour vs Chomley
59. NYCRO mic325; D/R Book EH, p410, r399
60. S/Soc 83; Rievaulx Chartulary, p149
61. YAS/RS 69; Yorkshire Deeds vol.5, p72
62. NYCRO mic 285; D/R Book BF, p433, r646
63. NYCRO mic 300; D/R Book CO, p393, r506
64. NYCRO mic 261; D/R Book D, p447, r521
65. YAS MD92-4
66. YAS MD92-3
67. YAS MD92-17
68. Yorkshire Fines 1522 Hilary Term 13 HEN VIII Percehay to Compton (and others)
69. NYCRO mic 269; D/R Book U, p160, r214. Dated 7th March 1750, this Newhouse was then occupied by James Spavin.
70. NYCRO mic 336; D/R Book FC, p469, r425
71. YAS MD92-3
72. NYCRO – Meridian Airmaps Ltd, Sortie ref. 49/73, run no.61, frame 126 (Figure 2)
73. NYCRO – Kirby Misperton Parish Registers, 1658–72
74. YAS/RS 45; Yorkshire Star Chamber Proceedings, vol.2, p137
75. *Scandinavian Culture in Eleventh Century Yorkshire*, Matthew Townend (2007), The Kirkdale Lecture 2007
76. *Domesday Book Yorkshire,* Part Two (1986) (Phillimore), note 23N19
77. *Anglo-Saxon Bishops Kings & Nobles*, W.G. Searle (1899), p374. See also Prosopography of Anglo-Saxon England www.pase.ac.uk
78. NYCRO mic 268; D/R Book S, p451, r623
79. NYCRO mic 280; D/R Book AU, p17, r14
80. Calendar of Close Rolls Henry III, vol.1 1227–31, May 1229. Eboracum – Abbas de Rivallis vs Willelmum de Ros
81. S/Soc 83 Rievaulx Chartulary, Introduction, pxxxvi
82. *Jervaulx Abbey*, English Life Publications Ltd (1972), p18
83. YAJ 73; Yorkshire Fines, Easter Term, 1533 William Percehay to Roger Cholmeley
84. YAJ 73; Yorkshire Fines, Easter Term, 1556 Richard Cholmeley and wife to Roger Sympson
85. NYCRO mic 295; D/R Book CE, p80, r130
86. NYCRO mic 350; D/R Book GD, p224, r275
87. S/Soc 83; Rievaulx Chartulary, p48; Ralph Neville's original gift to the monks at Rievaulx
88. S/Soc 83; pp143 & 152, Confirmations by Henry II dated 1159
89. S/Soc 83; p186, Papal Bull of Protection by Pope Alexander III dated 21 December 1160
90. S/Soc 83; p261, Confirmation by Henry II
91. S/Soc 83; p125, Confirmation by Richard I dated 17 Sept 1189
92. NRRY/NS vol.2; The Honor and Forest of Pickering, p215 Payment of 15s made by 'De Villata de Rigeton'
93. Calendar of Charter Rolls vol. 1226–57, p395 10 July 1252 at Clarendon confirming Neville's gift to Rievaulx
94. S/Soc 83; p401 confirming Assize Rolls Ebor Trinity term Edward 1 (1272–73) re free warren
95. YAS/RS 65; Yorkshire Deeds vol.4, p139
96. NYCRO mic 287; D/R Book BM, p265, r417 Wm Garforth to Joseph Wardale
97. *Domesday Book Yorkshire*, Parts 1&2, (1986) (Phillimore), SN. Ma2 and associated note
98. *Domesday Gazetteer,* H.C. Darby & G.R. Versey (1977), p533
99. YAS MS 601; 'Part of a Terrar of Newburgh's Lordship' (see Figure 13)
100. Tenant names in this survey suggest a date of around 1680, possibly 1683 after the death of one of the tenants.
101. NYCRO ZDV VI 66 (see Figure 15)
102. S/Soc 83; Rievaulx Chartulary pp48–9, Charter no. 81 Ralph Neville's original gift
103. YAS/RS EYC Vol.1, p313, Charter no. 402 is dated to 1157–58 and includes this area in the 'Wastes below Pickering' concerning Rievaulx.
104. YAS/RS EYC Vol. 1, p315, Charter no. 406 names Lund for the first time and is dated to 1176–79.
105. S/Soc 83; Rievaulx Chartulary, p149, Charter no. 210 as an example
106. *Monasteries and Landscape of the North York Moors and Wolds*, Bryan Waites (2007), Footnote no. 71 quoting *Registrum Epp.*, J. Peckham (Rolls Series) ii, p726
107. NYCRO mic 344, D/R Book FS, p583, r517
108. *The Yorkshire Dictionary*, Arnold Kellett (2008), p162
109. NYCRO mic 276; D/R Book AK, p507, r695
110. An Ormr and Earl Siward both married daughters of Ealdred, an earlier Earl of Northumbria.
111. NYCRO mic 309; D/R Book DD, p329, r337
112. NYCRO mic 319; D/R Book DU, p250, r324
113. NYCRO mic 3989; ZDV, p225
114. NYCRO mic 3989; ZDV, p207
115. NYCRO mic 3989; ZDV, p212
116. S/Soc 146; Shields of Arms M S Ashmole, no.834, p112, no.69
117. *Scotland History of a Nation*, David Ross (2013)
118. NA C3/108/25, 1558 Humphrey Knight vs William Sylyarde
119. NYCRO mic 271; D/R Book Y, p219, r332
120. YAS/RS EYC vol.1, p315, no.406, dated to 1176/9
121. YAS/RS EYC vol.1, p313 no.402 is dated to 1157–58 and is the earliest known reference to Tacriveling.
122. YAS/RS 69; Yorkshire deeds vol.5, p72, no.194
123. S/Soc 151; Register of Wm Greenfield Lord Archbishop of York 1306–15, part 3, p60 no.1274 dated 7 April 1311
124. YAS/RS 70; Yorkshire Star Chamber Proceedings p62 Tailour vs Chomley
125. Yorkshire Fines, 1527 – Michaelmas term 19 Henry VIII Percehay to Todde
126. B.I. TER/L/Kirby Misperton. This list of assets of the parish is not dated but must precede the death of Conyers in July 1707.
127. Great and Little Barugh are transposed; Low Moors in Ryton is not correctly located; and the Aykeland beck is shown as running into the Rye, but it actually joins the Costa at a completely different location.
128. NYCRO mic 344; D/R Book FS, p583, r517
129. YAS/RS 17; Monastic Notes, p122
130. NYCRO mic 309; D/R Book DD, p143, r123
131. NYCRO mic 306; D/R Book CZ, p555, r744

Appendix 1

Key Sources

There are a remarkable number of documents available concerning both Ryton and the Percehays, but a few have been so enlightening that they require some explanation to put them into context and to appreciate fully their impact. Some were previously undiscovered, while others had not been identified with a particular person or area, but being able to cross-reference them with so many other documents, their part in the bigger picture becomes a little more obvious.

Barstow Plan of 1744 (Figure 7) *and later Valuations and Rent-books*

In February 1687/8 Michael Barstow took over the debt of Christopher Percehay no. 3 (see Chapter 2) and on Michael's death the debt passed to his son Thomas as part of his inheritance. By October 1705, as the debt has increased substantially and is unlikely to be repaid, Thomas Barstow forecloses and becomes Lord of the Manor of Ryton and takes possession of the remaining Percehay assets. These pass to his son, another Michael, when Thomas dies in 1709, and on his death in 1743 the whole passes to his cousin Benjamin's son, another Thomas. The will is contested by Benjamin's brother, another Michael,[1] but to no avail, so Thomas immediately has his new acquisition surveyed by Robert Bewlay. A copy of the plan produced from this survey is made by Robert Gilson in 1787, and it is approximately half of this later copy, covering the area from the village green of Ryton through to the edge of the old West Field, that still survives. However, the Tithe Award map of 1842 (see Figure 17) covers most of the missing part of the plan, and as the field names coincide, the appropriate layout can easily be deduced. A rent book relating to the original plan still survives, and also contains full details of a re-valuation of the Ryton estate by Robert Bewlay senior in 1766; a further valuation by John Moiser in 1786; and yet another valuation in 1808 by William Dawson. Copies of all this information, combined with other documents kindly provided by the Barstow family, are now available at NYCRO. Obviously having so much detail about the extent of the Percehay estate at Ryton at the end of their tenure has been invaluable, as has the confirmation of the true size and location of the actual village in 1744. Unfortunately the part of the plan covering the centre of the village is lost, but the written detail does make up for this. The Barstow record is not complete, but tenants and rents are recorded right up to 1969, nearly the end of their tenure. Technically the Barstow family still hold the title 'Lord of the Manor of Ryton'.

Plan of Lund Forest in the Township of Ryton 1849 (Figure 15)

This plan is part of the extensive collection of documents from the Newburgh Priory estate held at NYCRO under the reference ZDV; the plan reference is ZDV V1 66 and is available to view on microfilm 1504 p516/7. At first glance it is disappointing as only the farmsteads are named, with the fields numbered and their area noted. However, on 25 January 1858, Sir George Wombwell of Newburgh, Baronet, and other interested parties, sold the Lund estate to the Lund family from Keighley, as detailed in the Deeds Registry at NYCRO (mic.382 Book IM, p162, record 248). While a plan of the estate is referred to but not copied into the register, a full schedule of all the fields on this plan is, including their names and corresponding numbers on the plan, along with the current cultivation and their areas. Fortunately this detail coincides almost exactly with the 1849 plan, so it is now possible to name all the fields. This in turn allows equivalent plans to be re-created for the earlier surveys of the Lund estate in 1796 (Figure 14), carried out by Edward Watterson and Thomas Rodwell,[2] and an even earlier survey carried out around 1683 (Figure 13).[3] Although the numbering schemes are not identical, and Lund Moor is ultimately completely enclosed, the field names, shapes and sizes are relatively easy to correlate, especially as all the plans begin their numbering schemes in the top left-hand corner with No.1 being named Moorhead Close on all three plans. The field names, coupled with their precise locations, are then critical in pinpointing old river crossings and tracks and ultimately revealing the location of the 'lost' Salescale. The plan of 1683 also shows very clearly why the additional land acquired for the estate in 1665 is referred to as Dicky

Ground,[4] because it looks just like a 'dicky' added to an area of land that resembles an enclosed carriage when drawn on a plan (see Chapter 5 and Figure 13).

Yorkshire Archaeological Society – MD 92 Nos 1 to 28
(These include the sale of the West Field of Ryton in 1535 and the Percehay distribution of 1604)

The relevance of this set of documents is only now being appreciated as they can be related to so many other sources of information. Originally catalogued as '1523 – 1622 Ryton Deeds, 28 items and 2 letters', they did not come into the possession of the YAS until the 1930s, too late to be inspected by Victorian scholars or the compilers of the VCH. The source of the documents is not known, but they all concern land that eventually came into the possession of John Garforth, although he is not mentioned in any of them (he is a witness once, on MD 92-25). The real connection to John is his father-in-law, James Boyes, the father of Alice, his wife; it is Alice who inherits most of the lands concerned on the death of her father. The documents concern four blocks of land. One is in Kirby Misperton and was given to Joan Percehay as part of her settlement when she married John Pickering some time before 1516. Another block of land is named Cholmeley Moors and it this area that became Shotton Hall farm. This land had been part of the Malton Priory estate and was referred to as Brodes or Broates; it was bought by the Cholmeley family after the Dissolution. Probably the most significant area, at least for its relevance to understanding the demise of Ryton, is the West Field (West Felde or Oxfelde). MD 92-3 is the original Indenture, dated 6 August 1535, detailing the sale by William Percehay and his wife Elizabeth to William's sister Isabell and her husband Robert Crayke, of the West Field of Ryton. The area is very clearly defined, with the boundaries still obvious on modern maps, and the ownership can now be traced from 1535 all the way through to today. As part of the deal, an annual rent of £7 is retained for William Percehay; on his death this benefit seems to pass to the heirs of his three daughters, Joan (Ellis), Maud (Emmerson) and Margaret (Cheseman). This accounts for the obscure amount of 46s 8d (being one third of the £7) still being documented as late as 8 March 1607/8 by Richard Ellis, a descendant of Joan (MD 92-24). The final block of land eventually becomes the subject of the Garforth distribution of 1655 (see below). It began as the benefit of Anne Percehay, widow of Robert, and after his death she married Robert Bower, hence she is then referred to as Anne Bower. After Anne's death, with her second husband already deceased, an Indenture (MD 92-16) dated 1 January in the first year of the reign of James 1 (1604 in today's calendar) carefully sets out how this land is to be divided between the offspring of Leonard Percehay, the recently deceased head of the family. There are six offspring: Thomas is son and heir with his second wife Mary (Wyvill); Robert is second son and has married a lady (first name unknown) called Cusand, which explains the use of this name in 1655; sons Henry and Leonard; youngest son Richard who is still a minor; and daughter Anne (becomes Johnson). Conveniently, tenants of part of this land are named as Nicholas Hutchinson and Edward Welbanke, these names helping to cross-reference with the 1655 distribution. From the signatures it is even possible to identify MD 92-16 as the copy originally held by Henry Percehay.

The Garforth distribution of 1655 (Figure 12)
(NYCRO microfilm 3989, pp199–205)

The records of the Newburgh Priory estate (NYCRO reference ZDV) include indentures concerning their acquisition of lands in Ryton. The earliest relevant document is a later copy of the original purchase from Henry VIII by Roger Cholmeley and his wife Christiana of the 'Manor and Grange in the Marish called Lund' that had been the possession of the 'monasterio de Ryevalles' (mic3989 p160/1) dated 23 August 1544. This even includes a defence of Henry's right to claim ownership of Rievaulx and to re-assign their possessions as he chooses. The purchase of Lund by Sir William Belassis of 'Newbroughe' from descendants of Roger Cholmeley is detailed in NYCRO 3989 pp165–6 dated 6 November 1599. The area that became known as Dicky Ground is purchased by Sir Rowland Bellassise in July 1665 (NYCRO mic3989 p230) from a John Cooke, and multiple indentures detail his purchase from John Bennett, who in turn had purchased from John Taylor and Lewis Darcy, who had purchased from Alice Garforth. The most informative document is the one giving the detail of how Alice came to own that land. It is an indenture dated 14 September 1655 (NYCRO mic3989 pp199–205) containing over 4000 words, and it explains in detail how John Garforth had acquired all the land from what we now know is the Percehay distribution of 1604. Of necessity he had to make multiple purchases as the land had been dispersed. Some of these are identifiable, specifically from Anne Percehay and William Cusand, but some are not. John's intention had been that he and his wife Alice should have the benefit of this land for the whole of their lives, and after the second death the benefit was to pass to all their non-inheriting children. However, after John's death Alice makes an agreement with her children that the land can be divided in her lifetime. As there are eight children concerned it is agreed that the area should be divided into ten equal parts, with Alice being given absolute ownership of two parts to compensate her for the loss of her life-interest of the whole, with the children receiving one part each. The document details the existing names for each close, complete with adjacent landholders (see Figure 12), and also the new names to be given to each newly created close with the appropriate acreage and the name of the new owner. The fact that we know the exact location of Alice's allocation enables all the other locations to be deduced. Unfortunately, of the new names only White Lilly and Brass Castle survive, although others may still be referenced in existing deeds. There are fifteen people involved in this complex document, and as there are only fourteen signatures (or marks) it is clear that the copy actually belonged to Henry Garforth, as his name is the one missing. The 'marks' rather than signatures for four of the ladies involved is a sad indication that the family did not think it was worth the money to educate some of the daughters as their only expectation in life was to marry well and produce heirs. However, this is a very 21st-century view and ignores all the other talents and achievements these perhaps very gifted ladies may have contributed to their society.

Note regarding other sources

Endnotes are used to allow referenced information to be verified, although the text can easily be followed without interruption if preferred. Not every single piece of information is referenced as that would have been obtrusive, but all the text is based on documented information rather than published speculation and assumptions, with originals consulted where possible. However, previous scholars have published the contents of many original documents via institutions such as the Yorkshire Archaeological Society (now the Yorkshire Archaeological and Historical Society), the Surtees Society and the Harleian Society, and as their publications are easily accessible at many locations, it is these publications that are quoted most frequently. All sources of information must be read bearing in mind the times in which they were written. There has been considerable misunderstanding of some of the terms used for family relationships that have very specific meanings today, but were not necessarily used in exactly the same way in earlier times (see details in Chapter 3). However, there is no doubt that business was invariably conducted either with relatives, friends (who themselves were probably related in some way), friends of relatives, or members of the same 'club' (such as the Merchant Adventurers) so it helps if these connections can be made, although it is not always possible. Care also needs to be taken with some of the descriptions used in documents as outlined in Chapter 5, Place-Names. Following deeds for a particular property over a long period of time, it is sometimes apparent that the wording used to describe it can remain unchanged for generations. The result is that a 'messuage lately builded' may actually be rather old, or even non-existent, and it may be adjoining 'Thomas Mold on east'[5] and similarly described over 86 years later,[6] despite the fact that all the Mold family are long gone. The term 'Fine' can also mislead: it is an abbreviation of the Latin for a final agreement and was a legal document used to transfer property.[7] Part of the legal process included recording the transfer in the records of the court, and as this required use of the lower part of the legal document (the foot) the records became known as the Feet of Fines. The records relating to Yorkshire have been collated and are available via British History Online's website www.british-history.ac.uk. Many original deeds and indentures have survived and detailed references for these have been given when appropriate.

Notes

1. NA E134/18Geo2/Mich9 Barstow vs Barstow
2. NYCRO mic 1285; p3038 onwards
3. YAS MS 601 – undated but estimated to be no later than 1683 because of the named tenants
4. NYCRO mic 3989; p230
5. NYCRO mic 269; D/R Book T, p440, r593 Thos Rowntree to Jacob Layland 30 March 1752
6. NYCRO mic 357; D/R Book GP, p100, r119 Thos Bickers to Robt Spanton 12 November 1838
7. See preface to the first volume of Yorkshire Fines

Appendix 2

Percehay of Ryton – Coats of Arms

The recording of coats of arms can be traced back to the time when the identification of knights at tournaments could only be made using their apparel as faces were obscured by protective visors on the helmets. However, coats of arms were in use well before the days of tournaments, primarily for identification in battle, and they were used increasingly to show descent from particular ancestors at a time when surnames were not in general use.[1] The formal recording of coats of arms began in the 13th century and eventually led to 'Visitations' by representatives of the Crown, the Heralds, who regulated their use and also the right to be called knight, esquire or gentleman. Consequently, pedigrees were also recorded at these Visitations and these have been invaluable when constructing the Percehay pedigree (see Chapter 3). There were five of these formal Visitations in Yorkshire covering the period 1530 to 1665 and 'Percehay of Ryton' features in each one. The reports from these, together with other references for the Percehay coats of arms, follow, along with notes about the sources of the records being quoted. The earliest reference, from around 1300, gives the family coat of arms as a silver (argent) shield with a red (gules) cross with each limb splayed into three at the ends (patonce), giving 'argent, a cross patonce gules' in heraldic terminology. This coat of arms, with or without variations, continues in use right through to the last known male descendant who died in 1711. It can still be seen on the Percehay shield at the top of the 'heraldic tree in the frieze of the arms of the gentlemen of the Wapentake of Rydale cum Pickering Lythe' in the 'Great Chamber at Gilling Castle'. This was photographed and featured in the centre pages of the very informative guide book of the same name by the late Hugh Murray.[2] Although all the known existing representations of the Percehay coat of arms can be described as argent, a cross patonce gules, none is identical. This is probably because each one reflected the style of that particular period, rather than conforming with any later set of rules. There is also much confusion about the subtle differences in the design of a cross when described as paty, patonce, formy, fleury, flory, fleuretty, crosslet, bottony (etc)[3] – the references following emphasise this confusion.

Unfortunately there does not appear to be any record for the Percehay coat of arms earlier than the reign of Edward I (1272–1307), but we do know that there were knights in the family as early as 1213–20 (see Chapter 2) and probably before that, so it would be expected that they did have a coat of arms by then. Indeed, information referred to in a footnote to the 1584/5 and 1612 Visitations, probably from that of Robert Glover in 1584/5, suggests that they did indeed have an earlier, but slightly different, coat of arms, but bear in mind that this information from the family was already at least 300 years old. This earlier one was given as 'gules, a [blank] between 15 cross crosslets argent', but an article entitled 'Ancient Heraldry in Deanery of Ryedale',[4] supposedly quoting the same source, gives 'their paternal coat, stated to have been gules crusilly [scattered with cross crosslets] and a fess [broad horizontal band across the centre of the shield] argent', suggesting that the 'blank' could have been a fess. The 'cross crosslet' is usually depicted as a cross but with each arm also being a cross, and in the earliest times each arm of the cross had ends 'rounded off buttonwise'[5] (like a clover leaf). It is not too unrealistic to think that this cross crosslet form of cross developed into the cross patonce on the later Percehay shield; but why change at all? Both the sources quoted seem to agree that 'at the sight of their evidences that one of them matching with a daughter and heir of Vesci, his posterity [descendants] left their old arms and have henceforth borne the arms of Vesci as their own proper coat'.[6] This statement is not factually correct. The Percehay coat of arms is the same as that of Vesci but with the colours reversed (or alternatively that the Vesci coat of arms is the same as that of Percehay with the colours reversed). The interpretation depends on which, if either, came first. The one marriage that is known to link the two families is that of Robert Percehay with Joan Vesci, who was daughter and heir to John Vesci, but by then the Vesci coat of arms is or (gold), a cross sable (black). In fact this coat can be traced right back to the Tyson family who were Lords of Alnwick and Malton, and the last male of the line – William Tyson – had or, a cross sable as his coat of arms. Both the titles and the coat of arms passed to Ivo de Vesci when he married the daughter and sole heir of this William Tyson. The descent of the Vesci family is well documented, but not all sources agree on the detail. All that can be said for certain is that at some time before Eustace de Vesci (1169–1216) the family arms have changed to gules, a cross fleury/patonce argent, as this is on the shield attributed to Eustace de Vesci when he was one of the barons who signed Magna Carta in 1215. No explanation has been found for this change, and no known marriage would account for the source of the new arms. However, the 1610 edition of Camden's *Britannia*[7] suggests that the father of Eustace, William son of Eustace son of Fitz John, 'being ripped out of his mother's [Beatrice de Vesci] womb, assumed unto him the name Vesci and the armes, a cross flory argent in a shield gules'.[8] His mother's arms, being daughter and sole heir, were 'or, a cross sable' (a plain black cross on a gold shield), and his father's 'quarterly or [gold] and gules [red]', so the reason for the new design is not immediately obvious. Whatever the reasons, 'gules a cross flory (patonce) argent' (a silver flory cross on a red shield) became the new family coat of arms. However, two generations later both John and his brother William 'changed the arms of their house into a shield or with a cross sable',[9] thus reverting back to the original arms of Ivo de Vesci.[10]

So, why did both the Percehay and Vesci families change their coats of arms at around the same time, why did they choose a cross patonce, and what really was the earliest connections between the two families? Until more reliable and detailed information is available it is not possible to give definitive answers, but some ideas are worth considering.

Earliest connections: There can be little doubt that Robert Percehay married Joan de Vesci some time before her father's death in 1289. At that time the Percehay arms were the later argent, a cross patonce gules, and those of Vesci were or, a cross sable. If the earlier changes had occurred as a result of another Percehay/Vesci marriage, then it is unlikely that their common ancestors were closer than great-grandparents. This assumption is based on the fact that the pedigree of the Percehays clearly shows that they did not (in general) marry close relatives (see Chapter 3). This would take them back to the era of Magna Carta and the Eustace de Vesci whose father seems to have instigated their change of coat of arms. There would be an obvious logic at that time for the Vescis, who had just married into the most important family in the area (Tyson) and were relative newcomers, to enhance their position even further by marrying into the next most important family, the Percehays, being also their immediate neighbours and with a lineage that went all the way back to France. This is also well before the formal recording of coats of arms so any resulting changes did not need to be explained or justified to anyone. Not enough is known to confirm this idea.

The cross patonce: Why change to this particular type of cross? Both families were based at or near Malton. Just before the conquest Siward, Earl of Northumbria, was one of the people who held Malton, as detailed at Domesday. There is also a more direct connection with Ryton, where there is reference to 'Siward's House' (Siwardeus) in the 12th-century gifts to the Priory at (Old) Malton, although it cannot be stated for certain that it referred specifically back to the Earl. The coat of arms of Siward is quoted as sable with a silver cross flowered at the ends, so this could be described as patonce. It is even possible that the Tyson family were related to this Siward, but the records seem quite confused. An even earlier Earl of Northumbria was Oswald, who became St Oswald. He was instrumental in the conversion of the area to Christianity, and his cult was very popular in the area. In fact it now seems that the Percehay oratory at Ryton was dedicated to St Oswald (see Appendix 3). The cross sometimes given in the arms of St Oswald would now be termed patonce – Tonge's Visitation suggests patee (in the monastery at Nostell) and flory (the monastery at Durham). Association with the same style of cross as Earl Siward and St Oswald would have been understandable for both the Percehay and Vesci families. Another coat of arms that was significant at around the time of the changes was that of the Knights' Templar who wore white tunics with a red 'moline' cross. This cross is very similar to the patonce/flory cross but with the limbs splayed into two at the ends rather than three.

Again, association with these crusaders, implied or actual, may have influenced the choice of the new coat of arms for both families. Finally, there is even the possibility that a connection with a third important family could be relevant. The 'proof of age' of William, son and heir of Sir William Latymer, taken at Scampston in 1351[11] shows that Walter Percehay was a god-parent to this William. The basic Latymer coat of arms is 'gules a cross patonce or' (red shield with a gold patonce cross), so perhaps earlier association with this influential family had some bearing on the new coats of arms chosen.

Whatever the reason, the Percehay and Vesci families do seem to have changed their coats of arms at around the same time, and as one is the reverse of the other, the changes would seem to have been co-ordinated, but it is not possible to say with any certainty why they did so, or why the Vesci family reverted back to their old coat of arms after only two more generations.

Although the Percehay family coat of arms remained 'argent, a cross patonce gules', they did display other coats of arms that clearly showed their connections to other families in the area (see Chapter 3). One connection was to the Spencer family and is given by Glover (1584/5) in the description of 'a funeral Escocheon in Mr Percehay's house', as explained in the following notes and reproduced on the back cover of this book. The Herald seems unimpressed by the modification of the Spencer family, then of Old Malton, to their ancestors' arms. They were 'descended oute of the [Spencer] house of Cople in Bedfordshire', as noted by Flower in his Visitation of 1563/4, but they do not seem to have sought authority to create their own modified coat of arms; consequently Glover instructs the Percehays to quarter only with their historic connections of Lound, Fauconberg and Darcy. The following Visitation, by Dugdale in 1665, confirms that they complied with this instruction and the modified Spencer coat of arms had been dropped. Ironically, in 1595 a later Clarenceux King of Arms, Richard Lee, was persuaded to 'discover' the descent of the original Spencer family from the ancient family of Despencer, a descent now known to be fictitious.[12]

Reference to declared coats of arms allows another, more important, connection to be made to the Percehay relatives in the West Country. The Harleian Society had already made the connection with a Sir Walter Percehay at Caundel Haddon in Dorset at around 1300,[13] and this does now seem to be the same Sir Walter from Ryton. Fortunately there are two references for the coat of arms of Henry Percehay, who was born at Kitton, near Holcombe Rogus close to Tiverton in Devon, and died in 1380; these are given as the same silver shield with a red patonce cross as the Ryton family, but with a black chess rook in the top right-hand corner for difference. Without this information it would not have been possible to confirm the link between these two families.

Percehay Coats of Arms – References

This list, in an estimated chronological order, gives the known references to the Percehay coats of arms with notes about the sources of the records quoted. Some of these are very specific, especially the details from the Visitations of the Heralds who recorded both coats of arms and pedigrees, but some are general lists whose dates and origins are still a matter for debate. Most of the references are written, rather than pictorial, and reflect the heraldic language of the day, so the same cross may be described using different terms.

Pre-1292 Percehay 'Ancient Arms' – Information provided by the family in 1584/5 suggests their earliest coat of arms was 'gules, a [blank] between 15 cross crosslets argent', and a later interpretation is given as 'gules crusilly and a fess argent',[14] so perhaps the blank was a fess. It is known that Walter, father of Robert Percehay, already had the later coat of arms (see 1272–1307) when Robert married Joan de Vesci, as their son, another Walter, added his mother's arms into the 'new' Percehay coat of arms (see 1322/1319). Both Robert and Joan seem to be deceased by 1292.

1272–1307 Percehay of Rydal – Argent, a cross patonce gules: This is an addendum to the 1584/5 and 1612 Visitations, and is headed 'Nomina et Arma Equitum qui cum Edwardo primo, Rege, stipendia merebant in Scotia et alibi'. This is very non-specific. Sir Walter, father of the above Robert, was called to serve in Scotland in June 1300, so it is not unreasonable to think that this is his coat of arms. This is the coat of arms underlying all future coats of arms, and is still in use in 1705 without any embellishment.

1322 / 1319 Sir Walter Percehay – Argent, a cross patonce (tricked patee in Ashmole MS)[15] gules and in the dexter chief point, an inescucheon or, a cross sable: This is always referred to as the Boroughbridge Roll from the battle in 1322, but new research suggests that this was from a tournament held during the Berwick campaign of 1319; it is unlikely to be renamed. Sir Walter's mother, Joan Vesci, was daughter and heir to John Vesci and entitled to give the family coat of arms 'or, a cross sable' to her son. This Walter was the grandson of the Walter above.

1327–77 EIII Rolls There are four Percehay entries in rolls vaguely dated to Edward III:

Walter Percehay – Argent, a cross patonce (flory) gules: The family coat of arms borne by Sir Walter.

Walter Percehay – Argent, a cross patonce (flory) gules, in the cantel a lozenge of the second [gules] all within a bordure engrailed of the last [gules]: The border suggests this was Walter, a younger son of the above Sir Walter and brother to William. The lozenge could be from his mother Agnes and indicate that his father is still alive. It is possible that Agnes was from the Greystoke family[16] who had or, 3 lozenges gules (Jenyns Roll).

Walter Percehay – d'Argent, a une crois patey de gules, a une border gules recersele: Again, this is probably the younger Walter, and recorded some time after his father's death with the border to distinguish him from William, the eldest and inheriting son. However, it is also possible that it could be William's eldest son, another Walter, again with the border for difference.

William de Percehay – d'Argent, a une crois patey de gules, a une lozenge de gules en le quartre devant: Eldest son and heir with an addition perhaps from his mother's arms[17] to distinguish him from his father who is still alive at that time.

1346–47 Sir Walter Percehay – Argent, a cross patonce (flory) gules, in the cantel an inescocheon quarterly sable and or: This is taken from a list of the knights at the capitulation of Calais in 1347, a Walter being knighted at that time. Closer examination shows it to be from the 'accounts kept by Walter (de) Wetewang, treasurer of the (King's) Household, of the wages of those present at the siege of Calais in 1346–1347'. One Sir Walter is known to have died and his will proved on 4 December 1346, so it is possible that either his younger son, Walter, or his grandson, yet another Walter, has taken over his duties at the siege of Calais. The inescutcheon may belong to the wife of one of these Walters; she has yet to be identified. A connection with the West Country Percehays is also possible.

1356 Sir William Percehay – Argent, a cross patonce gules. Crest – a bull's head couped azure: There is a remarkable seal, still attached to the original document at the Merchant Adventurers Hall in York, that was the impression left by Sir William Percehay when he granted the site of the existing hall 'on the Friday next after the feast of St Lucy the virgin in the year of our Lord 1356' (Friday 16 December in 1536). The arms of the Percehay family can still be recognised as a cross patonce, although the arms of the cross are wider than a standard patonce cross of today – more like a hybrid of the old 'paty' or 'formy' but with fleur-de-lis ends. This probably explains why at that time the arms were described as either patonce or flory, when in fact they were perhaps technically neither. Obviously the colours are assumed. (See Figure 6.)

Pre-1384 Sir William Percehay (died 15 August 1384) – Argent, a cross patonce gules: By an amazing coincidence, metal detectorists found the 'seal matrix' (now also in the Merchant Adventurers Hall) almost certainly of this William on land he acquired by marriage to Isabel, daughter of John de Melsa (sometimes referred to as Meux from the ecclesiastical connection to Meux in France). Again the colours are assumed, but there can be no doubt about the arms depicted or that it was 'The seal of William Percehay knight' as it states. This is probably a slightly later matrix lost by Sir William on a visit to his manor of Levisham. It is not quite identical to the one he used in 1356, with the main differences being the shape of the shield, now with a broader base reflecting the known changing fashion, and the arms of the cross are narrower, conforming more to our modern description of patonce. (See Figure 6.)

Pre-1380 Henry Percehay (died 1380) – Argent, a cross flory gules, in the dexter chief a chess-rook sable: From 'The note-book of Tristram Risdon, 1608–1628'. Page 264 gives this detail for Knights of Somersetshire, and page 102 gives similar for Devon. This is the conclusive proof that the 'Sir Henry Percehay Knight, born at Kitton in the parish of Holcombe Rogus, Sergent at Law, Baron of the Exchequer, Justice of the Common Pleas'[18] was indeed related to the Ryton family. The chess-rook, not a particularly common device, may have been included for difference and could be from the Rogus family, in the adjacent township of Holcombe Rogus, who had 'azure, a chevron argent between 3 chess-rooks or' but the connection has not yet been verified. The connection may even be closer to the Percehay Yorkshire possessions, with Anlaby of Etton given by Dugdale as 'argent, a chevron between three chess-rooks sable' – Alice

Percehay did marry Richard Anlably of Etton, but that was some four generations later; there may have been an earlier connection yet to be discovered.

Circa 1400 J Peyrchay[19] – silver a cross patonce gules

William Percihay – silver a cross patonce gules an escutcheon gold charged with a cross sable, in the quarter

R Percihay – silver a cross patonce gules a border indented gules

S Ashmole no. 834, published by Surtees Society no. 146, 1932. Some of the notes refer to Jenyn's Ordinary *circa* 1410. Although this information is all on one manuscript, it could be from different eras. The 'J' is probably John, the grandson of William, who took over from his father Robert (hence the 'R') when he died in 1427. Robert's border suggests that his arms were recorded during his father's life. William's arms are those recorded earlier for his father with the Vesci arms included.

1530 Tonge's visitation – Argent, a cross patonce gules: 'This ys the petigre of Willyam Percehay, esquier' [five generations listed]

1563 & 64 Flower's visitation – Argent, a cross fleury Gules: 'Crest of Percehay on a wreth Argent a bulle's hed raced Azure hornes typped Or & coller abowt the necke Or.' [seven generations]

1584/5 & 1612 Visitations of Yorkshire – Argent, a cross patoncee gules: 'Crest: a bull's head couped azure, attired per fesse or and azure' [twelve generations]. This is the combination of Robert Glover's visitation of 1584/5 and that of Richard St George in 1612. The actual wording is:

Arms: Quarterly, 1. Argent, a cross patoncee gules, Percehay. 2. Azure, a fret argent, Lound. 3. Argent, a lion rampant azure, debruised by a bend or, Fauconbridge. 4. Argent, an escocheon sable, within an orle of cinquefoyles gules, Darcy. Another Coat: 1. Percehay. 2. Lound. 3. Fauconbridge. 4. Darcy. 5. Gules, a chevron between 3 hinds heads or, Hynde. 6. Gules, 3 chaplets in bend between 2 cottises sable, Saxton.

The pedigrees declared at these and the previous visitations clearly show the family connections justifying these coats of arms (see detail in Chapter 3). Intriguingly there is a note added to this visitation as follows: 'That the ancient arms of this Percy [sic] were gu., a [-----] between 15 cross crosslets argent, wherefore it seems one of them matching with a daughter and heir of Vesci, his posterity [descendants] left their old arms and have now thenceforth borne the arms of Vesci as their own proper coat.' This then refers to a footnote that this information came from (Harleian) MS. 1487 (this is thought to contain a copy of all the visitations of Tonge, Flower and St George). Also included are four 'charters' concerning Joan Vesci, her son Walter Percehay, his son William, and a gift of his house in York to Robert Percehay by John de Vesci. It is then followed by the statement 'I doe gather by these several deeds that Percehay marrying an heir of Vesci doth assume and bear the arms of Vesci as his own proper coat' but there is no indication of who made this comment.

As a separate note with these Visitations is a list of 'The Arms taken out of the Churches & Houses at the Yorkshire Visitation 1584/5':

In the House of Mr Percey, alias Percehay, of Ryton
Argent, a cross patoncee gules [Percehay]
The same, impaling, or, a cross sable [Vesci]
Argent, an inescocheon sable, a border of the first, within an orle of 8 roses[20] gules [Darcy]
Argent, a cross patoncee gules, impaling, argent, a chevron sable between 3 fetter locks or (*sic*), a bordure of the first entoyre of roses gules [the fetter locks are almost certainly hinds heads, as this is for Hynde, hence the *sic* added]
Or, a plain cross sable [Vesci]

'A funeral Escocheon in Mr Percehaye's house.' Quarterly, 1 and 4, argent, a cross patoncee gules [Percehay]; 2 and 3. argent, a lion rampant azure, debruised by a bendlet or [Fauconbridge], impaling quarterly, 1 and 4, azure, fretty argent [Lound]; 2 and 3, azure, a fesse engrailed ermine between 3 leopards heads cabossed or [Spencer][21].

In the Church of Kirkby Misperton these two.
Quarterly, 1 and 4 argent, a cross patoncee gules; 2 and 3 azure, fretty argent [John Percehay = Alice d&h of Lound]
Quarterly, 1 and 4 argent, a cross patoncee gules; 2 and 3 argent, an inescocheon within an orle of 8 cinquefoils sable [Robert Percehay = Elizabeth Darcy]

Circa 1585 Leonard Percehay Esq – Argent a cross flory gules: This is listed as 'the Copy of Sir William Fayrfax' booke of Arms of Yorkshire'. It is still possible to see the actual coat of arms referred to in the Great Chamber at Gilling Castle, where the Percehay coat of arms is literally at the top of 'The heraldic tree in the frieze of the arms of the gentlemen of the Wapentake of Ryedale cum Pickering Lythe'.

The Percehay Family of Ryton

1665 Percehay of Ryton – Argent, a cross fleury gules [adds four more generations to the 1612 Visitation]: Crest: - A bull's head couped Azure, horns per fess Or and Azure. This is from Dugdale's Visitation of Yorkshire. The full entry for the arms is:

Argent, a cross fleury gules (Percehay) [added by Clay]

Argent, fretty Azure (Lound)

Argent, a lion rampant Azure, over all a bendlet or (Fauconbridge)

Argent, an inescutcheon sable within an orle of cinquefoils pierced gules (Darcy)

1705 Argent, a cross patonce gules: Crest: A bulls head. The last known surviving male Percehay, Christopher, with his wife Susannah, gave a silver chalice to the church of St. Michael's in Malton in 1705. Engraved upon it are the family coat of arms and their crest. This clearly shows a patonce cross but obviously no colours are given.

Circa 1700 The above Christopher may also have been the person who donated a pewter alms dish (see Figure 4) to the parish church at Kirby Misperton as one of his last acts. It was dedicated to St Oswald, probably in memory of the family chapel in their house at Ryton. This connection with St Oswald may be one of the reasons for the change in the family arms to a cross patonce, as this is the cross associated with St Oswald.

Notes

1. For a more detailed treatise on Heraldry see *The Story and Language of Heraldry* by Stephen Slater (2012), an inexpensive but informative introduction to the subject.
2. *The Great Chamber at Gilling Castle*, Hugh Murray (Saint Laurence Papers), (1996)
3. *A Grammar of English Heraldry* by the late W H St John Hope; 2nd edition revised by Anthony R Wagner, (Cambridge University Press) (1953), p89 gives a background to the confusion.
4. Yorkshire Archaeological Journal no. 28, p41
5. *A Grammar of English Heraldry*, W H St John Hope (1953), p90
6. See 1584/5 & 1612 Visitations detailed later.
7. *Britannia*, William Camden (1610 edn), p722
8. Camden's comments are significant because at this time he was Clarenceux King of Arms, and thus the final arbiter on all things concerned with Heraldry and Pedigree.
9. *Britannia*, William Camden (1610 edn), p722
10. The early Vesci descent and some of their coats of arms are detailed in the Eure pedigree given in the additional pedigrees in 1584/5 & 1612, p607.
11. Calendar of Inquisitions Post Mortem, EdwIII file 113, no.671
12. www.baronage.co.uk, The Spencers and Despencers
13. Harleian Society, Knights of Edward I vol.4 (P–S), p45
14. Yorkshire Archaeological Journal 28, 'Ancient Heraldry in Deanery of Ryedale', p41
15. See p89 of *A Grammar of English Heraldry* by the late W H St John Hope, second edition revised by Anthony R Wagner, Cambridge University Press 1953 for an explanation of paty/patonce/flory and reasons for confusion.
16. S/Soc 4, York Wills, p165 Will of Agnes de Lockton (granddaughter of Walter and Agnes Percehay) names Baron de Greystok as one of her executors. She also makes a bequest to Lady Greystok. A footnote suggests this is Catherine, daughter of Roger Lord Clifford of Somerset – yet another West Country connection.
17. This is before the rules on the use of heraldry that we assume today. His mother need not necessarily have been an heiress to pass on her family coat of arms, or even part of them.
18. Plymouth and West Devon Record Office; ref.373/2, 1716
19. The spelling variations and misinterpretation of the Percehay name is common, the arms are not.
20. The Darcy coat of arms is usually given as cinquefoils, sometimes sixfoils, and occasionally misread as roses.
21. This coat of arms bears a distinct resemblance to the Spencers of Bedfordshire. Sir John, knighted in 1553/4, had azure, a fess engrailed ermine between 3 eagles heads erazed argent, and an earlier member had the same but with 'six sea-mews [gulls] heads erased argent', so the various offshoots seem to have identified themselves by varying the number and style of heads included. Leonard Percehay married Prudence, daughter of Thomas Spencer of Old Malton, and that family was noted in Flower's visitation of 1563–64 as being 'descended oute of the house of Cople in Bedfordshire', so this coat of arms probably came with Prudence. Interestingly, the Spencer family eventually produced Princess Diana, but along the way they changed their coat of arms to claim descent from the ancient family of Despencer, although this is not now thought to be credible. As this information was recorded during the life of both Leonard and Prudence, the funeral Escocheon can only have belonged to Leonard's father, William. It reflects the coat of arms created when Edmund Percehay married Isobel Fauconberg, uniting the Percehay and Fauconberg coats of arms with those of Lound and Darcy, but for some reason the Darcy coat of arms are replaced by those of Spencer, perhaps to celebrate the marriage of Leonard and Prudence some time before 1566.

Appendix 3

The Chapel of St Oswald at Ryton in Ryedale

There is a pewter alms-dish in St Laurence's church at Kirby Misperton that suggests the existence of a 'Chapel' at Ryton sometime in the distant past dedicated to St Oswald. However, an inspection of *Yorkshire Church Plate* by T.M. Fallow and H.B. McCall in 1912[1] almost dismissed it as a fake, but not quite. Consequently, with the advantage of additional information that is now available, it is time to examine the possibility that this chapel really did exist at Ryton.

There is evidence for some kind of local church presence at Ryton as early as the twelfth century. At some date before 1157–58, Ralph Neville gave a gift of part of his lands in Ryton (later known as Lund) to the monks of Rievaulx Abbey.[2] No date is given in the details of the gift, but a later charter[3] confirming the boundary of the possessions of the monks in this area can be dated to 1157–58 and the Neville gift is clearly included. One of the witnesses to the gift was 'Elfwino, Presbitero de Rihtuna' or the priest of Ryton. His presence does not mean that Ryton had a physical church, but more likely the Lord of the Manor employed him to pray for him, his family, and the souls of his ancestors, probably in a private chapel in his house. Elfwino could also have held divine service for the Lord and the people of Ryton, but that may have been discouraged by the priest at Kirby Misperton, where the parish church was situated.

The next relevant reference comes from the Register of Archbishop Greenfield (1306–15)[4] that included a request from Joan Percehay, dated 5 March 1311, for an oratory in her manor of Ryton.[5] Current information now suggests that this Joan was a daughter of Sir Walter Percehay of Ryton, and sister to his son and heir, Robert, who had married Joan de Vesci, daughter and heir of John de Vesci Baron of Alnwick and Malton. By 1311 Sir Walter, Robert and his wife, and Joan's husband, Roger of Wrelton, had all died, leaving Joan in control of the Percehay lands in Ryton, hence the reference to her manor. On the death of her husband, Joan took the not unusual step of reverting back to her maiden name as the Percehays were the more important family. In 1311 she was described as relict (widow) of Roger, and requested an oratory at Ryton because of its distance from Kirby Misperton and the difficulty in sometimes making the journey there. Her request was granted on 7 April 1311, giving permission for her to hear divine service in her oratory at Ryton for three years with the proviso that any money collected there should be given to the rector of Kirby Misperton.[6] Her oratory was probably a small dedicated corner of her manor house, similar to a Lady Chapel in a church, rather than a separate building.

This oratory at Ryton seems to continue in use well after the three-year period agreed. In 1344 Walter Percehay mentions in his will 'Walterus capellanus de Ryton'[7] (Walter the chaplain of Ryton), confirming there is still someone conducting divine service at Ryton, and his wife Agnes later (1349) confirms the items being used when she bequeaths to her son William 'one chalice with all the equipment for a priest, one gilded bowl, one ivory image of Saint Mary'.[8] In fact this oratory seems to be still in use at the time of the Dissolution. As Henry VIII wanted to squeeze every last ounce of wealth out of his new possessions, including the oratories and private chapels, then collectively referred to as chantries, that had been previously licensed by the church, he sent out commissioners to value these assets. The Commissioners for Yorkshire were appointed on 14 February 1546 with the instructions that 'the proceeds of the sale of the chantry property should be devoted to the expenses of the French and Scotch wars'[9] (confirming another underlying reason for the split with Rome). At the time of this survey the chantry still existed in the Percehays' house at Ryton, and the reason given for its continued existence again concerned the distance from Kirby Misperton and the difficulty in getting there. At that time it was stated that mass and divine service were being celebrated by Robert Rome, the incumbent of Kirby Misperton, for the benefit of both the Lord and his servants; that situation may well have continued as the Commissioners suggested a payment of a tenth of the value of all the goods and lands associated with all the chantries in the parish to be paid yearly to the king rather than selling everything off. It is possible that the chantry at Ryton continued to be used as it had effectively become a 'chapel of ease', full control remaining with the parish church at Kirby Misperton. At some point this formal arrangement did cease, as 'Christopher Percehay of Ryton was presented as a non-communicant in 1663',[10] indicating that the then incumbent at Kirby Misperton was not visiting Ryton to perform services there. However, Christopher may have had his own covert 'Catholic' arrangements that did involve a (very) private chapel; in fact that may have been the root cause of the friction between him and the then rector at Kirby Misperton.

The findings of Messrs Fallow and McCall now need to be re-visited with the benefit of the foregoing information. Rather than paraphrase their detailed work it is probably best to include their report in full:

The pewter alms-dish is a very fine vessel, 16.5 inches in diameter. At the centre is engraved a representation of an Abbot in his mitre and robes. This is shown in a vesica, after the manner of a conventual seal, and surrounding it are the words: SIG. OSWALDI DE RICTUNE [sic].[11] Ryton is a place in the parish of Kirkby Misperton, and the implication seems to be that there was formerly a chapel there dedicated to St Oswald. But we do not think the inscription is ancient. The vessel itself looks like a production of the eighteenth century, and the device may have been copied from some old seal in order to perpetuate the memory of the almost forgotten chapel. But the whole thing is not, perhaps, free from the suspicion of being a 'fake'.

If read omitting the last sentence, the report could well have been correct in every detail. The dedication to St Oswald could easily be attributed to the person who instigated the chapel at Ryton, Joan Percehay. At that time St Oswald was one of the most important saints of the area, having been the King of Northumbria (an area that included, and was even centred on, York) who encouraged the spread of Christianity in the north-east. The most likely benefactor of the alms-dish would have been the Percehay family themselves, but the male line died out in 1711,[12] so it would probably have been presented sometime early in the eighteenth century. Their connection with the alms-dish may also be confirmed by what was thought to be a very small Maltese cross within the engraving but it is more likely to be a depiction of the 'cross patonce' featured in the coat of arms of both the Percehay family and of St Oswald (another connection that should not be ignored). This coat of arms can still be seen on a chalice presented to the church of St Michael in Malton in 1705 by Christopher, the last of the Percehay of Ryton line. This Christopher seems to have liked commemorative gifts, for in addition to this chalice, in his will he left money to his friend Sir William St Quintin to be 'bestowed in a piece of Plate in remembrance of me' and a gift with similar instructions to another friend, Thomas Longley. From these three gifts it seems distinctly possible that it may have been this last Percehay who donated the pewter alms-dish in remembrance of his family and their chapel.

From all the above evidence it would seem that the alms-dish is nothing like as old as the 'Chapel of Ryton' it commemorates, causing the original suspicions about its authenticity, but it is still probably over 300 years old. The interpretation by Messrs Fallow and McCall does seem to be correct and the alms-dish is exactly what it says on the pewter, celebrating the original oratory at Ryton that must now be assumed to have been dedicated to St Oswald. Surely it can now be confirmed, with a degree of certainty, that there is absolutely nothing 'fake' about this intriguing legacy of a long-forgotten age.

Notes

1. YAS Extra Series no. 3, vol.1, pp119–20
2. S/Soc 83; Rievaulx Chartulary, p49
3. YAS R/S; Early Yorkshire Charters, vol.1, p313
4. S/Soc 151; Register of Archbishop Greenfield, p59, no.1272
5. An oratory was a small chapel, especially for private worship.
6. S/Soc 151; Register of Archbishop Greenfield, p60, no. 1274
7. S/Soc 4; York Wills, p6
8. S/Soc 4; York Wills, p53
9. S/Soc 91; Yorkshire Chantry Surveys, vol.1, pxi
10. Aveling N/R; p356
11. The original letter they used was 'L but this is on the corner of the engraving and is more likely to be 'C'.
12. Will of the last Christopher Percehay was proved 4 December 1711 (Borthwick mic 988; vol.67, no. 313)